D1596007

SEX SEGREGATION IN SPORTS

Why Separate Is Not Equal

Adrienne N. Milner and Jomills Henry Braddock II

 PRAEGER™

An Imprint of ABC-CLIO, LLC

Santa Barbara, California • Denver, Colorado

Library of Congress Cataloging-in-Publication Data

Names: Milner, Adrienne N., author. | Braddock, Jomills H., author.
Title: Sex segregation in sports : why separate is not equal / Adrienne N. Milner and
    Jomills Henry Braddock, II.
Description: Santa Barbara, California : Praeger, an imprint of ABC-CLIO, LLC, [2016] |
    Includes bibliographical references and index.
Identifiers: LCCN 2015040363 | ISBN 9781440838101 (hard copy : acid-free paper) |
    ISBN 9781440838118 (ebook)
Subjects: LCSH: Sex discrimination in sports—United States. | Discrimination in
    sports—United States. | Sports—Social aspects—United States.
Classification: LCC GV706.32 .M55 2016 | DDC 796.082—dc23
LC record available at http://lccn.loc.gov/2015040363

ISBN: 978-1-4408-3810-1
EISBN: 978-1-4408-3811-8

20 19 18 17 16   1 2 3 4 5

This book is also available on the World Wide Web as an eBook.
Visit www.abc-clio.com for details.

Praeger
An Imprint of ABC-CLIO, LLC

ABC-CLIO, LLC
130 Cremona Drive, P.O. Box 1911
Santa Barbara, California 93116-1911

This book is printed on acid-free paper (∞)

Manufactured in the United States of America

Contents

Figures

CHAPTER ONE

Introduction

Is Separate Equal in Sports?

In 2011, standout high school wrestler Joel Northrup refused to compete against Casey Herkelman in the Iowa state wrestling tournament for one reason: her sex. He was applauded for his decision to forfeit the match, and even Casey's father stated that he understood and respected Joel's choice.[1] However, what would have happened if Joel, who is white, refused to wrestle a black male, a Hispanic male, an Asian male, or a Native American male because of his race; a gay or bisexual male because of his sexual orientation; or a Jewish or Muslim male because of his religion? In any of these cases, there most likely would have been public outrage and the U.S. public would not likely have supported Joel's decision. So why is sex treated differently than race, sexuality, or religion in sports contexts?

Likewise, the general public would not accept a male employer firing a female employee at his company, a male university president denying a female student admission, or a male landlord refusing to rent an apartment to a prospective female tenant on the sole basis of her sex. So why is sex treated differently in sports than in other social institutions? Furthermore, what are the consequences of sex segregation in sports for women and for society as a whole?

This book attempts to answer the question of why sex discrimination seems to be acceptable in sports contests and to address other issues surrounding the motivations and consequences of sex segregation in sports. By examining the similarities and differences in the manner in which sex and race categories are constructed and maintained, we question whether sex integration in sports contexts is possible, and how it might best be achieved. Specifically, this book begins by addressing the issue of sex segregation in sports through an examination of two U.S. educational policies: Title IX, the federal law prohibiting sex discrimination in education;[2] and the *Brown v. Board of Education* ruling,[3] which declared the *Plessy v. Ferguson* decision "separate but equal" unconstitutional.[4]

When thinking about Title IX legislation that focuses on sex and *Brown v. Board of Education* legislation that focuses on race, a sociological perspective goes beyond the traditional understandings of these topics, demonstrating that the concepts of sex and race are similar and comparable because they are both social constructions real only in their consequences and not in and of themselves. In addition, the tactics that have historically been used to discriminate against women and racial minorities are similar, where both groups were formally and informally barred from voting, owning property, and serving in the military, and continue to experience discrimination in employment and educational contexts. In sports specifically, women and racial minorities have restricted opportunities for participation and both groups are significantly underrepresented in decision-making positions compared to their male and white counterparts.

Although we often discuss the concepts of sex and race separately throughout this book, we acknowledge the importance of intersectionality—the understanding that neither sex nor race exists in a vacuum and that multiple aspects of such individuals' identity characteristics as socioeconomic status (SES), sexual orientation, and age intertwine to shape life chance opportunities.[5] In addition, we acknowledge the unique experiences of women of color who endure interlocking forms of oppression associated with simultaneous membership in minority sex and race groups.

Both sex and race categories result from the division of individuals into "socially constructed" groups based on *perceived* biological differences. Examples of the social construction of race include the way in which the concept of "whiteness" has changed over time,[6] how mixed-race individuals are often labeled by the rule of hypodecent, where they are classified as members of the lesser socially advantaged group,[7] and the differential outcomes that result from group membership in such nuanced racial categories as black Hispanic vs. white Hispanic and African immigrant vs. African American. Examples of the social construction of sex include that many such individuals as those who identify as transgender, intersex, and hermaphrodite transcend the traditional binary sex classification system, and previously assumed such innate sex differences as those associated with childrearing and intellectual ability are declining as women have increased their participation in the workforce and expanded their employment into nontraditional occupations in every sector of the labor market.

The socially constructed concepts of sex and race are further complicated by their respective relationships with the concepts of gender and ethnicity. Like sex and race, gender and ethnicity are also socially constructed categories that result from the division of individuals into groups based on *perceived* cultural differences. Gender involves the normative cultural performance of traditional notions of sex roles associated with masculinity and femininity as reflected through dress, hairstyle, speech patterns, hobbies, career choice, and so on, and does not necessarily correspond with individuals' assigned sex. Ethnicity involves the cultural performance of ethnic group membership and is reflected in language, religion, values, food, and so forth and is often related to, but not necessarily entirely representative of, individuals' racial group membership. That gender and ethnicity are socially constructed is evident in the ways that definitions and performances of femininity and masculinity and of shared nationality and cultural traditions change across time and space. For instance, femininity in some cultures and time periods has been characterized by waifishness, and in others, it is epitomized by voluptuousness. In addition, whereas the colors pink and blue are currently viewed as feminine and masculine, respectively, in the early 20th century, men wore pink to project strength, whereas women wore blue because it denoted daintiness.[8] Similarly, identifying as Czech was defined differently before and after 1993 when the former Czechoslovakia separated into the Czech Republic and Slovakia, and currently, individuals who identify as Czech in Europe would most likely mean that they grew up in the Czech Republic, while Americans who identify as Czech would most likely mean that they had ancestors who were from Czechoslovakia.

Stereotypes associated with sex, gender, race, and ethnic categories are also social constructions without scientific basis. That is to say, because these concepts do not exist naturally, there are no inherent commonalities between individuals who are placed in categories relating to such constructions as woman/man/feminine/androgonous/masculine/Black/White/Hispanic/Asian/Arab/Irish/Jew nor are there inherent or biologically meaningful distinctions between individuals who are placed in different categories. For instance, people from Israel, Korea, India, Laos, and Russia do not all have something naturally in common because of politically created geographical barriers that designate them to be "Asian," while at the same time, a Native American male and a Latina woman who both have lung cancer may have both been biologically, environmentally, and socially predisposed to the disease. Similarly, all women do not naturally conform to uniform performances of femininity in terms of their appearance, interests, and objectives simply because they are labeled female, and some women do not conform to traditional notions of femininity at all.

Although categories associated with sex and race are not naturally occurring, membership within these categories, whether through self-identification or through the labeling of others, affects individuals' life chance opportunities where affiliation with different groups is associated with social privilege and disadvantage. The application of how socially constructed group membership results in differential treatment in sports contexts specifically is exemplified by the fact that white people believed that Blacks were biologically inferior to Whites, and Blacks were subsequently barred from athletic teams and events. Many people, especially males, continue to believe that women are not just biologically different from men; they also believe that women are biologically inferior to men and thus they are relegated to separate teams and rules for competition.

Blacks were historically excluded from many sports because they were perceived to be biologically and intellectually inferior, and consequently, they were thought to be unable to compete with Whites, and this ideology was supported by informal norms of exclusion as well as through legislation. Although Blacks participated in both amateur and professional sports after the Civil War into the late 1800s, legal segregation had a significant negative impact on their opportunities in athletics during the early 20th century.[9] Specifically, in the South, legislation forbade athletic interaction between Blacks and Whites, and it severely limited Blacks' sports participation opportunities. For instance, a 1933 Texas Penal Code provision prohibited boxing and wrestling between different races, an Atlanta City ordinance passed in 1932 banned black and white amateur baseball clubs from playing within two blocks of one another and, in 1956, Louisiana and Mississippi adopted ironclad segregation policies that made any form of interracial athletic participation illegal.[10]

At the college level, not only did prohibition of Blacks from attending certain white universities serve to limit their opportunities in college sports but also both formal and informal rules frequently resulted in Blacks' athletic exclusion in schools to which they were admitted. The power of informal tradition in baring Blacks from college sports is evident in "gentleman's agreements" between teams in certain conferences that prevented Blacks from playing in interleague competition, the establishment of unwritten quotas that restricted the number of black athletes on a team, and the fact that Northern schools would often travel without black team members for fear that their opponents would refuse to play against black players.[11]

Although the great majority of Northern colleges achieved at least some measure of integration in sports by the end of World War II, Southern schools only began to incorporate Blacks into their athletic programs in the late 1960s. When integration occurred, this change was most likely attributed to Title VI of the Civil Rights Act of 1964, which prohibits discrimination based on race, color, or national origin in programs or activities that receive federal financial assistance.[12] After Title VI was passed, black students and, consequently, black athletes became more prevalent at Southern universities. For instance, in Southern colleges, participation of black students in collegiate basketball increased from 22 percent to 61 percent from 1970 to 1985.[13] Interestingly, this trend had an unfortunate impact on historically black colleges and universities (HBCUs), as Southern universities began capitalizing on newfound black football prospects in their recruiting, ultimately resulting in the decline of many HBCU football programs.[14]

The "old-fashioned" racist ideology, which deemed Blacks biologically inferior, led to the establishment of discriminatory practices that clearly inhibited their access and success in sports. However, so too does current "modern" racist ideology that deems Blacks to be athletically gifted. The racialized conceptualization of Blacks' physical superiority has been coupled with a flawed ideology that Blacks are simultaneously intellectually inferior.[15] Rarely in the United States are athletically inclined individuals perceived to be smart, exemplified by common themes in media and education that play on notions of "brains vs. brawn" and the stereotypical "dumb jock."[16] This dualism is damaging for Blacks within sports because they are perceived not to be as adept at such high-pressure, less-physical sports as golf, and even in team sports Blacks are often stacked into peripheral positions that are thought to require less intellectual ability than others (e.g., football wide receiver and baseball outfielder), whereas white players are overrepresented in central or thinking positions (e.g., football quarterback and baseball pitcher).[17] Ideology suggesting false biological racial differences also results in biased attributions regarding perceptions of athletes' accomplishments and failures; when black athletes succeed, they are often thought to have had a natural advantage and, therefore, their hard work and skills are diminished, whereas when black athletes fail, they are thought to be squandering their innate potential or not putting forth enough effort.[18]

Like false attributions, perceptions, and misconceptions about race, sex segregation in sports is also a consequence of presumed innate biological differences between male and female athletes, which creates and reproduces a dominant sexist ideology that women are physically inferior, although there is no scientific or biological proof that a sex binary exists.[19] If women were able to procure the same opportunities in sport as men throughout their lifetimes, differences in ideology about physical ability between the sexes might dissipate similarly to how ideology associated with the athletic inferiority of Blacks has changed dramatically in the past several decades. Current racial ideology suggests that Blacks are physically superior to Whites, although empirical evidence has of course disproven the idea that genetically distinct muscle or skeletal structures make Blacks more suited to particular types of sports (e.g., basketball, rather than swimming; sprints rather than distance running in track), since both racial categories and sports are social inventions rather than naturally occurring entities. It is not inconceivable that like Blacks and Latinos, who were once banned from such sports as baseball, basketball, and football but are now overrepresented in those very same sports, women could conceivably achieve athletic success at rates similar to men if there existed a truly egalitarian gender ideology regarding their ability, if they were afforded equitable resources in coaching, facilities, and equipment, and if women modified their diets and exercise patterns to support athletic success. This book seeks to compare the ideologies associated with the concepts of sex and race to explore how the corresponding educational policies of Title IX and *Brown* have affected inequities in sports contexts and the larger society.

Most scholars, as well as the American public, recognize the impressive impact that Title IX has had on increasing athletic participation among girls and women. However, there exists disagreement about the extent to which Title IX has furthered sex equality and its potential to do so in the future. Most discussion about Title IX focuses on either implementation or lack thereof and whether Title IX policy has had a negative impact on men's sports; rarely is sex integration discussed as a feasible or necessary solution to end inequities in sports.[20] Although most academics argue that to achieve sex equity in sports, Title IX should be reworked or more strictly enforced,[21] this book discusses how dismantling Title IX's contact exclusion clause, in favor of sex integration, may solve problems associated with disparities in athletic contexts.

Working within the framework that sex equity in sports and in society is desirable, the current argument against applying the rule of *Brown* to sports is that this would decrease, if not eliminate, opportunities for women in athletics. We, however, disagree that sex integration in sports would necessarily result in diminished opportunities for women (and believe that specific policy measures should be taken to prevent the elimination of women's opportunities in sex-integrated sports), but even if women's participation were to decline somewhat in integrated contexts, it does not mean that segregation is acceptable. For instance, there are fewer opportunities for lower SES individuals to play such sports that require expensive facilities and equipment as ice hockey or equestrianism, but that does not mean that poor individuals who do compete should be relegated to separate leagues. In this book, we suggest that different policies can promote opportunities for girls and women, which they are currently denied, especially in such contact sports as football and wrestling, without diminishing the positive impact that sex-segregated teams have afforded women. We specifically look to women's colleges and HBCUs as examples and consider how these institutions have existed simultaneously with coed and predominantly white universities (PWUs) in a diverse higher education system and have consistently provided excellent educational opportunities to women and racial minorities, particularly in the areas of science, technology, engineering, and mathematics (STEM) fields. For example, neither HBCUs nor PWUs exclude students on the basis of race, rather, they provide different learning and social environments, while creating more equitable opportunities for access and success in higher learning. Similarly, both majority-female and majority-male sports teams and competitions may serve the particular interests of different players, coaches, and staff with varying abilities and needs, resulting in increased, rather than decreased, opportunities for sports participation for everyone. In addition, the promotion of female-only teams in conjunction with coed teams in a sex-integrated sports system is a feasible means for preserving opportunities in sports, similarly to how women's-only colleges have functioned to provide additional opportunities for higher education within an overarching sex-integrated system of higher education. In this book, we address concerns that the elimination of Title IX's contact sports exclusion clause would result in diminished opportunity for girls and women and provide specific recommendations for ensuring equity in terms of participation and success.

Aside from its focus on legislation, this book uses a sociological perspective to challenge biological, cultural, and social arguments that women cannot and should not compete with men. The book also considers why and how sex integration in sports may be beneficial *and* possible. We were motivated to write this book because sports arenas are one of the final places where sex segregation and the labeling of women as inferior are regarded as socially acceptable. Women in such other male-dominated institutions as the military and those working in STEM fields experience sexism, but it is no longer socially acceptable to assert that they are inferior or to legally deny them employment in these domains. For instance, in 2013, the Pentagon announced that it would integrate women into ground combat positions by 2016, although some specialties in the army and marine corps remain closed.[22] In addition, Nobel Prize-winning biologist, Sir Tim Hunt, sparked public indignation in June 2015 during his speech at the World

Conference of Science Journalists when he referred to female scientists as "girls" claiming: "Three things happen when they are in the lab: You fall in love with them, they fall in love with you, and when you criticize them, they cry." After intense condemnation, he resigned from his position as an honorary professor at University College London and his other professional appointments.[23] Whereas the general public expressed disapproval over Hunt's comments about mixed-sex laboratories, an athlete, commentator, or coach making similar statements about problems associated with mixed-sex sports most likely would not have experienced comparable criticism and repercussions.

Dominant sex and gender ideology suggesting women's perceived athletic inferiority and the subsequent relegation to inferior treatment in sports still too often goes unchallenged. This fact is especially interesting when one considers that sport is simultaneously viewed as meritocratic and unequal, especially when it comes to men's and women's interests and abilities. The institution of sport is unique in that most people view it as fair and egalitarian; the pressure to win ensures equity where the best people for the job get to start the game, play the most minutes, and serve as coaches and referees, where such idealized sporting principles as fairness and cooperation actually happen in real life. However, and although often unrecognized, inequalities exist in every aspect of sport where sex, race, class, and sexuality politics play a large role in forming and controlling both policy and practice, affecting who gets to play and under what circumstances.

Cyd Zeigler provides a recent example of how social inequalities are manifested in sport but are not generally viewed as problematic in his analysis of the differential treatment of two National Football League (NFL) Draft prospects, Michael Sam in 2014 and Shane Ray in 2015. Both Sam and Ray played the position of defensive end at the University of Missouri and were awarded the Southeastern Conference (SEC) Defensive Player of the Year, are of comparable physical size, performed similarly at the NFL scouting combine in the 40-yard dash, bench press, and vertical leap drills, and both had comparable amounts of sacks, tackles, forced fumbles, and touchdowns in their college careers. The major difference between the two players was that leading up to their respective drafts, Ray was charged with drug possession while Sam came out as gay.[24] Ray was drafted 226 spots ahead of Sam, yet there was limited public awareness or anger regarding the homophobia that Sam experienced, resulting in his loss of millions of dollars and possibly the end of his football career.[25] Instead, both Ray's and Sam's draft experiences were rationalized by commentators, coaches, and players who crafted distinct story lines that legitimized their differential treatment; commentators focused on why Sam's skills and size would not translate to the NFL and minimalized his college success while they did the opposite for Ray, diminishing his disappointing combine performance and pointing to his college career as the reason for why he was a top NFL prospect.[26]

Another illustration of how sexism is manifest in sport contexts involves Diana Nyad, who on August 31, 2013, at 64 years old became the first confirmed person to swim from Cuba to Florida—without a shark cage. The way in which Nyad's historic achievement was portrayed by her alma mater, Emory University, in a magazine article[27] highlights the sexist treatment female athletes frequently experience in the media, where their femininity rather than athletic prowess is emphasized and their physical accomplishments are ignored or diminished. When examining this article in particular, it is important to note that Emory is not an unbiased source and has a vested interest in portraying their alumni in the most positive way possible to attract top students and donors.

Nevertheless, in the Emory Magazine online article, Nyad is depicted in a head shot wearing a pink shirt and looking out into the distance; she is not pictured in her uniform, swimming, or breaking the record. The first sentence of the article suggests that outside factors rather than her athletic ability and personal determination were responsible for her achievement, emphasizes her past failures rather than the impressiveness of her swim, and includes a typo about her age, indicating that this story may not have been a priority for the publication: "Good luck and favorable current buoyed 64-four-year-old Diana Nyad (Emory College, 1971) this time around, as she became the first person confirmed to swim from Cuba to Florida without the protection of a shark cage." In the mere 350-word story, the third paragraph mentions that Nyad was dismissed from the university for attempting to parachute out of her dorm window, while the sixth paragraph alludes to the idea that because of her fast time, Nyad may have received unlawful assistance during her swim.[28] Instead of discussing positive contributions Nyad made to the university or lauding her extraordinary accomplishment, the article portrays her as a delinquent and perhaps even a cheat. Although there are no comparable cases to date, it can be argued that if a male alumni had broken the same record, Emory magazine would have reported on his training and nutrition regimen, his thoughts during the 53 hours he spent in the water, and on why the feat was rare and meaningful; these critical themes were not mentioned, at all, in the piece about Nyad.

Sam's and Nyad's experiences demonstrate how the pervasive homophobia and sexism that permeate the larger society are manifest in sports contexts, despite the common perception that sports are meritocratic. In addition, Sam's treatment may likely reinforce sexual inequality both ideologically, where his story will serve as an example that gay players cannot make it in the NFL, and in practice, where gay athletes may hesitate to come out for fear of similar mistreatment and gay individuals may be discouraged from playing football and other sports. Similarly, skepticism concerning Nyad's momentous swim may make women less motivated to break records or promote their accomplishments for fear of negative publicity and character assassination. Because dominant sex and gender ideology are related to the way in which events in sports are constructed and associated with future outcomes, it can be argued that social inequality is both reflected and reproduced in sports contexts, and sports provide a prism through which to examine broad societal patterns on inequality.

Most people generally understand that social institutions, other than sport, are unequal. For instance, in government, it is easy to see sex inequality as we have yet to have a female president of the United States; in education, it is fairly obvious that there exists socioeconomic and racial disparities between schools in various neighborhoods; and in the criminal justice system, it is clear that the severity of punishment, justice, and fair treatment is often related to the racial characteristics of the perpetrators and victims involved in a crime. However, the dominant perception of sports organizations as meritocratic prevents questions, understanding, and challenges surrounding sexist, racist, homophobic, and classist sports ideology and practices. This book examines the false meritocracy and perceived egalitarian structure of sports to examine how covert and overt discrimination against women in athletics at the individual and institutional levels is not only harmful to women but to society as well.

Sport is not always viewed as a serious setting for academic research, although sport involvement has been associated with a number of important social, economic, political, and physical outcomes of interest to scientists, including self-esteem and self-efficacy, obesity and eating disorders, drug and alcohol use, sexual activity, socialization, character development, formation of relationships, and civic engagement. Furthermore, on a macrolevel, sport as an institution has important links to such other social institutions as the family (e.g., parents of all backgrounds invest considerable time and resources in supporting their children's sport involvement because sport is seen as a key context for positive youth development); education (e.g., a great deal of youth participate in school-based sport; National Collegiate Athletic Association (NCAA) championships in football and basketball have increased the number of applications universities received); law (e.g., court cases surrounding sport and the rights of athletes have affected federal and state legislation associated with privacy, freedom of religion, and commerce); and economics (e.g., countless jobs and businesses are created by sport; cities have spent millions of taxpayers' dollars building stadiums). On a microlevel, sport is deeply meaningful where millions of people devote massive amounts of time, energy, and resources to playing, watching, and consuming sport. The way in which sport profoundly affects individuals' lives is evidenced by the fact that fans who oftentimes have no direct connection to a team—they do not know any of the players personally and have no vested economic interest in the organization—internalize wins and losses as if they were their own successes and failures. In addition, because it is one of the last remaining legally sex-segregated institutions, and because sport is widely perceived to be both egalitarian and meritocratic, sports contexts, in particular, offer a valuable framework for examining sexist ideologies, practices, and differential returns on participation for women and men who expose and reify sexism in the larger social structure.

For us, the institution of sport is not only fertile ground for investigating social inequality but it also provides an exciting setting for achieving large-scale social change. Similarly to how inequities in social structures are mutually reinforcing, so too are social victories. In fact, sport as a social institution has served as a historic avenue for social and political protest and change. For example, in the majority of Olympic games from 1956 to 1988, certain countries boycotted or were banned for political reasons,[29] Jackie Robinson broke the baseball color barrier in 1947, years before U.S. schools were integrated and many expected that the elimination of the color line in baseball—the national pastime—would spur similar changes outside of sports, and despite its conservative contingent of fans, in 2015, the National Association for Stock Car Auto Racing (NASCAR) publicly condemned Indiana legislation that legalized religious discrimination against lesbian, gay, bisexual, and transgender (LGBT) individuals[30] (about a year earlier, the NFL threatened to pull the 2015 Super Bowl out of the state of Arizona if similar legislation was passed there).[31] The goal of this book is not only to explore how sex integration in sports may result in the advancement of women's overall social status but also to consider potential societal benefits, as well as to recommend strategies for achieving integrated sports competition.

The topic of sex integration in sports is timely because women are continuing to shatter previously held expectations regarding their athletic ability, and their place in athletics. For instance, U.S. female athletes outperformed their male teammates, even in such traditional male-dominated or masculine-type sports as boxing, judo, shooting, and wrestling in the 2012 London Olympics.[32] Despite her 5'0", 100 lb. frame, Kacy Catanzaro was the first woman to complete the final American Ninja Warrior course on July 14, 2014.[33] Mo'Ne Davis, at 13 years old, became the first female athlete to pitch a shutout in Little League History on August 10, 2014 and the first little leaguer (male or female) to grace the cover of *Sports Illustrated*.[34] The San Antonio Spurs hired Becky Hammon to be the first female assistant coach in the National Basketball Association (NBA) on August 5, 2014 and Hammon became the first female head coach in summer league history in 2015.[35] (Natalie Nakase served as an assistant coach for the Los Angeles Clippers in 2014.)[36] In July 2015, the Arizona Cardinals hired Jen Welter to coach inside linebackers, making her the first woman to hold an NFL coaching position of any kind.[37] Michele Roberts was named executive director of the NBA Players Association in July 2014, becoming the first woman to hold that position and the first woman to head a major professional sports union in North America.[38] In September 2014, Noora Räty became the first Finnish woman to play in a men's professional ice hockey league,[39] and in December 2014, Elana Meyers Taylor (United States) and Kallie Humphries (Canada) became the first women to pilot four-man bobsleds in a World Cup race.[40] Women's basketball teams averaged 69.5 points per game in the first round of the 2015 NCAA basketball tournament, while men's teams averaged 67.8,[41] and in the 2015 NCAA overall three-point shootout, female guard/forward Cassandra Brown of the University of Portland beat Gonzaga's male guard, Kevin Pangos.[42] In the summer of 2015, 12-year-old Sam Gordon, who had become an Internet sensation for her peewee football performances against boys, founded America's first girls tackle football league for fifth and sixth graders.[43] Finally, Pat Summitt still holds the record for the most all-time wins for a coach in NCAA basketball history of either men's or women's team in any division.[44]

It is important to point out that these accomplishments occurred in a world where women are consistently viewed and treated as biologically, physically, and athletically inferior to men. Women are socialized to believe they are naturally disadvantaged in sports, often are afforded fewer coaches, substandard equipment and facilities, have limited opportunities for participation, and receive a fraction of the return on their accomplishments, in terms of financial and social accolades, compared to their male counterparts. In this book, we attempt to lay out the potential for sex integration in sports to increase success for women both in sports and in society and to offer recommendations for why and how sex integration may be a better alternative to segregation for the greater good, socially, legally, and ethically.

The book is structured as follows: Chapter 2 outlines the history, implementation, results, and controversies surrounding Title IX. Chapter 3 presents background on the *Brown* ruling and compares the intentions and consequences of *Brown* and Title IX as national educational equity policies. Chapter 4 provides a sociological perspective on the concepts of sex and race and addresses reservations about sport integration regarding assumed biological differences between females and males. Chapter 5 compares the objectives of Title IX and *Brown* and presents evidence of why sex integration is necessary within the current opportunity structure in the United States. Chapter 6 discusses potential benefits of sex integration within and beyond sport in such domains as the workforce, family, media, and education systems and highlights potential benefits of sex integration for nongender-conforming individuals. Chapter 7 outlines specific steps to initiate the desegregation process in sports, and also offers recommendations for policy makers on how to evaluate and ensure the continued success of athletic sex integration.

CHAPTER TWO

Title IX

History, Results, and Controversies of "Separate but Equal"

The civil rights movement and the women's movement have spawned decades of debate on the concept of equality. Sometimes the answers have been glaringly obvious; other times they have been elusive. In the early days of these movements, discrimination was often blatant, with jobs reserved for only whites or only men. Such explicit, facial distinctions have all but vanished in the face of constitutional claims . . . One significant exception, however, is sports, where we continue to accept, expect, and even defend sex segregation as the status quo.

—B. Glenn George[1]

Background

Social justice legislation is never conceived or established in a vacuum, and Title IX emerged in the context of domestic, international women's, and civil rights movements. Feminists in the United States, like U.S. civil rights activists, made discrimination and equality the major political issues. Thus, the passage of Title IX and the Women's Educational Equity Act of 1974 (WEEA), which provided programmatic funding to implement many of the principles set forth in Title IX[2]—like *Brown v. Board of Education* and the civil rights legislation of the 1960s—represented major achievements for social justice advocates seeking an end to the systemic inequities that permeated the U.S. educational system.[3]

Title IX was intended to address broad societal sex disparities rooted, at least in part, in educational inequities. For example, before Title IX, sex stereotypes in school textbooks defined very limited "gender appropriate" roles for girls. Indeed, the textbook roles typically defined as appropriate for girls, constrained their access to mathematics and science courses in high school, STEM majors in college, and scientific careers in adulthood. Sex sorting in schools affected female opportunities at every level of education. Even in high school vocational programs, most girls could only take courses that trained them for such low-wage, traditionally female jobs as cooks or cosmetologists, not such better paying "male" jobs as mechanics or electricians. In addition, teenage girls who became pregnant often faced expulsion from school because of the prevailing social norms. Before Title IX, female educators mainly taught in elementary and secondary schools and women had very few faculty or administrative opportunities in higher education. Girls and women also had little recourse for addressing sexual harassment in all its varied forms. Sex bias in standardized testing resulted in lower female performance. Females' access to computer technology and technical training was also limited by gender stereotypes in a society that defined technology as a masculine, and thus exclusively male, domain.

Considerable progress has been achieved in the post-Title IX era: gender stereotypes are slowly but steadily changing, girls can now pursue career training in such courses as aviation or automotive repair and have access to upper-level STEM courses required for pursuing a college major in these fields at the same rate as boys, and in most disciplines, women are more equitably represented among college faculty. In addition, women now constitute about half (47 percent in 2011) of medical school matriculates,[4] and women received 45 percent of PhDs in biology awarded from 1999 to 2003.[5] Nevertheless, significant sex disparities persist, and the playing field remains uneven in many respects. Indeed, on the 30th Anniversary of Title IX, a sex equity report card by the National Coalition for Women and Girls in Education (2002) assigned the following areas specific to sex equity progress grades: Access to Higher Education (B), Athletics (C+), Career Education (D), Employment (C−), Learning Environment (C−), Math and Science (B−), Sexual Harassment (C), Standardized Testing (C), Technology (D+), and Treatment of Pregnant/Parenting Students (C+).[6] A decade later, the Title IX 40th Anniversary Report of the National Women's Law Center noted some continuing progress, but significant challenges remain, including sex wage gaps and glass ceilings.[7]

Title IX and Athletics: A Brief History

Historically, females' athletic participation opportunities have been limited. Beginning with their early development in the 19th century, organized sports in the United States aimed to develop and nurture among young males such socially desirable qualities as cooperation, strength, assertiveness, and responsibility.[8] In this context, girls were neither encouraged nor allowed to participate in most sports, as traditional gender attitudes did not include a role in sports for females. Consequently, sports have typically been characterized as a male-dominated and hypermasculine space,[9] where competitiveness, physical prowess, heteronormativity, and other traditional values associated with masculinity prevail.[10] Clearly, before the enactment of Title IX, women's athletic opportunities were severely limited by widespread sex inequalities. Thus, Title IX advocates expected that this legislation would assist in leveling the playing field in athletics as well as in nonsport educational contexts.

Ironically, and perhaps surprising to some, athletics was not a prominent focus in most discussions of sex inequalities in education, nor was athletics specifically mentioned in the original Title IX legislation. The way in which Title IX regulations applied to athletics was generally an afterthought until after enactment. For example, even Senator Evan Bayh (IN), one of the leading sponsors of the legislation, who later became known as the "Godfather of Title IX," deflected attention away from the subject when the issue of sports was mentioned in floor debates before Title IX's passage.[11]

However, after Title IX was enacted, the Department of Health, Education, and Welfare (HEW) pointed out that the law did apply to athletics.[12] This led to intense lobbying by Title IX opponents to amend the law to exempt sports generally or, at the very least, to exempt men's revenue-producing sports.[13] For example, the NCAA initially sought to have athletic departments exempted from Title IX, its executive director condemned the legislation as the "possible doom of intercollegiate sports," and a number of high-profile college football head coaches also lobbied against the legislation.[14] Senator John Tower (TX) twice proposed amendments to exempt revenue-producing sports from Title IX compliance; both were defeated. Senator Javitz (NY) proposed a successful alternative amendment requiring HEW to "include . . . reasonable provisions considering the nature of the particular sports" in Title IX's application to intercollegiate athletics.[15] In 1975, HEW issued regulations that specified how Title IX applied to educational athletic programs and subsequent information on eliminating sex discrimination in athletics, which was distributed to school officials.[16] In the same year, HEW also issued regulations that gave elementary schools one year to comply, and high schools and colleges three years to comply with Title IX. Attempts in Congress seeking to reject the HEW regulations and to amend Title IX failed to pass, such as an update of the Tower Amendment. In addition, Sen. Jesse Helms (NC) also twice sought, unsuccessfully, to implement legislation that would prohibit the application of Title IX regulations to athletics, where student participation is not required by the school's curriculum.[17] In 1976, the NCAA filed a lawsuit challenging the Title IX athletic regulations, which was unsuccessful.[18] Since its inception, the legality and interpretation of the Title IX statute have been repeatedly contested, not just because it represented a major challenge to dominant ideology regarding sex, gender, and sports but also because the legislative language was quite broad and lacked specificity, especially with regard to its application to athletics.[19]

In practice, a major challenge for Title IX has been ensuring that schools comply with the law. In 1979, HEW's policy interpretation provided three ways for schools to be Title-IX compliant, which became known as the "three prong test."

> Prong One requires schools to provide females athletic participation opportunities that correlate with their share of the student enrollment. This requirement or condition is met when male and female participation opportunities, in comparison to their respective enrollments, are "substantially proportionate." This is commonly referred to as the "proportionality test."

> Prong Two requires schools to demonstrate a continual expansion of athletic opportunities for the traditionally underrepresented sex (typically female). This requirement or condition is met when a school has demonstrated a history and continuing practice of program expansion that parallels the developing interests and abilities of the underrepresented sex.

> Prong Three requires schools to accommodate the interest and ability of the underrepresented sex (typically female). This requirement or condition is met when an institution can provide evidence that it is meeting the interests and abilities of its female students, regardless of whether there are disproportionately fewer female sports participants or opportunities for female participation in sports.

Although Title IX only requires schools to comply with any, not all, of the three prongs, many high schools and colleges have yet to achieve equity.[20] The first prong—proportionality test—has become the criteria through which most schools attempt to achieve compliance with Title IX regulations. Unfortunately, to meet the proportionality compliance standard, many schools have cut men's programs, even though reducing men's sport participation opportunities was not the objective of Title IX nor the manner in which the Office for Civil Rights (OCR) desired compliance. Furthermore, proportionality or equity was not the only option for Title IX compliance. Athletic departments can demonstrate that they are complying with Title IX, simply by showing that they are making efforts to achieve, rather than by actually achieving parity, in sports participation, treatment, and financial assistance.

Despite the fact that Title IX prohibited sex discrimination in schools and universities receiving federal funds, implementation was decelerated by both the gendered practices of educational institutions and the Supreme Court's 1984 Grove City decision, which took away Title IX coverage of athletics, except for scholarships, thus weakening the law.[21] In 1987, Congress passed the Civil Rights Restoration Act, despite President Ronald Reagan's veto, to reverse Grove City and restore Title IX's institution-wide coverage.[22] Therefore, in schools that receive federal funds for any program or activity, all of those schools' programs and activities must be Title IX compliant.

After HEW's Title IX regulations were implemented in 1975, over a six-year period the number of girls participating in high school sports grew from 300,000 in 1972 to more than 2 million in 1978. In a similar manner female participation in college sports increased twofold, from 32,000 in 1972 to more than 64,000 in 1977.[23] Although this early growth was significant, it was not equitable. For example, in 1979, the sports participation rate for high school girls was less than half that of boys (i.e., nationally, girls were only 48 percent as likely as boys to be involved in interscholastic athletics).[24] Opposition to Title IX and inadequate funding have continuously hampered full enforcement of the act. As a result, females remain underrepresented in both high school and college sports and still do not enjoy the same resources as their male counterparts.[25]

The slow pace of implementing Title IX, in the face of both public resistance and legal challenges, has also been quite similar to what occurred with implementing school desegregation following *Brown*. For example, nearly a decade after the Court's ruling, 99 percent of Blacks in the South still attended schools that were completely segregated and most Southern school districts had done nothing to implement the law.[26] It required the power of President Lyndon Johnson and the historic 1964 Civil Rights Act to achieve meaningful enforcement of school desegregation by threatening districts with a loss of federal funds or lawsuit if they failed to desegregate.[27] Desegregation requirements were subsequently raised yearly and a 1968 Supreme Court ruling mandated that desegregation be comprehensive and immediate in states that were traditionally segregated, which actually caused Southern schools to become the nation's most integrated.

Nevertheless, despite becoming "the law of the land," school desegregation was constantly challenged, both in judicial courts and in the court of

public opinion. As a consequence of continuing legal challenges to the principles of *Brown*, the nation's schools have become increasingly resegregated.
Two major factors have contributed to resegregation in public schools:
First, starting as early as 1986 in a Norfolk, VA school desegregation case,
the federal courts began ruling that once a school district has fully implemented the policies and practices imposed by court order, the district would
be declared "unitary" and thus would no longer be bound to continue court-
mandated desegregation policies and practices, even if discontinuing them
resulted in the district's schools once again becoming segregated.[28] Second,
as more conservative justices were appointed, the Supreme Court's guiding
philosophy on school desegregation shifted from a focus on remedying
individual harms as was done in *Brown* to a philosophy where *limited* desegregation remedies would be permitted only when there exists a compelling
state interest. In effect, school desegregation and student diversity advocates
now have to demonstrate that communities, rather than individuals or social
groups, are harmed by segregation and racial isolation in schools.

Title IX has also faced continuing challenges in the courts. Many of the
athletics-focused lawsuits and legal challenges to Title IX have come from
males in such nonrevenue sports as wrestling, or swimming and diving,
which face elimination, or have been eliminated. However, there are still a
number of cases where female plaintiffs have been compelled to file lawsuits
to gain, or protect, their access to athletic opportunities. For example, in
2009, female volleyball players filed, and won, a lawsuit against Quinnipiac
University (CT) when the institution dropped volleyball and replaced it
with cheerleading, which the court ruled, violated Title IX as cheerleading
did not count as a sport.[29] Fort Valley State University (GA) dropped its
women's volleyball team in 2012, but was forced to reinstate the team and
players' scholarships, because dropping the team caused the institution to
fall out of compliance with Title IX proportionality requirements.[30] These
two cases are examples of the broad and complex challenges facing Title IX
proponents. Even though faced with persistent resistance and legal challenges, Title IX has had a major impact on women and society. The impact
of Title IX has been the subject of extensive research and legal analysis. It
is ironic, however, that although exponentially more females play high school
sports, most analyses of the impact of Title IX have focused on college sports.
In the following section, we consider the effects of Title IX on sex equity
in both high school and college athletics, for women and men, as well as
its impact on U.S. society, writ large.

Title IX's Effect on Females

Female Participation Opportunities

High School Sports

According to the High School Athletics Participation Survey conducted annually by the National Federation of State High School Associations (NFHS), the number of participants in high school sports increased for the 25th consecutive year.[31] Figure 2.1 shows the number of girls and boys participating in high school sports over time. In 2013–2014, overall high school sports participation reached a record high of 7,795,658, and this growth—a net increase of 82,081 from 2012 to 2013—represented the highest single-year gain since 2009–2010. Among girls, high school sports participation also increased for the 25th consecutive year. Female high school sports participation growth—with a net increase of 44,941—reached a record high of 3,267,664. Likewise, boys' high school sports participation also reached an all-time high—with more than 4.5 million male participants for the first time (4,527,994).

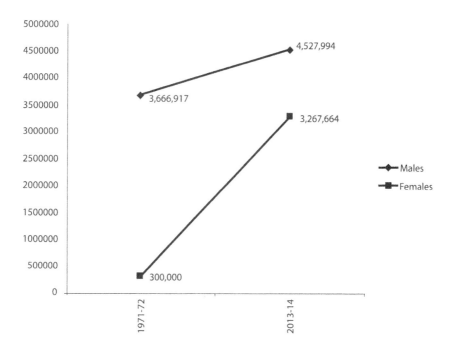

Figure 2.1 Number of Boys and Girls Participating in High School Sports: 1971–2014.

For the top 10 boys' high school sports, the largest increase in participation was in baseball (+7,838), followed by football (+6,437) and soccer
(+6,437), during the past year. In terms of overall participation numbers
across all sports, the top 10 boys' sports were football (1,093,234), outdoor
track and field (580,321), basketball (541,054), baseball (482,629), soccer
(417,419), wrestling (269,514), cross country (252,547), tennis (160,545),
golf (152,647), and swimming and diving (138,373). Among girls, the top
10 sports were outdoor track and field (478,885), basketball (433,344),
volleyball (429,634), soccer (374,564), softball (364,297), cross country
(218,121), tennis (184,080), swimming and diving (165,779), competitive
spirit squads (120,593), and lacrosse (81,969). During the past year, volleyball was the female high school sport, showing the greatest participation
increase (+9,426), followed by track and field (+5,946).

As the data in Figure 2.1 indicate, since the passage of Title IX, girls have
made tremendous participation gains in high school athletics, yet female
athletes remain significantly underrepresented in most sports. In addition,
despite the fact that 6 of the top 10 sports for boys and girls are the same—
track and field, basketball, soccer, cross country, tennis, and swimming/diving
in high school (and postsecondary school)—each of these specific (along
with most other) sports remains largely sex segregated and, as such, represents an important institutional context for examining sex equity in society.

One of the more disappointing aspects of female advances in athletic participation in the post-Title IX era concerns the unevenness of the increased
opportunities across demographic population subgroups. For example,
compared to white females, girls of color have not experienced comparable growth in participation opportunities. In addition, as intersectionality
theory would suggest, sports participation opportunities also differ with
regard to schools' socioeconomic characteristics resources available to support extracurricular programs.[32] In public schools, girls continue to have
lower rates of sports participation than boys, girls of color have lower rates
of participation than white girls, and girls of color from low SES families
have the lowest overall participation rates.[33] Thus, with regard to access to
sports participation opportunities, poor, minority females seem to face the
sort of triple jeopardy implied by intersectionality scholars. More specifically, these race, sex, and class differences in sports participation reflect
the lived experiences of black girls and white girls. Because of racial disparities in poverty, schools in which black girls attend often "have fewer
material resources (such as gymnasiums or athletic fields), human resources
(coaches or physical education teachers), or programmatic support (such
as fewer intramural and extramural sports programs)."[34] In addition, black
female participation in high school sports has often been limited to such

sports as basketball and track and field, which are the least expensive for both the athletes and schools.[35]

Research also shows that such individual-level factors as students' SES and academic achievement affect their sports involvement. For example, higher SES students are more likely to participate in sports than their lower class counterparts.[36] Higher SES students are also more likely to attend schools in higher status communities that offer more opportunities to play sports.[37] Likewise, racial differences in sports participation often occur because black students are more likely to attend schools in lower-status communities that offer fewer opportunities to play sports.[38] Furthermore, white students are more likely to attend private schools, located in more affluent communities that offer students more opportunities to play sports, and students in private schools compared to students in public schools are almost twice as likely to play sports.[39] A recent report of high school freshman shows disparities in sports participation, whereas 58 percent of white girls participate, only 42 percent of black girls participate.[40] As research has shown, this participation disparity likely reflects differential access to school-based sports, more than different levels of interest in sports between black and white girls.[41] In addition, compared to their white counterparts, black girls receive less support from teachers to engage in physical activity.[42]

Nationally, racial and economic school segregation has resulted in diminished opportunities for students of color and students from poor families to participate in both academic and such extracurricular activities as sports.[43] Thus, all students at high-poverty and high-minority schools have limited opportunities to play sports, especially females. Sports participation among girls of color is not only substantially lower than that of white girls but it is also significantly lower than the participation rates for boys, regardless of race.[44] These intersectional variations in athletic opportunities have not received public and policy attention because there has been very little research examining the issue. However, in a recent study, the National Women's Law Center and Poverty and Race Research Action Council used data from schools with student bodies that were either 90 percent or more white or 10 percent less white to document sports opportunity disparities related to race and sex. The results demonstrated that relative to their enrollment, girls of color receive far fewer opportunities to participate in athletics, in terms of available spots on teams, than white girls, white boys, and boys of color. From a policy perspective, the researchers suggest that these disparities not only deprive girls of color the benefits associated with sports participation but also that this systematic failure for equitable treatment violates legislation prohibiting discrimination by sex (Title IX) and race (Title VI).[45] These results also parallel Tracy Richmond et al.'s findings of similar levels of physical activity among black, Hispanic, and white adolescent girls attending the same schools, where disparities between white girls and girls of color emerge overall because girls of color are more likely to attend poor, racially isolated schools with lower rates of physical activity,[46] although these patterns are not found for boys.[47]

Moneque Walker Pickett et al. report that in 1972, black females were slightly (14 percent) more likely to participate in high school sports than white females, but this trend has changed over time, where in 2002, black females were less likely to participate in high school sports (20 percent).[48] They also found that compared to white females, black females' high schools were less likely to offer such sports as soccer, crew, volleyball, or softball. These high school sports, sometimes referred to as "growth sports," provide opportunities to develop skills and experiences leading to college scholarships, because they are the same sports that colleges have adopted to expand female athletic opportunities to achieve Title IX compliance.[49] The NCAA Committee on Women's Athletics defines a "growth" or "emerging" sport as one "that is intended to help schools provide more athletics opportunities for women, more sport sponsorship options for institutions and help that sport achieve NCAA championship status."[50] Notable examples of the success of growth sports include women's crew and soccer. Across all three divisions, NCAA data show that between the 1981–1982 and 2013–2014 academic years, the number of women's crew teams tripled— increasing from 43 to 145. During the same time frame, the number of women's soccer teams grew exponentially—from 80 to 1,022.[51] From the outset, when colleges began to recruit females in those sports, to comply with Title IX, athletic scholarships in soccer, volleyball, crew, or softball have also been disproportionately awarded to white females. Thus, the way high schools expanded female athletic opportunities in response to Title IX benefitted white girls by offering a broad array of new sports teams, but black girls' high schools continued to constrain their participation opportunities to two low-cost sports, basketball and track and field, exacerbating racial inequities in access to school sports among girls.[52]

College Sports

Figure 2.2 shows NCAA data illustrating the growth in the number of females and males participating in intercollegiate sports since Title IX.[53] In the school year (1971–1972) preceding enactment of the law, fewer than 30,000 women participated in intercollegiate sports. By 2013–2014, however, the number of college female athletes exceeded 200,000—almost seven times the pre-Title IX rate. In their efforts to comply with Title IX, NCAA institutions have adopted an ever expanding array of sports available

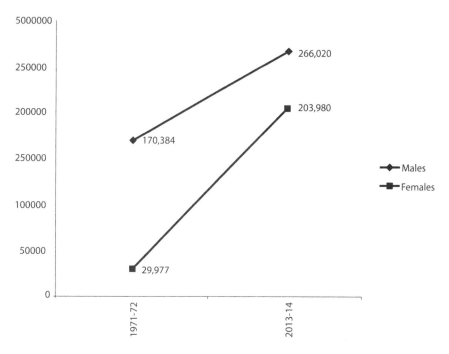

Figure 2.2 Number of Males and Females Participating in College Sports: 1971–2014.

for female college athletes. Among females, outdoor track and field has traditionally been the largest women's sport, followed by soccer, indoor track and field, softball, volleyball, basketball, and cross country, respectively. This pattern remains generally consistent today across all divisions of the NCAA, except that soccer has overtaken track and field as the top female sport in Divisions II and III.[54]

Among NCAA female athletes, NCAA data show that the top 10 sports in terms of participation numbers during the 2013–2014 academic year were outdoor track and field (478,885), soccer (374,564), indoor track and field (478,885), softball (364,297), volleyball (429,634), basketball (433,344), cross country (218,121), swimming and diving (165), lacrosse (81,969), and tennis (184,080). Among male athletes, the top 10 sports were football (1,093,234), baseball (482,629), outdoor track and field (580,321), indoor track and field (580,321), soccer (417,419), basketball (541,054), cross country (252,547), lacrosse (81,969), swimming and diving (138,373), and golf (152,647).[55] Like the situation noted for high school sports, 5 of the top 10 sports for men and women are the same—outdoor track and field, indoor track and field, basketball, soccer, cross country, tennis, and swimming/diving—yet, these *in common* intercollegiate sports also remain largely sex segregated and continue to serve as barriers to true sex equity in sports and society.

The NCAA offers both championship and nonchampionship sports. Data from the 1981–1982 to 2013–2014 NCAA Sports Sponsorship and Participation Rates Report show that the number of championship sport teams available to females has increased steadily over the past 30 years. According to NCAA reports, females gained slightly more championship teams (140) than men (111) over the past three decades. Nevertheless, more male student-athletes (56.6 percent of the total) than female student-athletes (43.4 percent) participate in championship sports, and during the 2013–2014 academic year, the average NCAA member institution had approximately 187 female and 243 male student-athletes.

Since the 1981–1982 academic year, the most offered women's championship sport has been basketball, and other highly sponsored women's sports include volleyball, cross country, soccer, softball, tennis, and track and field, respectively. Similarly to women's basketball, NCAA data show that men's basketball is the sport offered most for men, although because interest and appropriateness of sport type is thought to differ by sex, the other frequently sponsored men's championship sports differ slightly from women's: cross country, baseball, golf, soccer, tennis, track and field, and football, respectively. These patterns are generally consistent across Divisions I, II, and III of the NCAA for both women and men.[56]

In their efforts to comply with Title IX, many institutions of higher education have focused on adopting "growth" sports to increase female participation opportunities. NCAA statistical data show that between 1988 and 2014, member institutions have gained an additional 2,703 women's varsity athletic teams. During that period, the most frequently added sport has been soccer; however, golf, indoor track and field, cross country, outdoor track and field, and softball have experienced growth as well.[57] Another frequent strategy for increasing female sport participation involves adopting such "emerging" sports as archery, badminton, equestrian, rugby, squash, synchronized swimming, and team handball.[58] As in the case of high school athletics, focusing on growth sports in higher education also results in constrained athletic participation and scholarship opportunities for women of color as a consequence of their limited access to these activities in the high schools they attend.[59] For example, since 1995, some of the key emerging sports adopted by NCAA member institutions include ice hockey, water polo, rugby, and equestrian.[60] Current participation data show that these sports continue to draw a vast majority of white female participants, where white females constitute the majority of sports on teams: ice hockey

(75 percent), water polo (68 percent), rugby (64 percent), and equestrian (91 percent).[61] Thus, females overall have made considerable progress in increasing athletic participation; a long-standing black–white female participation gap in intercollegiate athletics has not abated and indeed continues to widen as a result of growing differential sports access opportunities, which deprives black females from returns on the benefits of sports participation.[62] To increase women's athletic opportunities and to meet Title IX mandates, most colleges and universities have strategically added nontraditional sports for women. An important, but perhaps, unintended consequence of this approach has been that the nontraditional sports most often recruit female athletes from a primarily white talent pool. Because of their disproportionate attendance at urban, high-minority, low-income schools—which offer only a very limited range of sports—black females face a pipeline problem. In their high schools, black female athletes are primarily concentrated in basketball and track and field and receive little, if any, opportunity to participate in nontraditional sports. As a result, they lack opportunities to develop the skills and experience sought by coaches and recruiters of the most-offered growth sports, volleyball, soccer, and crew. Thus, the expansion of teams and scholarships in these sports disproportionately benefit white female athletes, whereas female athletes of color are less well positioned to reap the benefits of expanded sports opportunities resulting from Title IX.

For example, the NCAA reported that in 1999, across all divisions, 9 percent of all female college athletes were black, but black women were overrepresented in basketball (22.5 percent) and underrepresented in most growth and emerging such sports as soccer (3 percent), lacrosse (0.7 percent), and crew (0.6 percent). More than a decade later, in 2014, NCAA data reveal that little has changed: black female athletic participation across all divisions (10.9 percent) had increased by a little more than 1 percent, but their overrepresentation in basketball (23.4 percent) and both indoor (23 percent) and outdoor (25 percent) track and field persisted.[63] From these data, it is apparent that compared to white women, black women remain underrepresented in college sports overall and the progress in women's sports participation rates has been inequitable. In addition, according to NCAA statistics, not counting football and baseball that have no female athletes, black females continue to be underrepresented in 24 of the 27 other sports.[64]

Taken together, the evidence presented here demonstrates two things: First, since Title IX was passed, both female high school and college athletes have made dramatic gains in the overall participation numbers, the range of sports available to them is much more extensive, and females increasingly participate in contact sports, and second, the benefits of this historic gender equity legislation have been unequally distributed, with female athletes of color receiving fewer sport participation gains than their white counterparts. Thus, for females of color, both sex discrimination and race–ethnic discrimination remain significant barriers to achieving the objectives of Title IX—full equality of opportunity for girls and women in sports. Legal scholars have noted that the precedent of support for sex equity in athletics set by Title IX and equal protection litigation, including Title VII, is clear; however, it is also clear that Title IX has not adequately addressed issues of equity in athletics for women of color.[65]

Developmental and Other Outcomes for Females

Sport participants, in general, may derive social, economic, health, and academic economic benefits from their involvement. Therefore, it is imperative that females—to receive the same life-chance opportunities as males—be given equal opportunities for participation in athletics. In addition, because the benefits of sports participation are far reaching and persist throughout the life course, it is important not just for girls and women but also for our society as a whole that females have equitable access in sports. The empirically documented benefits of sports participation are outlined in this chapter,[66] while the potential benefits of integrated sports contexts, for both girls and women and for society in general, are discussed in Chapter 6.

Social Benefits

In general, sports are perceived to provide children with such social skills as interacting with both peers (e.g., teammates and opponents) and authority figures (e.g., coaches and referees), learning how to graciously win and lose, and developing qualities associated with leadership and cooperation that translate to other social contexts.[67] Research shows that sport is an important popularity indicator for boys.[68] However, for girls and black males compared to white males, sport does not mean as much in terms of popularity.[69] In addition, Casey Knifsend and Sandra Graham examined how ninth grade sports participation relates to perceived sex discrimination from peers and adults at school over four time points spanning throughout high school. They found that girls who played sports perceived greater sex discrimination as well as accelerated peer sex discrimination than girls who did not play sports.[70] In addition, researchers have found that playing sports can teach and reinforce positive social behaviors.[71]

Research also shows that both females and males derive long-term employment and economic benefits from sports participation in schools.[72]

Thus, sports participation can play a vital role in women's, as well as men's, academic and professional success, as well as the success of our society, where large-scale improvements in academic and employment contexts contribute to collective benefits.

Physical and Mental Health Benefits

Sports contexts serve as a space and opportunity to commit to engagement in exercise that ultimately leads to improved individual and collective physical health. Youth sports participation is negatively associated with obesity and positively associated with sports participation in adulthood, leading to the reduction of obesity and such other poor health outcomes as cardiovascular disease and type 2 diabetes, which are related to physical inactivity throughout the life course.[73] Therefore, the process of socialization into sports and the continued modeling of sports participation in social contexts positively affect the physical health of our society. In addition, for females specifically, sports participation may also act as a buffer against body dissatisfaction and disordered eating[74] and teenage pregnancy.[75]

Aside from improved physical health, sports participation has been linked with mental health benefits and, specifically, positive returns on self-esteem and efficacy,[76] and psychological health, well-being, and management skills.[77] The Association for Applied Sport Psychology (AASP) lists several other psychological benefits obtained through physical activity related to improvements in mood, ability to cope with stress, and energy levels, and decreased symptoms of depression.[78] Because of the association between sports participation and positive mental health outcomes in addition to the reduction of negative mental health outcomes, perhaps through the mechanism of improved overall mental health, researchers have suggested that playing sports may reduce the chance of suicide among teens and young adults.[79]

Academic Benefits

A number of studies have found that athletic involvement improves academic performance in youth of all grade levels.[80] In particular, school sports have been associated positively with children's physical, cognitive, and moral development,[81] higher grades and examination scores, decreases in dropping out,[82] and positive effects on girls' achievement in such traditionally masculine subjects as science.[83] In addition, compared to students who do not play sports, minority female athletes earn higher grades and black female athletes are almost a third more likely to graduate from college.[84]

Title IX's Effect on Males

In the face of the sexism evident in sports in terms of the lack of opportunities and discrimination females experience, the controversy surrounding Title IX remains and is twofold: (1) it mandates equality for women and (2) there is public perception that the law negatively affects men's sports.[85] The backlash against Title IX centers on concerns about elimination of particular men's sports as schools seek to comply with the requirement to equalize male and female sports participation opportunities.

Participation Opportunities

In the post-Title IX era, males' sport participation opportunities, as determined by the number of male teams and athletes in the United States, continued to expand.[86] As previously noted, boys' high school sports participation continues to increase, although at a slower pace than girls' participation. For example, in 2013–2014, a record number of boys (4,527,994) played high school sports, leaving a substantial sex equity gap (1,260,330) in high school sports participation. As shown in Figure 2.2, men's overall intercollegiate sports participation has exhibited steady growth following the passage of Title IX. In 2013–2014, there were 62,040 more male athletes than female athletes. Indeed, males comprised 57 percent of college athletes, even though females accounted for roughly 57 percent of the total college enrollment in 2013–2014. Between 1988 and 2011, NCAA member institutions dropped 2,748 men's teams but added 3,727, and interestingly, more women's teams than men's teams were dropped in 2010–2011.[87] Changes in specific NCAA men's-sponsored sports offerings reflect broader trends in schools' dropping men's wrestling and gymnastics and adding track and field, cross-country, soccer, baseball, and lacrosse, with lacrosse (+18) being the most likely sport added in 2013–2014. Football has been the largest male sport for quite some time, and in 2013–2014, it had participation rates upward of 200 percent than those of the second most sponsored sport, baseball. With regard to participation level, the next highest men's sports are indoor and outdoor track and field, soccer, basketball, and cross country, respectively. Examining the number of men's-sponsored sports teams, NCAA data show that indoor track and field and lacrosse (+174 teams each) were the men's sports with the greatest increases in teams since 1988–1989; notable gains since 1988–1989 also occurred in men's cross country, outdoor track, soccer, and baseball. Contrary to public perception regarding how Title IX negatively affects men's sports, tennis (−1) was the only men's sport with an overall loss of teams in 2013–2014, although since 1988–1989, wrestling has been the men's sport most in decline (−104). Because women began at a significant disadvantage, they have made larger gains than men during the 1989–2014 time period, but sex equity has yet to be achieved in terms of the number of participants and opportunities for participation.[88]

Title IX's Broad Societal Impacts

Broadly speaking, sport can also serve as a catalyst for social change[89] and positive societal development and peace.[90] In the 1970s, sport began to be used as a venue to assert human rights, especially women's and civil rights,[91] leading to the passage of Title IX of the Educational Amendments to the Civil Rights Act in 1972, which requires that no person shall be denied on the basis of sex the opportunity to participate in sport.[92] On the basis of interviews of professional athletes who were social activists, Peter Kaufman and Eli Wolff found that athletes have been successful in using their status to promote ideals of social consciousness, meritocracy, responsible citizenship, and social interdependence.[93] Cynthia Pelak assessed interview, survey, and archival data collected in 1999–2000 and found that athletes and sports administrators alike were able to redefine a collective identity that bridged historical racial divisions in South Africa.[94] However, athletes who have spoken out about such polemical issues as war, racism, and inhuman labor practices, for example, have also endured harsh criticism and public backlash.[95]

Title IX and Gender Diversity Outcomes

While very little empirical research has been conducted on the topic, there appears to be a growing consensus that women's ever increasing accomplishments in traditionally male-dominated (nonsport) roles in society have been indirectly affected by their past participation in school sports. For example, numerous female corporate executives have acknowledged the influence that playing sports had on their careers. According to a recent global study of 400 female executives conducted by the EY Women Athletes Business Network and espnW, a background in sport can help accelerate a woman's career. The study found that roughly three-quarters (74 percent) of women surveyed believe that a background in sport can help a woman's leadership and career potential. The researchers note that of the female executives surveyed, 94 percent had a background in sport; more than half of women in the C-suite (52 percent), defined as serving on the board of directors at a company or in another C-level position (e.g., CEO, CFO, or COO), played at the collegiate level; nearly 7 in 10 women (70 percent) had participated in sports as a working adult; and 70 percent would be more likely to hire a candidate with a background in sport. This international group of female executives believes that former athletes make good professionals and that the self-discipline developed through athletic participation can translate into positive corporate qualities shaping determination and work ethics. They also believe that the ability to motivate others and a commitment to complete projects are beneficial outcomes of playing sports that can payoff in the labor market.[96]

International Sports Competition

Such sports mega events as the Olympics and the Fédération Internationale de Football Association (FIFA) World Cup are contexts through which nation-states exercise "soft-power."[97] Håvard Nygård and Scott Gates illustrate that mega sports events for nations are believed to (1) promote image building through returns on hosting mega events, (2) provide such platforms for dialogue as in promoting the Goodwill Games between the United States and the USSR, (3) improve trust building between nations, for example, by holding football matches between Israeli and Palestinian youth, and (4) create a catalyst for achieving reconciliation, integration, and the promotion of antiracism, evident in the case of Nelson Mandela's promotion of South African Rugby just after the fall of apartheid.[98] In addition, international mega sporting events provide both casual and ardent sport fans, and even nonfans, opportunities to experience a sense of collective identity in rooting for success of their nation's teams and individual athletes. For example, in identifying with TEAM-USA, all Americans, both home and abroad, can bask-in-the-reflected-glory (BIRG) of the team's success—a tendency of people to display or accentuate their association with successful others. In the context of most mega sporting events, TEAM-USA fans find themselves identifying with and rooting for racially and sexually diverse athletes who represent individual and collective self-interests. Thus, men who may not support Title IX or who may feel that males are superior athletes nevertheless, cheer for (and perhaps, on some level, identify with) individual female athletes and women's teams representing the United States.

Historically, for the United States, and many other nations, international sporting competitions have provided an important forum to showcase an idealized national character, as well as to demonstrate athletic prowess. For example, leading up to the 1936 Berlin Olympics, Adolph Hitler had viewed the Games as an opportunity to demonstrate the virtues of Germany's national character and commitment to Aryan superiority. In contrast, Americans pointed to Jesse Owens's four medals in track and field in the 1936 Olympics to portray to the world the virtues of the nation's diversity and democratic values to undermine Hitler and the Nazis' claims surrounding biological Aryan superiority. This was true notwithstanding the irony that, at the same time, segregation remained legally mandated in Alabama— Owens's home state. For the nation as a whole, Jesse Owens' second-class racial status was quite apparent following his victorious return to the United States as he was reduced to racing against horses to survive financially. Even in 1948 under Jim Crow segregation, United States Olympic Committee (USOC) official, Gustavus T. Kirby, stated that the U.S. Olympic flag bearer should always be featured beside two symbolic athletic figures, "one of whom should be a woman and the other a Negro" to depict the diversity of the U.S team.[99]

More recently, the U.S. media has emphasized similar virtues of our national character in highlighting the growing racial and ethnic diversity of U.S. Winter Olympic teams and the significant progress toward gender parity in the composition of our Summer Olympic teams. Thus, in all of these ways, the Olympic Games have provided a global stage for representing U.S. exceptionalism and superiority resulting from its exclusive title as "the land of the free." Other nations have also sought to use the global sports platform in such similar ways as how South Africa pointed to their 2007 World Rugby Championship and 2010 World Football Championships to symbolically demonstrate racial progress and unity, even though rugby previously represented the values associated with apartheid.[100]

The 2012 London Games were heralded as the "Year of the Woman at the Olympics."[101] For the first time, every participating country's delegation included at least one female athlete. Also for the first time, women competed in all 26 sports, including boxing. In addition, women's participation in the Olympic Games has increased significantly since 1960, when they represented just 11.4 percent of all athletes, to 2012 where they comprised 44 percent of Olympians. Because the men's soccer team did not qualify, TEAM-USA included slightly more women (268) than men (261), and U.S. female Olympians earned a disproportionate share of TEAM-USA medals. Overall, these patterns reflect a larger global trend toward sex equity in sports. As sport has historically been defined as a masculine turf, more equitable participation and increasing accomplishments by female athletes suggest that sports are experiencing sex and gender diversification. According to the USOCs report to Congress, "If Team USA's women competed as their own nation, they would rank tied for second in the gold-medal count—an impressive feat considering that London 2012 marked the first time in history where every nation featured a female athlete on its roster."[102] Overall, the U.S. women won 58 of a total of 104 medals while also earning 29 of the 46 gold medals secured by TEAM-USA.

A recent study further examined how sex diversity related to both the performance of the U.S. Olympic Team in the 2012 London Games and the success of TEAM-USA over an 80-year period in the Summer Olympic Games. Findings indicate a strong positive association between the number of women included on TEAM-USA and the number of medals won, supporting the notion that sex diversity is beneficial in sports contexts. Results show that relative to their participation, female athletes account for a disproportionate share (78 percent) of total medals won by the U.S. Olympic Team in the 2012 London Games. In addition, female athletes were more successful in a broader range of sports (including such traditionally male-dominated sports as boxing) than their male counterparts. Examining TEAM-USA's success over time, bivariate ordinary least square (OLS) regression analyses indicated that sex diversity was positively and significantly associated with total medals earned as well as the prestige of medals earned (i.e., gold versus silver or bronze).[103]

These results suggest that the U.S. National Olympic Committees should continue to promote women's Olympic participation since the benefits of sex diversity extend beyond the return to individual female athletes; TEAM-USA as a whole (medals are counted by nation not sex) earns both a greater number and prominence of awards, when female athletes are well represented. Furthermore, because the Olympics serve as an international arena to display national character, strength, unity, and pride, the nation benefits from this higher return and prestige of medals. That is to say that at the highest level of sport, the Olympic Games, the United States profits from sex diversity. Second, because of Title IX, the United States is one of the few nations to promote women's athletics through sex equitable access to school-based sports and collegiate scholarships; the increased representation of women on the Olympic roster provides the United States an advantage over most other countries that are yet to encourage women culturally, and support them financially, to compete at the highest levels of sports. U.S. women won gold medals in basketball, beach volleyball, soccer, gymnastics, and water polo, along with silver medals in volleyball and beach volleyball, which as a result of Title IX are frequently offered in U.S. schools and universities. The Olympic (and World Cup) success of TEAM-USA's female athletes has occurred mainly in such low-revenue, high school and college sports as basketball, track and field, soccer, and volleyball, where Title IX played a major role in creating and expanding female participation opportunities. In each of these sports, U.S. women have won a disproportionate share of Olympic medals, most of them gold. And in the case of soccer, perhaps the biggest beneficiary of Title IX in terms of expanded participation opportunities, U.S. women have now won three of the first Women's World Cup championships.

We have noted that since the passage of Title IX, girls and women have made tremendous progress toward achieving sex equity in society, in education, and in athletics. In making progress toward equity, women have faced numerous institutional and sociocultural obstacles. This progress can only be sustained, however, if Title IX supporters—regardless of sex—remain vigilant and committed to a long struggle. The struggle for sex equity has, in many ways, always run parallel to the ongoing battle to achieve racial equality. We discuss this commonality in greater detail as we compare the Title IX legislation and the *Brown v. Board of Education* ruling in the next chapter.

CHAPTER THREE

Title IX and *Brown v. Board of Education*

Intention, Implementation, and Outcomes of Sex-Based vs. Race-Based Policy

In May 1954, the United States Supreme Court ruled in Brown v. Board of Education that the "separate but equal" doctrine was an inherently disparate and unconstitutional means of delivering education to African-American children. Less than twenty years later, Congress legislated that women should have the same educational opportunities afforded to men at institutions that receive federal funds. Those two events on the spectrum of American law have had a dramatic effect on amateur sports in America.

—A. Jerome Dees[1]

There are some compelling similarities regarding the manner in which dominant race and sex ideology in the United States have structured and rationalized systemically inequitable systems of privilege for dominant social groups, Whites and males, respectively. Both racial and sexual stratification systems have been constructed to privilege white men and afford them power over people of color and women.[2] In many ways, race and sex inequality were institutionalized through the U.S. Constitution in a manner that has required constitutional amendments, congressional legislation, and judicial rulings, to ensure and protect each groups' most basic citizenship rights—including the right to vote and the right to own property, and labor rights—including the right to participate as wage laborers. Yet, as

Evelyn Glenn notes, in a society that proclaims freedom, individualism, and unlimited mobility, the persistence of rampant inequality along ascriptive lines of race and sex seems to be a contradiction.[3]

In this chapter we consider two historic federal interventions aimed at ameliorating sources of structural racial and sexual inequalities in education—*Brown v. Board of Education* and Title IX. *Brown* and Title IX were expected to enhance Blacks' and females' status in society, socially, educationally, and occupationally, as a result of improved access to equality of educational opportunity. Before these major systemic reforms, race and sex inequity in educational access and outcomes was not only commonplace, but, in many cases, also had the sanction of law. Both Title IX and *Brown* established legal frameworks and educational reform movements that had as their mission the creation of equal educational opportunity for women and racial minorities.

During the pre-*Brown* era in the South, and in many other areas of the country, unequal educational access and outcomes for Blacks and Latinos were sanctioned by law.[4] For example, in the South as late as 1940, per pupil expenditure for black students averaged only 45 percent of that in white schools.[5] In 1954, the Supreme Court, in a rare unanimous decision, determined that the Courts 1896 "separate but equal" ruling in *Plessy v. Ferguson* was unconstitutional under the "Equal Protection Clause" of the Fourteenth Amendment. Chief Justice Earl Warren wrote that the question in *Brown v. Board of Education* was not simply whether separate is equal but also rather: "Does segregation of children in public schools solely on the basis of race, even though the physical facilities and other 'tangible' factors may be equal, deprive the children of the minority group of equal educational opportunities?"[6] The Court answered this question affirmatively and proposed a policy framework requiring that racial inequities in education be addressed through "integration" instead of "equal segregation." The *Brown* decision was based, in part, on social science evidence indicating that segregation law denoted the inferiority of black children, which negatively affected their motivation to learn and, in turn, their educational and mental development, ultimately depriving them of the benefits they would receive in an integrated system.[7]

Early proponents of school desegregation anticipated that school integration would provide black and Latino students equitable access to the full benefits of schooling—the resources, experiences, and connections that facilitated full and equal participation in mainstream U.S. society. Indeed, as Amy Wells points out, in *Brown,* and especially in the higher education cases that preceded it, the plaintiff's emphasis was on the negative effects on black students of not only the resource inequalities experienced by segregated black schools but also because of their status in society and the social networks of faculty and students within them.[8] Ironically, most social science research on school desegregation, subsequent to *Brown v. Board of Education*, was not grounded in the same set of understandings that guided the plaintiffs and the Court.[9]

During oral argument before the U.S. Supreme Court in *Brown v. Board of Education,* Thurgood Marshall contended that "Equal means getting the same thing, at the same time and in the same place."[10] Thus, given the plaintiff's focus, and the legal ruling, one might expect that it would have been appropriate for researchers examining the impact of the Court's ruling to have made monitoring and evaluating parity in Blacks' representation in schools, classrooms, and courses the main educational equity outcomes of interest. Rather, the vast majority of post-*Brown* research focused mainly on cognitive and affective outcomes. As a result, those outcomes came to dominate the school desegregation research agenda. More specifically, instead of focusing on the learning opportunities and educational climates experienced by black and Latino students in desegregated schools—which have been shown to be inequitable both before and following *Brown*[11]—most studies instead focused almost exclusively on academic achievement outcomes that are, at best, indirectly linked to the desegregation policy. For example, 23 years after *Brown*, in a major review of the research on desegregation, Meyer Weinberg expressed surprise at how few studies had actually examined the influence of tracking and grouping on achievement in the context of desegregated schools. In essence, school desegregation researchers had done extensive examination of differences in achievement test performance without examining variations in associated student learning opportunities. This approach is questionable, especially because school desegregation was not itself an educational program (i.e., curriculum and pedagogical approach). For example, some researchers sought to compare the academic achievement effect of school or classroom desegregation (racial composition) to the amount and quality of instruction provided—even though desegregation *per se* is not an educational intervention.[12]

Why did researchers examine desegregation effects on learning as if racial mixing (to the extent it occurred) were, ipso facto, an educational intervention? There are multiple reasons of course, including the fact that test scores were readily available measures of student outcomes. Nevertheless, despite extensive historical evidence documenting the high value placed on education within the black community,[13] researchers were influenced by a dominant social science paradigm that assumed an educational values deficit among Blacks. As a result, much of the research on school desegregation assumed either explicitly or implicitly that this presumed minority student deficit could be offset by a "lateral transmission of values" from their white classmates. The lateral transmission hypothesis assumes that "the white majority in the classroom, through their achievement-related behavior both in word and by deed, would provide minority children with . . . a new benchmark toward which to strive."[14] Interest in this perspective has been rekindled directly among economists, with the recent focus of studies examining peer effects on the achievement gap[15] and, indirectly, with a growing interest in socioeconomic integration.[16]

Given the absence of an early research emphasis of monitoring and ensuring equitable learning opportunities for black and Latino students, the courts were later confronted with the so-called second-generation school desegregation problems like tracking and ability grouping, which in effect, resegregated black and white students within the same school building.[17] In retrospect, it seems clear that issues of equitable access to learning and extracurricular participation opportunities should have been addressed as first-generation *Brown* school desegregation problems. Put differently, researchers (and the courts) should have more appropriately evaluated school desegregation as a dependent variable—based on evidence regarding equitable access to learning opportunities. In this case, the voluminous body of research on school desegregation as an independent variable—including both its short- and long-term effects on achievement and other related outcomes—would represent important *value-added* basic research evidence of its efficacy as an educational policy. Thus, desegregation researchers might have shown that in addition to providing black and Latino students with equal educational opportunities, as mandated by the Supreme Court, schools also experience the added benefits of improved student academic performance, as well as better intergroup relations among students.

Wells and her colleagues[18] argue that the Coleman Report[19] came to have a huge impact on the conceptualization of equal educational opportunity by focusing on the distinction between educational resources and educational outcomes. Before the 1960s, equality of educational opportunity emphasized equal access to equivalent schools, but following the Coleman Report, the definition of equality of educational opportunity shifted to equal effects. Thus, equality of educational opportunity came to be associated with closing the achievement gap between Blacks and Whites.[20] This study also had a huge impact in deemphasizing the role of schools and resources in accounting for the achievement gap and shifted research attention to factors often assumed to be related to sociocultural deficits and differences. From a policy perspective, this reframing of equality of educational opportunity led to an emphasis on compensatory education rather than a reconfiguration of schools and learning opportunities through school integration.

Like black and Latino students, female students also confront persistent segregation. In contemporary U.S. schools, despite the passage of Title IX, sex segregation remains quite pervasive; for the most part, females and males use separate bathrooms, receive different forms of sexual and physical education, and are held to distinct standards of dress—that is when they are in the same school; sex-segregated schools are still quite popular. The issue of whether educational institutions should be sex segregated has sparked debate among legal researchers regarding the advantages[21] and disadvantages[22] of single-sex education. However, one of the most controversial topics surrounding sex equality and sex segregation in education involves Title IX implementation strategies in athletics.[23]

Although the concept of proportionality that characterizes Title IX was borrowed from early racial segregation cases involving schools, the ideological rationale behind Title IX is the opposite of that of *Brown*. With regard to Title IX, the Federal Government was determined to redress discrimination and equality issues in athletics, using a theory of "separate but equal."[24] However, opposition to Title IX and inadequate funding have continuously prevented the act from being fully enforced such that women remain underrepresented in both interscholastic and intercollegiate athletics, and do not enjoy the same resources as their male counterparts.[25]

Most scholars recognize the impressive impact Title IX had on increasing females' athletic participation, but among both academic and the general public, a consensus has yet to be reached concerning the extent to which Title IX has met the goals of sex equity and its potential to do so in the future.[26] Interestingly, scholars on similar sides of the debate could have conflicting reasons for their support of, or opposition to, Title IX. For instance, some supporters of Title IX favoring women's rights may feel that it has been and will continue to be a vehicle for creating opportunity in sport for women, whereas other supporters of the law may view Title IX as a means of maintaining sex segregation and, consequently, male superiority in sport. Similarly, individuals who feel ambivalent about women's rights may oppose Title IX because they fear the potential elimination of men's collegiate sports, whereas others with a vested interest in women's equality may oppose the law because they feel that an even more stringent policy is necessary to achieve sex equity in athletics.

Working within the framework that sex equity in sport is desirable, the debate surrounding Title IX focuses on whether applying the integration principles of *Brown* in athletics would serve to eliminate sex inequality or whether sex integration in athletics would diminish if not eliminate opportunities for women. In an attempt to reconcile this conflict of legal philosophies, it is useful to directly relate the Court's ruling in the *Brown* case to sex discrimination. Specifically, adapting the language of the Supreme Court in the *Brown* ruling, but substituting sex for race, the question that Chief Justice Earl Warren might ask is as follows: Does segregation of *women* in athletics, solely on the basis of *sex*, even though the physical facilities and other "tangible" factors may be equal, deprive *women* of equal opportunities?[27] Following the Court's logic in *Brown*, the sex segregation questions would be as follows: First, does sex segregation in athletics signify the inferiority of women? One would have to assume that the answer would be *yes*. Since women have been relegated to the subordinate sex category and "mainstream" sex ideology has historically labeled women as intellectually and physically inferior to men,[28] legal segregation has clearly served to support and reify these notions. Second, does this sense of inferiority affect women's motivation to play sports? Again, one would have to assume that the answer would be *yes*. Research has highlighted sex differentials in motivation to play sports, and presumed inferiority learned through gender-role socialization has been identified as a possible cause.[29] Third, taking together the answers from the first and second questions, does sport segregation serve to retard the development of women and deprive them of some of the benefits they would receive in integrated sports contexts? Here, the answer would also be *yes*. Denying women the opportunity to compete with men at the highest levels of athletic competition throughout their lifetime serves to prevent them from achieving their full athletic capabilities and, consequently, their full potential both individually and collectively.

Assessing Progress Toward Race and Gender Equity in Educational Opportunity

Both the 40th Anniversary of Title IX and the 50th Anniversary of *Brown v. Board of Education* provoked both widespread celebration and critical assessments among academics about the significance of these historic efforts to achieve educational equality. Social scientists and legal scholars have re-examined the role of the courts in educational equity cases and the appropriateness of litigation as a strategy to obtain equality of educational opportunity. These analyses reveal mixed assessments of the significance of Title IX and *Brown*. Some have offered compelling arguments that the Court could reasonably have rendered different decisions in key post-*Brown* and post-Title IX cases, leading to very different outcomes for school desegregation and sex equity policies and practice.[30] A central point in many of these assessments has to do with how even the Courts are not immune to the politics of race and sex.[31]

With regard to their efficacy and sustainability, a major distinction between Title IX (as a strategy to eliminate sex-based inequity in education) and *Brown* (as a strategy to eliminate race-based inequity in education) can be seen in the manner in which their impact has been assessed. Assessments of *Brown* as an educational policy intervention have mainly been *summative* evaluations. In this sense, the courts, researchers, educators, and the public have routinely made judgments about whether or not school desegregation—*as implemented* in schools, communities, and the nation— is working or has worked. As we discuss hereafter, "as implemented" is a key factor in understanding the problematic nature of using a summative evaluation strategy to assess post-*Brown* school desegregation. To a great extent, assessments of whether school desegregation worked relied heavily on evidence from standardized tests comparing whether black student performance has improved relative to white student performance. In many cases, school desegregation efforts were considered failed policy if black student test performance did not close or reduce the "achievement gap" relative to white student test performance, in a relatively short time span (e.g., one semester or one school year). In contrast, assessments of Title IX as an educational policy intervention have mainly been *formative,* not summative evaluations. Thus, with regard to Title IX, evaluative judgments—by the courts, researchers, educators, and the public—have focused mainly on whether or not the law is being implemented, *not* whether or not Title IX is working, or has worked.

Lessons Learned

There are important lessons to be learned from the case of school desegregation research. While social scientists have unquestionably made substantial contributions to equity and social justice in the U.S. society through their studies of school desegregation, questions arise regarding to what extent debates over the role and effectiveness of school desegregation as an educational policy may be related to social researchers having earlier asked the wrong questions. Unfortunately, virtually all of the post-*Brown* research adopted a *school effects* input–output model, the dominant paradigm in educational research, which in most instances defines such school characteristics as racial composition as the independent variable. If the *Brown* decision represented, as many people believe, a judicial ruling about Blacks' moral, ethical, and fundamental right of citizenship, it is appropriate to question whether much of the research on school desegregation should have been considered simply "formative" studies of the implementation of an important new development in education rather than "summative evaluations" of the efficacy and appropriateness of desegregation policies. More specifically, both scholarly and judicial assessments of the impact of *Brown* should have examined access to equal educational opportunities—in schools, classrooms, extracurricular activities, and the like—as the dependent or outcome variable.

In addition, most civil liberties are not typically evaluated in the same manner as we have assessed black children's right to attend any publicly supported school. For example, Blacks' voting rights or women's suffrage was not, nor should they have been, assessed in terms of racial or sex gaps in registration or turnout rates. Historically, in U.S. society, constitutional rights of citizenship are more often examined and fine-tuned, where necessary, to make them work well, not "evaluated" to determine whether they should exist. In the case of *Brown*, support for, and enforcement of, the principle of equality of educational opportunity for black and Latino students has been diminished as a direct result of social science research, suggesting that school desegregation has not worked or has not closed the achievement gap.[32] Thus, it is not unreasonable to suggest that had strong compelling research on access to learning opportunities—like that of Joyce Epstein, Maureen Hallinan, Roslyn Mickelson, Jeannie Oakes, and others[33]— become the dominant early paradigm for assessing the efficacy of school desegregation interventions, the nation might be in a very different place today with regard to race and equality of educational opportunity.

Consider the following analogy grounded in the principle of equality of educational opportunity. Title IX, like *Brown*, was conceived to address gender inequities in education (involving academic as well as athletic access barriers). Title IX, like *Brown*, has faced persistent opposition and efforts to undermine its legitimacy and impact. Both Title IX and *Brown* are, at their core, about equality of educational opportunity. How appropriate would it have been for social researchers and the courts to focus on women's athletic performance compared to men or on the consequences of women's athletic participation on social and psychological outcomes like gender role ideology, rather than on the extent and quality of their sports participation opportunities to assess whether Title IX is "working" or whether it should be abandoned? Most scholars (and the public) would likely consider such assessments of Title IX to be misguided.

In many ways, researchers' decisions, to summatively assess the efficacy of *Brown*, largely on the basis of reductions in racial standardized achievement test gaps, are akin to summatively evaluating Title IX on the basis of time performance disparities between men and women in the 100-meter dash, or male–female test performance disparities in mathematics. As a consequence of increased access to sports participation opportunities, resulting from Title IX, male–female performance gaps have indeed narrowed in many sports, as well as mathematics. Nevertheless, although most Americans would generally regard reducing sex disparities to be laudable outcomes of Title IX, we do not believe that women, or advocates of sex equity, would allow the nation's commitment to this particular dimension of educational equity to be tied to questions about athletic (or even mathematics and science tests) performance gaps. We contend that in *Brown*, as in Title IX, the important research issues should involve questions of *access* with a focus on implementation, and fidelity of implementation, of mandated policies and plans. Likewise, in *Brown*, as in Title IX, the important research issues should have involved questions of *equitable access*—focusing on implementation and fidelity of implementation of desegregation policies and plans.

Understanding the impact of major educational policy initiatives like *Brown* and Title IX in achieving race and sex equity requires evidence on *both* how effectively the policies are implemented and their consequences (short and long term) for individuals and communities. Social scientists commonly use cause and effect models, where sex equity or desegregation in schools can be either a dependent variable or an independent variable. When viewed as a dependent (or outcome) variable, the key research questions would examine whether and how efficaciously the policy initiatives are implemented. In the present case, the questions become are women (Title IX) and minorities (*Brown*) receiving equitable—classroom and extracurricular—opportunities in schools? In contrast, when viewed as an independent (causal) variable, the key research questions examine whether and how much the existence of Title IX (or *Brown*) results in improved educational outcomes for women (or racial minorities). More specifically, the questions become have the educational outcomes of women (Title IX) and minorities (*Brown*) improved as a consequence of Title IX and *Brown* as educational policies? Thus, when Title IX or *Brown* is framed as dependent variables, researchers are, in effect, conducting *formative* evaluations—measuring progress toward the laws expresses policy goal of equality of educational opportunity. In contrast, when Title IX or *Brown* is framed as independent variables, researchers, in effect, take equality of educational opportunity as a given and conduct *summative* evaluations—measuring whether Title IX or *Brown* led to educational achievement equity (e.g., comparable test scores).

We argue that the dominant approach in studies of *Brown* has been summative, framing school desegregation initiatives as the independent variable, whereas the dominant approach in studies of Title IX has been formative, framing sex equity as the dependent variable. The formative research focus, we believe, has been helpful in advancing the goals of Title IX and women, but the summative research focus has hindered the attainment of the core goal of *Brown*—equality of opportunity for racial minorities. Both *Brown* and Title IX sought to improve access to equality of educational opportunity. Both were conceived with the ultimate goal of creating equitable opportunities and status for social groups that have been discriminated against. The Supreme Court understood that improving the status of Blacks and Latinos in society required more equitable educational opportunities. Likewise, Congress was motivated to enact Title IX, in part, because it recognized that improving women's position in the labor force, and in society, required more equitable educational opportunities.

Figure 3.1 illustrates the different ways in which *Brown* and Title IX, as educational equity policies, have been assessed. For racial minorities, the upper panel of Figure 3.1 illustrates the processes through which the *Brown* ruling should create racially equitable learning (access), and participation, opportunities in schools and classrooms, leading to greater minority student

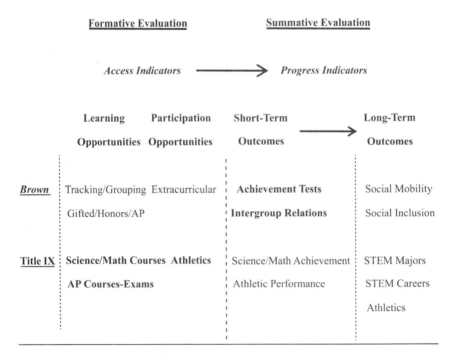

Figure 3.1   Major Emphasis on Research on *Brown* (Race) and Title IX (Sex) Equity in Education.

educational achievements (short-term progress), which in turn would result in improved adult social status for minorities (long-term progress). Likewise, for women, the lower panel of Figure 3.1 illustrates the processes through which Title IX should create sex-equitable learning (access), and participation, opportunities in schools and classrooms, leading to greater female student educational achievements (short-term progress), which in turn would result in improved adult social status for women (long-term progress).

The diagram distinguishes between major outcomes examined in formative and summative evaluations of these policy initiatives. The primary purpose of evaluation research is to measure a program's effects against its original to inform subsequent decision making regarding the program and how it might be improved.[34] Michael Scriven distinguishes between formative and summative evaluations. Formative evaluations are intended to provide feedback information for program improvement. Summative evaluations are usually done when a program is completed and serve to provide information about program impact that might inform further adoption or expansion of the program.[35] With regard to both Title IX and *Brown*, formative evaluations should reasonably focus on access outcomes that indicate whether or not females and racial minorities, respectively, are being provided equitable educational opportunities. For females, the appropriate access indicators measured should reflect outcomes that Congress intended to impact. For example, Title IX sought to provide females access to equitable learning opportunities, including improved access to science and mathematics courses. Title IX also sought to provide females access to equitable participation opportunities, including improved access to sports. Thus, Title IX research focusing on learning and participation opportunities is consistent with the goals of the legislation and with the interests of women and sex equity advocates. For Blacks and Latinos, the appropriate access indicators measured should also reflect outcomes the Supreme Court intended to impact. For example, *Brown* sought to provide racial minorities' access to equitable learning opportunities, including improved access to high academic track/groups and such enriched learning contexts as honors and gifted programs. *Brown*, like Title IX, also sought to provide black and Latino students the access to equitable participation opportunities, including equitable access to sports and other extracurricular activities in desegregated schools. Thus, the majority of *Brown* research—school desegregation—focusing on short-term progress outcome indicators (achievement test or intergroup attitudes) instead of learning and participation opportunities was *not* consistent with the goals of the Supreme Court ruling nor was it consistent with the interests of Blacks and Latinos and civil rights advocates.

As noted earlier, despite their similarities, Title IX and *Brown* have been evaluated and judged differently. The strategy adopted by most research-ers in evaluations of *Brown*—school desegregation—has typically been sum-mative evaluations. As indicated by the bold type in the upper panel of Figure 3.1, desegregation researchers have focused more on *progress indicators*—important short-term student outcomes like standardized achievement scores, but have largely ignored *access indicators*—variations in the classroom contexts that determine what, and how much, is learned. Obviously, what students learn is what they are taught. Students in enhanced learning programs (e.g., gifted, honors, and advanced placement) and high academic tracks or ability groups have qualitatively (better teaching) and quantitatively (richer, more advanced content) different learning experi-ences. As a result, students with access to the enhanced learning programs and high academic groups/tracks experience better learning outcomes (e.g., higher standardized test scores).

Because black and Latino students' access to enhanced learning programs and high academic groups/tracks has not been routinely monitored in stud-ies of school desegregation and because many desegregation rulings have not held school districts accountable for providing equitable access to black and Latino students, they are often disproportionately underrepresented in these contexts.[36] Lacking comparable opportunities to learn (access), black and Latino students' standardized test performance (progress) lags behind students with better access. Students' academic achievement in school, to a great extent, shapes their career and social mobility opportunities in adult-hood. Thus, students with enriched learning opportunities earn higher test scores, are likely admitted into more prestigious colleges, and get better and more rewarding jobs. In this way, the lack of monitoring (by researchers) and accountability (by the courts) to ensure racially equitable learning opportunities (access) has lifelong implications. Inadequate attention to access has not only been a major difference in evaluation methodology between *Brown* and Title IX researchers; we argue, it has contributed to making school desegregation efforts less sustainable.

In contrast, the strategy adopted by researchers in most evaluations of Title IX—sex equity—has almost exclusively been formative evaluations. As indicated by the bold type in the lower panel of Figure 3.1, sex equity researchers have focused more on *access indicators*—female enrollments in mathematics and science courses, for example, but have largely ignored *pro-gress indicators*—differential student sex outcomes like boys and girls sci-ence and mathematics standardized achievement scores. Female and male students also learn what they are taught. Students in advanced science and mathematics courses—who have often been disproportionately males—

experience qualitatively (better teaching) and quantitatively (richer, more advanced content) different learning experiences than students in regular and lower level courses. As a result, male students with access to more advanced science and mathematics opportunities experience better learning outcomes (e.g., higher mathematics, and science, standardized test scores). However, because female students' access to advanced science and mathematics opportunities has been routinely monitored in assessments of sex equity, and because Title IX legislation and court rulings have held schools and districts accountable for providing equitable access to females, they have become more equitably represented.

Before gaining comparable learning opportunities (access), females' standardized test performance (progress) in mathematics and science had lagged behind their male peers who had better access. Females' science and mathematics achievement in school, to a great extent, shapes their career and social mobility opportunities in adulthood. Thus, females with more advanced science and mathematics opportunities earn higher test scores in these subjects, are more likely to pursue STEM majors in college, and gain greater access to higher paying STEM careers. In this way, the strong emphasis on monitoring (by researchers) and accountability (by the courts) to ensure sex-equitable learning opportunities (access) has lifelong implications for women. We argue that by focusing attention on access—through formative evaluation research, rather than short-term progress—as would be measured in summative evaluation research, Title IX researchers have contributed to making sex equity efforts much more sustainable than school desegregation efforts.

Despite entrenched, and persistent, opposition, it is undeniable that both Title IX and the *Brown* decision had a tremendous impact on the education of female and minority student populations. Nevertheless, substantial barriers remain in the path toward racial and sexual equity in education. Specifically, for females in athletics, the problem of challenging and overcoming a dominant sex ideology defines the sports domain, as male turf still looms as one of the most formidable obstacles yet to be overcome.

CHAPTER FOUR

The Social Construction of Sex and Race

Concepts Real Only in Their Consequences and Why This Matters in Sports

I never say that I'm incapable of beating anybody, because I don't believe in putting limits on myself. So I mean, I would have to say if you're just talking about what's in the realm of possibility of what's possible of who I could beat, well, I could beat 100 percent of [men]. But, um, you can't tell me that there's a zero percent chance that I can beat anyone on the planet, so I'm never gonna say that.
—*Ronda Rousey*[1]

[Rousey fighting a man is] a stupid idea. Seriously, that's a stupid idea. I'm as much a feminist as anyone but the fact is that biologically, there's a difference between men and women. Hello. Duh. A woman who is 135 pounds and a man who is 135 pounds are not physically equal.
—*AnnMaria De Mars, former judo world champion and mother of Rousey*[2]

Ronda Rousey, arguably one of the best mixed martial arts (MMA) fighters of our time, was recently labeled by *Sports Illustrated* as "the world's most dominant athlete,"[3] winning her last four fights before losing to Holly Holm in a combined total of 130 seconds. Ultimate Fighting Championship (UFC) analyst Joe Rogan commented that she would be able to beat 50 percent of males in her weight class. Rousey responded by saying that it is possible that she could beat 100 percent of males in her weight class. However, Rousey's mother, AnnMaria De Mars, publicly stated that it was a senseless idea for her daughter to fight a man, implying that women and men are inherently physically unequal.[4] Rousey herself later qualified her statement to say that she will not fight a man in the UFC, because she does not believe there should exist a setting where a man hitting a woman is condoned and that no athletic commission would allow it.[5] Although we agree that violence against women and individuals in general should not be tolerated, in a fighting competition specifically, why is it socially acceptable for men to hit men and women to hit women, but it is not socially acceptable for men to hit women? Furthermore, why is it socially acceptable for Rousey or another woman to hit a man in competition but not socially acceptable for him to hit her? Shouldn't a fair fight, whether it is inside or outside a ring, be determined by size and experience rather than genitalia, since individuals do not fight with penises and vaginas, but rather, fists, arms, and legs? Moreover, wouldn't a man be at a disadvantage during a fight with a similarly sized and trained woman because of his external organs that make him more vulnerable? Lastly, is Rousey's mother correct: are there biological differences between men and women that make integrated sporting contexts, and especially those that involve high levels of contact unfair?

Gender Ideology vs. Reality: Questioning Dominant Sex Categories and Assumptions in Sport

Dominant sex ideology suggests that men are physically superior to women; however, women on average live longer, are less likely to die at birth, and are able to carry and bear children.[6] Similarly, dominant gender ideology suggests that such traits traditionally associated with masculinity as rationality and aggressiveness are more valuable than such traits associated with femininity as emotionality and passivity,[7] even though the construction of masculinity may result in men's health risks and disparities.[8] Sex, and to a certain extent gender, can be thought of as social statuses in which they represent a hierarchy of inequality. Because U.S. society is a patriarchy, maleness and masculinity are valued, whereas femaleness and femininity are devalued. In U.S. society, physical prowess is also valued, and thus, it logically follows that men are not only viewed as physically advantaged as a group but that they also receive a greater return on possessing strength, speed, endurance, balance, and agility in the form of respect, admiration, perception of attractiveness, and monetary compensation than their female counterparts.

The notion of male physical superiority is evident in sports contexts where dominant gender ideology deems men's sports to be better than women's. However, it is important to note that because the institution of sport is socially constructed, sexed rules and performances in athletics are not inherently better or worse. Sports are human social inventions and not naturally occurring phenomena, and therefore one group, whether biologically defined or not, cannot be better or worse at sports. To put it another way, there is no such biological marker of any sport that exists in humans as a gene that makes certain individuals more prone to success or failure, because sports are made up of games that do not exist organically. It is akin to saying that men are naturally better drivers than women (they are not; studies consistently show women are better drivers because they are socialized into less aggressive behavior),[9] even though cars are human inventions and once again, sports are not played and cars are not driven with genitalia. Michael Burke explains that men, through authoritative positions in sports, have defined sports excellence in ways that permit men, rather than women, the opportunity to embody excellence and continue to occupy authoritative positions, and subsequently make moral and legislative judgments in athletics.[10] With regard to the dominant gender ideology associated with men's and women's athletics, it is often the case that such particulars in men's sports as dunking in basketball and checking in ice hockey are viewed as better simply because men do them. That is to say that if women dunked and men did not, public perception may be that the women's game is boring because they have close-up opportunities to put the ball in the basket rather than having to shoot the long ball, that women's poor defense leads to dunks, and that women are less capable at passing because it is not a necessity when dunking characterizes the game. We should also point out that women's style of basketball could also be considered more "fundamentally sound." In the absence of a male-dominant gender bias, the more fundamentally sound style of play would likely be considered as superior. Significantly, this same type of distinction regarding basketball teams' fundamental soundness in men's basketball was frequently invoked to infer that such all-white teams as the University of Kentucky were superior to such all-black teams as the University of Texas-El Paso when they played for the NCAA championship in 1966. Similarly, if women checked in ice hockey and men did not, public perception may be that women possess poorer stick and skate skills than men, where all they do is knock each other over instead of playing with the finesse of the men's game. Women's sports are perceived to be inferior solely because women do them! One comparable example is the perception of historical familial sex roles of men as providers and women as nurturers. Anthropologists have proven that in hunter/gatherer societies, women were the ones who sustained their tribes because men would often not have success at hunting large game for months, so the small game and foraging done by women resulted in the family's survival.[11] Thus, women were the actual providers, but their contributions are devalued because breadwinning is still viewed as a male domain and valued more than caregiving, and the perception of women as breadwinners would discredit a dominant sexist ideology in which men have been portrayed as having a more valuable familial role throughout history.

Just as it is inappropriate to say that individuals are naturally predisposed, or not, to socially constructed sports, it is even more indefensible to suggest that such groups that are themselves socially constructed as sex or race groups are naturally better, or worse, at sports. Both sports and the groups themselves are social constructions. Not only can the intent and outcomes of dominant sexist ideology that deems men athletically superior be questioned, so too can the underlying notion that men and women are separate sexes and thus should compete separately in sports contexts.

Sex Categories as Social Rather Than Biological Phenomenon

What determines someone's identity as a woman or man? Most people would say that it is chromosomes (XX for female vs. XY for male) or genitalia (vagina vs. penis) or hormones (estrogen vs. testosterone) or the ability to give birth (women) or not (men). However, transgender individuals, intersexed individuals, those with triple and quadruple X syndrome, XXXXY syndrome, pentasomy X, Klinefelter's syndrome, Turner's syndrome, XX gonadal dysgenesis, XX male syndrome, XXYY syndrome, and XYY syndrome, women who are infertile or menopausal, individuals who were born without or have injured their genitalia, and those with polycystic ovarian syndrome, hirsutism, late-onset congenital adrenal hyperplasia, and testosterone deficiency, despite not conforming to traditional notions of fixed sex categorical constraints, still often identify as women or men and, therefore, *are* women or men. The wide range of individuals who do not biologically conform to the traditional sex binary classification system demonstrates that an inherent male/female dichotomy does not exist in nature. Dominant ideology suggests a "natural" and complementary sexual division of women and men, but there are many such counterfactual examples in nature as hermaphrodite animals (e.g., snails), animals that change sexes during their lives (e.g., clownfish), and animals that reproduce asexually (e.g., komodo dragons).

Furthermore, the fact that individuals sometimes identify and publicly pass in sex categories independently from their genetics and anatomy indicates that in terms of the way in which people feel and recognize sex, processes apart from biology are taking place. Even individuals who biologically conform to traditional sex categories do not necessarily focus on their genetic and anatomical makeup when contemplating their own sex. If most people were asked how they experience their sex, very few would discuss chromosomes or hormones because those entities are not actually felt. Rather, sex is a social concept where individuals come to learn and comprehend their own and others' sex through socialization and their own social, not biological, experiences. For example, such biological events as hair growth or breast development are viewed and interpreted through a social lens, where overarching sexist ideology shapes the way people understand sex processes and characteristics.

However, this is not to say that biology plays no role at all in behavior but that the relationship among social, biological, and psychological processes is complex, where various theoretical and interdisciplinary approaches to understanding sex and gender characteristics, roles, stereotypes, and behaviors are needed.[12] Gene–environment interplay has become an emerging area of research in the social sciences and we do not dispute that investigation into the relationship between the social environment and biology is important. However, as sociologists studying the social institution of sport, we are primarily concerned with how social factors shape ideology and behavior at both the individual and structural levels. In terms of sex and gender specifically, we are interested in moving away from a dominant ideology, which posits biology as the primary and most significant detriment of sex, and toward a social explanation for the invention and maintenance of sex categories, identities, and performances.

When most people think of sex and gender, they argue that sex is the biological and gender is the cultural and that sex comes first and gender comes afterward. However, the Sapir–Whorf hypothesis establishes that culture always comes first, even before biology. Although language is often thought of as simply a human tool, the Sapir–Whorf hypothesis illustrates that language is more than a tool; it is the most important part of culture because it structures perceptions of reality.[13] People think, feel, and live in language and the social world is constructed and experienced through language. Without language, the word "biology" would not exist and people would have no knowledge of what "biology" is or entails. Thus, culture comes before biology, because without the cultural component of language, there is no sex or chromosomes or organs or division of individuals into categories based on these markers. It can be argued that sex is as much of a social construction as gender.[14] Sex classifications, similar to such other socially constructed categories as those associated with race, socioeconomic status, and sexuality, change across time and space and are not real in and of themselves, but are very real in their consequences because of their social construction.

Simone de Beauvoir famously argued that "one is not born, but rather becomes, a woman."[15] De Beauvoir contended that through sex classifications, women learn to regard themselves not only as "other" but also as inferior because the meaning of what it is to be a woman is given by men. Therefore, in a patriarchal society, women begin to see themselves and their such female experiences as menstruation and pregnancy as a burden and disadvantage. However, because women are not intrinsically inferior and nor so is their biological condition, De Beauvoir believed that women are capable of transcending their subordinate position that has been prescribed to them by men.[16]

In order for sex equality to be achieved, sexist ideology must be disrupted. Specifically, it is important to dismantle the idea of men and women as naturally occurring, separate groups, as well as provide alternative ways of thinking about sex categories. For instance, when most people think of lesbians, they think of women who are primarily attracted to other women. However, Monique Wittig argued that lesbians are not women, because they defy the economically, politically, and ideologically oppressive relationship that defines men and women. Wittig contended that because of the intrinsic link between sex and sexuality, lesbians do not conform to the definition of "women" as a class of people, because lesbians do not have traditionally sexed relationships with men, which require their reliance on men to fulfill sexual, monetary, and emotional needs. Therefore, for Wittig, the difference between men and women does not lie in the biological, but rather the cultural. Like De Beauvoir, Wittig poses women not as a group that is naturally separate but merely politically divided from men, where women are not born, they are socially imagined.[17]

Wittig's contention that women as a class of people only exist in their relationship to men is not exaggerated. In fact, the word "women" essentially does not exist on its own and cannot be spelled and defined separately from "men." Although the word "man" was sex neutral until the 13th century, it currently indicates both "human adult male" and "humanity" (e.g., "human" and "mankind" both use the root word "man"),[18] whereas the word "woman" also uses the root word, suggesting that "men" are the default in the human race and "women," the other; men are the standard human beings and women are the abnormal, a mere subcategory of the normal, of men. The literal translation of the words "women" and "men" implies that women do not exist on their own terms without men and need men to be complete. This has prompted some feminists to use the alternative spelling "womyn," reclaiming the term and symbolically stating that women as a group exist apart from men.[19]

Applying sexed language to other common examples of categorization demonstrates the implications. For instance, in the case of the fruits, "apples and oranges" and the letters, "A and B," "oranges" and "B" would cease to exist where instead "men and women" more closely translates to "apples and sub apples" and "A and sub A," or "apples and other apples" and "A and other A." Relying once again on the Sapir–Whorf hypothesis to highlight the importance and power of language, the linguistic distinction between men and women is not an arbitrary one, because it structures individual and social realities surrounding sex and gender.

De Beauvoir, Wittig, and other feminist theorists demonstrate that within a patriarchy, the way in which the category of "women" has been constructed strictly in relation to men results not merely in the reality of difference but rather in domination and subordination.[20] In a similar way, race scholars have begun to use language that more accurately reflects the racist hierarchy rather than conveying sheer racial difference in the titles of the courses they teach. For instance, instead of relying on such names of race courses typical at most universities as "Race and Ethnic Relations" or "Diversity in America," in 2015, Arizona State recently offered a course called "U.S. Race Theory and the Problem of Whiteness,"[21] whereas a class entitled "White Privilege Seminar: An Introduction to the Intersections of Privilege" was taught at Notre Dame.[22] Using language in a similar vein to reflect the sexist social structure, courses habitually called "Sociology of Sex and Gender" or "Sex and Gender Relations" would be more aptly named "Sociology of Male Privilege and Supremacy" or "The Patriarchy."

Feminist legal scholar Catherine MacKinnon argued that sex equality law should be shifted from understanding sex categories as difference to understanding them as dominance, because the constructed sex binary is a hierarchy. Under the guise of difference, sex legislation, including Title IX, serves to benefit men because sex neutrality is in essence the male standard where women's equality is judged according to their measured distance from being the same as men.[23] To demonstrate the point that sex neutrality reflects the male standard, MacKinnon cites the example of medical school anatomy models depicting the male body as the human body, where women's bodies are subjugated as only suitable objects of study in obstetrician/gynecology (OB/GYN) settings.[24] An example of how this classification system manifests in modern society is that in cases of infant sex assignment of babies born with ambiguous genitals, female bodies are not understood on their own attributes but are defined through a lack of a penis."[25]

Another example of the sexist ideology evident in the construction of sex categories surrounds the presentation of disease. Although the number one killer of women in the United States is heart disease and lung cancer is the leading cause of cancer deaths among women, breast cancer and cervical cancer receive a great deal more national attention.[26] In sports contexts specifically, NFL players wear pink helmets, sweat bands, and cleats during October, breast cancer awareness month, whereas NCAA women's basketball players wear pink jerseys. Both the pinkification of breast cancer awareness and the push for human papilloma virus (HPV) vaccines for girls highlight the perceived imperfections of women's anatomy as disease causing to the general public and simultaneously diminishes the problems associated with the heart, an organ all people possess. Unfortunately, the distinction of false biological sex categories and the conventional thinking that breast cancer is a women's disease has resulted in men dying at higher rates of breast cancer, because they too have breasts but are less likely to screen themselves or seek medical attention when they notice a problem.[27]

The notion of men as the default, and therefore, superior sex category is similar to the notion of Whiteness as the default, and thus, superior racial category. By comparing the socially constructed categories or sex and race, John Stoltenberg uses a theoretical argument to debunk the notion of sex categories as natural. Specifically, he compares the idea of the male sex to the idea of the Aryan race to demonstrate that ideology influences perceptions of reality, although that does not make the ideas real:

> The Nazis believed that from the blond hair and blue eyes occurring naturally in the human species, they could construe the existence of a separate race—a distinct category of human beings that was unambiguously rooted in the natural order of things. But traits do not a race make; traits only make traits. For the idea to be real that these physical traits comprised a race, the race had to be socially constructed. The Nazis inferiorized and exterminated those they defined as "non-Aryan." With that, the notion of an Aryan race began to seem to come true. That's how there could be a political entity known as an Aryan race, and that's how there could be for some people a personal, subjective sense that they belonged to it. . . . The force and violence created a racial class system, and it created those people's membership in the race considered "superior." The force and violence served their class interests in large part because it created and maintained the class itself. But the idea of an Aryan race could never become metaphysically true, despite all the violence unleashed to create it, because there simply is no Aryan race. There is only the idea of it—and the consequences of trying to make it seem real. The male sex is very like that. Penises and ejaculate and prostate glands occur in nature, but the notion that these anatomical traits comprise a sex—a

discrete class, separate and distinct, metaphysically divisible from some other sex, the "other sex"—is simply that: a notion, an idea. The penises exist; the male sex does not. The male sex is socially constructed.[28]

Similar to Stoltenberg, Judith Butler uses the notion of a value system assigned to sex conformity through the perceived linear relationship among sex, gender, and sexuality to illustrate the construction of these categories, rejecting the notion of a sex binary that feminists unintentionally reified by positing women as a group with common characteristics and interests. Specifically, Butler argues that gender is physically imposed and internalized where the performance of gender affords individuals cultural returns on their identification in terms of feelings of belonging to a sex group. Thus, individuals' core identities do not cause the gender performance, but rather are the result of it.[29]

Male Superiority and Female Inferiority: The Irrationality of Biological Determinism

Aside from theoretical arguments that dismantle dominant understandings of sex categories as inherent naturally occurring phenomena, Anne Fausto-Sterling, who received her PhD in developmental genetics, famously made a biological argument in 1993 that there should be five rather than two sex categories and, in 2000, explained that the focus should in fact be moved away from genitalia because sex and gender are best conceptualized as points in a multidimensional space rather than on a continuum or categorically.[30] Fausto-Sterling's recent work demonstrates the irony and unnaturalness of what humans perceive to be "nature" and as "natural" and continues to dismantle notions of inherent sex-based difference, arguing instead that biological difference is socially and environmentally produced and not naturally occurring.[31]

The conception of sex categories as social rather than biological concepts is also evident through the way in which biological processes are constructed differently to place value on those associated with men and devalue those associated with women. Often in modern culture, the way in which biological sex processes are conceived can be illogical; exposing irrationalities surrounding the way these processes are regarded further reveals how they are socially constructed to reinforce a dominant patriarchal ideology. For instance, in modern U.S. slang "having balls" and "having big balls" implies strength and bravery although having testicles at all and having bigger testicles makes people more susceptible to pain and injury. Although modern conceptions of male genitalia suggest otherwise, the possession of such external organs as gonads and penises in general heightens individuals' vulnerability to injury, and this exposure to danger increases by organ size. Interestingly, blue whales, which possess the largest genitalia in the animal kingdom, hide their penises inside their bodies because if left exposed in open water, penises would produce drag and could easily be bitten off by predators.[32] In contrast, the patriarchal practice in U.S. culture of labeling someone to be "a pussy" denotes weakness, although vaginas are physiologically strong and resilient; they are self-cleaning, have a rich blood supply that promotes rapid healing, and can stretch up to 200 percent during sexual intercourse or childbirth.[33] Although scientific convention equates male anatomy with weakness and female anatomy with strength, dominant social ideology affirms the opposite. Even though this type of sexist ideology is not logical, it is strongly reinforced by language, and through such socialization processes in institutions as the family, medicine, education, and media, it continues to shape popular beliefs that reify the superiority of men and inferiority of women.

Gloria Steinem in her piece, "If Men Could Menstruate," also emphasizes how sex concepts are not logical, but rather serve to reinforce the existing social structure. Steinem contends that "logic is in the eyes of the logician," arguing that the power of giving birth makes "womb envy" more logical than "penis envy" just as white skin does not make people more superior, just more susceptible to skin cancer. Women's inferiority and lack of political power are currently justified by the phenomenon of menstruation, where women are thought to be overemotional and incapable of leadership because of their menstrual cycles. Steinem posits what the world would be like if men, rather than women, could menstruate and proposes that menstruation would become an "enviable, worthy, masculine event" that men would use to justify their power and superiority. Steinam suggests that men would brag about how long and how much they menstruated, sanitary supplies would be federally funded and free, menstruation would be a commonly discussed topic in media, and women would be denied access to such fields as medicine and mathematics because they would be viewed as not being able to handle the sight of blood and without possessing a natural biological gift of measurement.[34]

The social construction of sex is also shown in Emily Martin's work, in which she describes how the manner in which children are taught in biology classes about reproduction relies on stereotypes central to cultural definitions of femininity and masculinity rather than scientific evidence. Specifically, she shows that scientific schoolbooks imply that female biological processes are less worthy than male biological processes, which reinforces conventional beliefs that women are less worthy than men. For example, language commonly used in textbooks often characterizes the process of menstruation as "dying," "losing," or "expelling" and as wasteful, whereas the process of ejaculation is described as "triumphant," "impressive," and "remarkable." Furthermore, textbooks repeatedly depict the egg as passive, whereas sperms are portrayed as vigorous penetrators of the egg despite overwhelming research that shows that the sperm and the egg are mutually active partners in reproduction.[35] The existence of "the money shot" in pornography that deems the male orgasm and release of semen to be the ultimate achievement and culmination of sexual activity further underscores the point that biological processes associated with men are emphasized as culturally more important and desirable than those of women. Semen is comparable in consistency to both female ejaculate and menstrual fluid; however, in contemporary culture, these substances are commonly viewed as disgusting or as burdens rather than revered, and rarely are female orgasms or the clitoris mentioned in sexual education classes or materials.

Questioning Dominant Ideology of Women's Biological Athletic Inferiority

Not only is female-specific biology devalued but also physical characteristics that both women and men share are distinguished, even though they are not directly related to sex. For instance, both men and women have breasts and the majority of people experience heightened sensitivity in their nipples, but only women's breasts are eroticized, deemed inappropriate for public display, and covered with bras, which research suggests may be linked with breast cancer.[36] Both women and men have fat and muscle, but dominant gender ideology and research emphasize than men have more muscle and women have more fat, not because muscle and fat are sexed, but because muscle is valued and fat is devalued. Interestingly, the fat/muscle distinction is often explained through hormones, where the hormone associated with maleness, testosterone, is culturally linked with the valued attributes of strength and muscle growth, whereas the hormone associated with femaleness, estrogen, is culturally linked to the devalued attributes of emotion and fat development. Although both men and women possess varying levels of testosterone and estrogen, testosterone is often associated with aggressive behavior, although this is not commonly viewed as problematic because testosterone and aggressiveness are associated with men and masculinity, even though emotions associated with estrogen are socially constructed as debilitating for women. Another socially defined difference for men is reflected in gendered notions regarding the appropriateness of occupying social and physical space. Women are encouraged to physically take up less space than men, not only feeling the pressure to conform to societal ideals of thinness but also evidenced by the existence of the size 0 in women's but not men's fashion (literally that women should aspire to be nothing, or double nothing, in the case of the size 00).[37] The way in which women are not physically expected to take up space is also evident in how their actions are socially constructed, where women are not supposed to affect their surrounding environment. For instance, although stomachs and intestines are not sexed, gas emission is seen as more natural and socially acceptable for men than for women. This is also evidenced in the case of snoring, where men changing their auditory environment is viewed as natural, whereas women's snoring is not socially accepted. Such false biological designations of separateness can be harmful to society. For example, in the case of alcohol consumption, women are told to drink less than men; however, the metabolization of alcohol has nothing to do with sexed characteristics, but rather individuals' size, stress level, nutrition, drinking patterns, and so on. It is a public disservice to suggest that men and women should consume a different amount of drinks per day to remain healthy, because this may result in smaller men over consuming alcohol and perhaps engaging in such dangerous behavior as drunk driving when they have had the prescribed amount of drinks for men. In addition, Catherine Palmer suggests that assumptions based on male drinking as normal and drinking behavior as a means for reinforcing hegemonic masculinity result in a lack of research on the relationship among women, sport, and alcohol consumption.[38]

Research in the area of biological sex differences in sports performance outcomes in general should also be reconsidered, especially notions of inferiority associated with cause and effect should be reexamined. For instance, the only reason that men were "better" ski jumpers at the 2010 Winter Olympic Games is that women were not allowed to compete in the event and there was no comparable women's competition. In fact, Linsdey Vonn holds the record for the longest jump off Whistler, British Columbia, built for the 2010 Vancouver Olympics.[39] After a law suit brought by female ski jumpers, the International Olympic Committee (IOC) announced that a women's ski jumping event would be added to the 2014 Sochi Olympic Winter Games program. However, women still had only one event (normal hill competition), whereas men had three (normal hill, large hill, and team competition).[40] To combat these inequities, Mika Hämäläinen recommends implementation of either mixed-pair or integrated competitions.[41] Because there is no biological or physical rationale for sex segregation in ski jumping, Mark Stoddart suggests that the current policy is ideologically and implicitly sexist, as ski landscapes are still constructed as masculine and the mountainous terrain is viewed as a site for performing athletic, risk-seeking masculinity, resulting in different power relations in terms of sex and place.[42]

Like the sexism evident in Olympic ski jumping, Nadav Goldschmied and Jason Kowalczyc argue that the sex segregation of Olympic shooting was a blatant sexist response to Chinese skeet shooter, Zhang Shan, who set a new world record and became the first woman to win a gold medal in the 1992 Olympic Games in a nonsegregated shooting event. In their study of NCAA Rifle Championships from the 2007 to 2013 seasons, the researchers found no sex differences in performance and recommend that the Olympic Committee should reconsider its "separate and (un)equal" policy.[43]

Scholars have argued that sports researchers should understand the methodological limitations of studies conducted in a patriarchal and capitalist social system.[44] Vikki Krane argues that feminist theories and methodologies are necessary in sports research because feminist research recognizes that knowledge production is a social process.[45] She cites Jack Nelson et al.'s study of differential throwing behavior of boys and girls to show that the authors, even after finding sex differences in environmental factors that affect throwing behavior, chose to conclude that physical differences were responsible for boys' throwing superiority,[46] thus confirming the dominant gender ideology and resulting in subsequent outcomes reflecting this ideology.[47] In fact, Fontini Venetsanou and Antonis Kambas found that home and school environment and facilities and level of permissiveness and acceptance of behaviors within those environments, along with SES, existence and absence of siblings, and movement programs, affect preschoolers motor development, and also suggest that the living environment (urban vs. rural) and technology time should also be considered in future research on physicality.[48] Andrew Smiler explains that the relationship between theory and measurement is particularly important in masculinity research because not only does the psychological construct of masculinity reflect researchers' underlying theoretical preferences but their measures also reflect these preferences where they serve as both subject and object, symbolically representing the construct while also becoming the focus of investigation.[49]

That is to say the research on biological difference in sex performance in sports is conducted within and because of a dominant sexist ideology that privileges men, and most studies do not consider how factors other than biology may influence results. Typical thinking about causality of biology and sport is disrupted in Irwin Silverman's research on visual reaction time, where he found that sex differences are narrowing and will likely continue to decrease. Specifically, he suggests that sport participation improves reaction time, so instead of women's exclusion from sport being due to their inferior performance, the lack of participation was causing the poor performance, and because women's sport participation has increased, their reaction times have improved.[50] Heinz Krombholz also found that for preschool girls, participation in sport outside of school, as well as having an older sibling, served to positively affect physical performance, disrupting the causal linear thinking evident in most research on sex performance differences in older individuals.[51] In their presentation of the case of Little League vs. Maria Pepe and the National Organization for Women, Joe Torg and Jeff Ryan disprove much of the dominant ideology of sex differences in prepubescent children, suggesting that girls are 100 percent as strong, quick, and reactive as boys and that female bones are actually more mature, making girls less susceptible to injury.[52] Although they believe that disparities develop during puberty, it can also be argued that the changing societal expectations and treatment of boys and girls that occur during puberty account for such differences. In addition, Debra Lewis, Eliezer Kamon, and James Hodgson document important physical similarities between men and women despite commonly accepted ideas that highlight physiological and morphological sex differences. For instance, these researchers found that men and women experience similar relative strength gains when training under the same program; there are no differences between sexes in central or peripheral cardiovascular adaptations to aerobic training; no differences in relative increases in the maximum volume of oxygen an athlete can use (VO2 max) for men and women when they are trained under the same intensity, frequency, and duration; the menstrual cycle phase makes no difference in performance; and when men and women are matched for surface area:mass, VO2 max, and percentage body fat, the major disadvantages women have in hot temperatures disappear.[53]

Lynda Birke and Gail Vines argue that in sports research, biology should not be viewed as "fixed," and a truly feminist understanding of women and sport must rely on the acceptance of the notion that physiology is transformative.[54] Whereas research suggesting innate biological difference in sex reifies sexist disparities as fixed, studies that do consider alternative explanations in sex sport performance are important because they provide avenues for combating inequality. Gerturd Pfister found that similar to other public social environments where women do not claim much space, they seldom appropriate and use the natural environment for sport, and these differences can be changed, because they are caused by such social factors as familial and peer-group socialization and differential sporting facilities.[55]

A 2015 *Women's Health* online article, "9 Female Athletes Speak Candidly About Their Body Hang-Ups," featured such elite sportswomen as Olympic gold medalist swimmer Natalle Coughlln and FIFA World Cup champion Megan Rapinoe discussing parts of their body they dislike, even though these features may contribute to their athletic success.[56] Shari Dworkin shows that both female nonweight lifters and moderate weight lifters negotiate traditional notions of femininity, resulting in limiting their bodily agency through avoiding, adjusting, or holding back during weight workouts.[57] Interestingly, Mari Sisjord and Elsa Kristiansen found that elite female wrestlers were policing their own strength and muscularity to conform to dominant ideals of femininity.[58] Female judokas in Anna Kavoura, Marja Kokkonen, and Tatiana Ryba's study also were "doing" femininity, even though it served to inhibit their athletic performance.[59] In Jesse Steinfeldt et al.'s study of college student athletes, although all of the male athletes reported a desire for muscularity, some female athletes did not want to be muscular, suggesting that women as a group are not reaching their potential for muscular development.[60] In their study on sex and physical self-concept, Anne Klomstem, Skaalvik Einar, and Geir Espnes found large sex differences in the global physical self-concept of endurance, strength, appearance, and body fat, whereas they found smaller differences in health self-concept of flexibility and coordination dimensions. These differences between girls and boys were largely attributed to perceptions of physical appearance, and the researchers cite such differential uniforms as those evident in gymnastics and beach volleyball, as one avenue for improvement.[61] Herbert Marsh and Susan Jackson also found differences in the self-concepts of male and female high school athletes and suggest that one avenue for change is through altering the way in which masculinity and femininity are viewed as bipolar, linear, and opposite concepts, where being more of one suggests that an individual is less of the other.[62]

Although dominant sexist ideology assumes biological differences in competitiveness linked to differential levels of testosterone, Anna Dreber, Emma von Essen, and Evan Ranehill found no sex difference in reaction to competition in any tasks and suggest that studies in different environments with different types of tasks are important to make generalizable claims about sex differences in competitiveness.[63] Howard Nixon also did not find sex differences in attitudes of toughness or in thresholds for pain among athletes and nonathletes, demonstrating that even though men are more prone to pain because of higher rates of participation in high-contact sports, they are not more tolerant of pain.[64] In addition to research refuting notions of sex difference in inclination toward competition, Shelly McGrath and Ruth Chananie-Hill present the irrationality of the paradox that women are simultaneously taught that they cannot develop big muscles but at the same time are taught not to lift weights because they will get bigger, and thus become unattractive to males, showing the complex relationship among sports, sex, and sexuality.[65]

Sexuality, Sport, and the Social Construction of Sex and Gender

It would not be fair to examine the social construction of sex in sports contexts without also discussing the social construction of sexuality because, as Butler, Stoltenberg, and Wittig have explained, sex and sexuality are intrinsically tied. Similar to how dominant ideology related to men's biological superiority and women's inferiority is often irrational, so too is dominant ideology associated with sexuality and sports. For example, football is perceived to be one of the most masculine and heteronormative sports in U.S. society, but Alan Dundes argues that football is actually homoerotic; the goal of the game is ultimately to penetrate the other team's end zone, there exists such position names as "tight end," the ball is shaped like a testicle, and each play climaxes in a pile of men laying on top of one another.[66] In addition, football commentators often sexualize the players and their bodies using slow motion technology, which is hardly used in television outside of pornography.[67] Conversely, males participating in ice skating are often labeled to be homosexual, when in fact the sport of ice skating relies on heteronormative ideology: male ice skaters are usually fully clothed, whereas even though they are performing on ice, female skaters wear leotards that expose their legs, and in the partners competition, men lift and throw women but women do not lift and throw men.

Most people believe that sex determines one's sexuality where individuals are defined by whether they are attracted to similarly sexed, other-sexed, or multiple types of sexed individuals, which results in individuals being defined as heterosexual, homosexual, bisexual, queer, pansexual, omnisexual, gay, lesbian, and beyond (although this definition of sexual orientation does not apply to asexual individuals and object-sexual individuals). However, it is important to recognize that sexuality also affects individuals' sex and gender, where to whom one is sexually attracted often determines their own sex and gender performance. For example, girls in school may not answer questions aloud because they fear that if they do, boys will not like them because intelligence is not a trait consistent with dominant notions of femininity and is not traditionally viewed as attractive in girls and women. The link among sex, gender, and sexuality is important in sports contexts, specifically because men, and especially those in masculine sports, who excel are often perceived as attractive, whereas women who excel at sports, and especially at the very same masculine sports, are frequently perceived as unattractive. This is important because differential returns on sports involvement in terms of popularity and sexual desirability result in such sex disparities as those associated with motivation to take up and continue to participate in sports and in large-scale inequities in media coverage and sponsorships.

Sexuality is one of the main ways that maleness and femaleness and masculinity and femininity are constructed. This is seen in the popular notion that boys become men through their sexual conquests of women (but not of other men) and are expected to continue to prove their manhood throughout adulthood by being sexually skilled and experienced. Conversely, girls are often assigned the task of sexual gatekeeping to preserve their femininity, and female sexuality in general is feared or ignored.[68] Kathleen Miller et al.'s study demonstrates how the connection among sex, sexuality, and gender performance is evident in sports contexts, where the researchers found important sex differences in how sports participation affected adolescents' sexuality. For girls, athletic participation afforded empowerment, social support, and a less traditional feminine orientation that may have enabled them to resist sexual pressure, whereas for boys, athletic participation reified sexist notions that males are the primary initiators and consumers of sex and, thus, desiring and partaking in sexual activity are expected.[69]

In her study of accounts of tomboyism, C Lynn Carr highlights the connection among sexuality, sport, and gender conformity and resistance. She finds that when scholars presume that women reject tomboyism in adolescence, they presume conformity and heterosexuality. However, she found that some women, and especially heterosexual women, who are not afforded the benefits of such alternative gendered identifications as "butch" and "dyke," which have been reclaimed by queer communities, secede from tomboyism, because of the lack of positive language for competent, active, muscular, assertive, androgynous, athletic, strong, and independent girls and women.[70] In addition, Thalma Lobel, Michelle Slone, and Gil Winch used a tomboyism questionnaire and found that Israeli preadolescent girls who reported traits and behaviors considered to be traditionally masculine were less popular, had lower social self-esteem, and were less satisfied with their gender.[71]

Past research on sex, sexuality, and sports shows the relationship among dominant sex ideology, notions of femininity and masculinity, and perceived sexual orientation and attractiveness. Mary Jo Kane found that both women and men afforded females involved in sex-appropriate sports significantly greater status than females involved in sex-inappropriate sports.[72] Using interest in sports as a male-valued behavior, Donald McCreary found strong support for the sexual orientation hypothesis that, for males, there is a stronger perceived link between gender roles and sexuality and that a male acting in a feminine way is more likely to be considered a homosexual than a female acting in a masculine way.[73] Eric Anderson in his research on male cheerleaders and masculinity demonstrates the role of sexuality in determining how athletes view their own and others' masculine self-worth.[74] In their study on the sexualization of female athletes, Elizabeth Daniels and Heidi Wartena found that boys appeared to objectify sexualized athletes more than sexualized models, which they argue demonstrates that sexualized images of female athletes may contribute to the devaluation of female athleticism.[75]

Sex categories are constructed to suggest differences in needs, desires, and experiences of sexual pleasure for women and men, although it is evident that all such aspects of sexuality as what is seen as desirable, what constitutes sex, and what sex partners and acts are socially acceptable are culturally, not biologically, determined, and therefore, sexuality is not naturally sexed. In fact, in a recent study, neuroscientists found that regardless of sex, age, sexual orientation, nationality, and race, participants rated erogenous sensitivity of 41 different body parts at similar intensities. Interestingly, the researchers stated that the result that surprised them most was that sex differences in eroticism were not evident, even though anatomically there was nothing to warrant such a finding because sex categories and eroticism are socially constructed.[76] However, the example does show how deeply ingrained the dominant ideology suggesting biological sex differences is in society and within the scientific community. In fact, neuroscientist Gina Rippon has recently received a great deal of media attention for dismissing studies in her field that rely on sex essentialism, claiming that if someone examined a male brain and a female brain, they could not tell them apart.[77] Rippon contends that there are very few sex differences in the brain and any differences can be attributed to what she calls "the drip drip drip of gender stereotyping," which are environmentally, not naturally, caused.[78]

Sport and the Social Construction of Race

The essentialist view that there exist natural sex differences still evident in neuroscience and other academic disciplines is comparable to conducting scientific research based on false notions of racial essentialism. Similar to how there exist countless biological similarities and comparably few anatomical variances among differently sexed individuals, there are far more biological commonalities than differences among individuals across racial categories. The existence of biologically determined racial categories has been consistently disproven empirically, where it is now well documented that there is greater genetic diversity within designated racial categories than between them.[79] Ichiro Kawachi, Norman Daniels, and Dean Robinson explain that even though "science" intending to prove such racial differences as studies that attempted to expose cranial size differences between Blacks and Whites to justify the notion of white intelligence superiority has been discredited, the completion of The Human Genome Project in 2003 gave rise to new biologized notions of racial disparities and promoted research aimed at pinpointing genetic racial differences.[80] An entire issue of one of the world's most cited scientific journals, *Nature Genetics* (2004), was devoted to examining the possible implications of The Human Genome Project and cautions scientists against oversimplifying the concept of race. The issue Editorial stated as follows:

> The use of race as a proxy is inhibiting scientists from doing their job of separating and identifying the real environmental and genetic causes of disease. . . . We are not going to be able to solve the social problem of racism scientifically, because its source lies with racists and not in the intrinsic biology of their victims.[81]

Not surprisingly, over a decade of genetic studies inspired by The Human Genome Project did not reveal inherent race-based biological differences between groups, although research in this area continues to be financially supported and conducted. In a recent *Atlantic* article, Jason Silverstein provides an overview of the political and economic reasons for why genetic research of racial health disparities continues to be funded despite the lack of significant findings that a genetic component of inequality exists.[82] For instance, in their review of 68 published articles from 2007 to 2013, Jay Kaufman et al. found no significant genetic explanations for the disparity in cardiovascular disease between African Americans and Europeans.[83] Silverstein uses interview quotations from Kaufman and other prominent researchers as well as articles published in such world-renowned academic journals as *Nature* and *Science* to argue that genetic research on racial disparities remains socially acceptable because it is a way to divert the responsibility of disease away from social institutions and onto racial minorities themselves, alleviating the necessity for action on the part of governing bodies to reduce social inequality. On the basis of his interviews and literature review, Silverstein also debunks the biological existence of the concept of ancestry, showing how ancestry is constructed by scientists through its relation to race and serves simply as a gentle proxy rather than provides meaningful insight into health disparities. Citing a 2005 editorial in *Nature*

Biotechnology, which stated "pooling people in race silos is akin to zoolo-
gists grouping raccoons, tigers, and okapis on the basis that they are all
stripey," Silverstein contends that genetic research on racial health disparities is not only scientifically flawed but morally flawed as well.[84]

Bruce Link and Jo Phelan's theory of fundamental causes outlined the
association between social factors and disease outcomes and showed how
disparities are continuously reproduced.[85] Social scientists continue to provide evidence that racial health disparities in such areas as obesity, heart
disease, diabetes, and life expectancy can be attributed to such social rather
than biological factors as SES, the built environment, and large-scale segregation, racism, and discrimination, which affect access to and treatment
in health care, health-related behaviors, and psychological and physical outcomes.[86] For instance, in two recent studies, David Chae and colleagues
found that racism, racial discrimination, and the internalization of negative racial group attitudes are related to cardiovascular disease risk and the
acceleration of the aging process for black men.[87] In his most recent study,
Chae quantified community-level racism through Google searches contain-
ing the "N-word" and found a significant association between racism and
Blacks' mortality rate as well as risk for heart disease, cancer, and stroke,
even after controlling for socioeconomic factors.[88] In her study on racial
and ethnic disparities in medical care, Irena Stepanikova found that under
high time pressure, physicians are more likely to rely on implicit racial
biases, which for black and Hispanic patients resulted in a less serious diagnosis and lower likelihood of referral to specialists.[89] Because race and
ancestry are socially constructed rather than natural categories, Matthew
Anderson et al. argue for removing race from the forefront of patients' medical
charts and instead recording race as an aspect of patents' social history.[90]

This is not to say that we dispute empirical research suggesting that racial
group membership is associated with differential health outcomes and
proneness to disease. Rather, similar to how culture comes before biology
in the case of sex and gender, so too does it for race and ethnicity. The social
processes in which racial and ethnic categories are produced and maintained result in biological outcomes. Geographical boundaries, conceptions of attractiveness and acceptable mating partners, medical knowledge
and education, access to birth control and abortion, slavery, internment
camps, incarceration, rape, genocide, and freedom, stress and comfort, war
and peace, and poverty and wealth are culturally constructed phenomena
that affect biological and genetic processes and realities. Racial and ethnic
categories and differential outcomes, biological and otherwise, associated
with group membership, are produced and reproduced through social, not
natural, mechanisms.

Like sex, race is a social, rather than biological category that people experience socially, not bodily. Such perceived genetic markers of race as skin color are not physically felt, but rather socially felt. In addition, racial categories change across time and space and the concept of "whiteness" has transformed over time.[91] For instance, such immigrant groups as Jews, Irish, and Italians were not considered to be white in the early 1900s, and a person of color currently traveling across countries would likely be labeled in different racial categories depending on where they were. Classifying people by skin color and their other perceived racialized physical characteristics is as arbitrary as dividing them by eye color, as Jane Elliot so famously did in 1968 to teach her third grade class about racism. Similar to how biological justifications of superiority and inferiority are concocted to support the prevailing sexist ideology, so too are racial justifications that support white supremacy. To rationalize the ideology that blue-eyed people were superior, Elliot lied to her students that melanin, the pigment only present in blue-eyed children, was linked with higher intelligence and learning ability. Elliot also segregated the blue-eyed children, gave the blue-eyed children special privileges, and emphasized the positive attributes and performances of specific blue-eyed students while underscoring the mistakes and poor behavior of brown-eyed students. In only a few days, Elliot's experiments resulted in internalized notions of superiority and inferiority reflected in children's differential behavior, treatment of one another, and examination scores.[92]

Although the implementation and justification of racial divisions are social inventions, racist ideology has manifested more than hundreds of years, and even in the 21st century, race remains one of the, if not the most important, factors in determining individuals' life chances.[93] Similar to sex categories, race categories are not simply about difference, but rather dominance, where racial categories exist in a hierarchy. James Loewen explains that in Western societies, racial categories and racism originated from the interplay between slavery as a socioeconomic system and racial ideology as an ideal system, justifying the taking of land from indigenous populations and enslaving Africans to work that land. Although Loewen emphasizes the complexity of the historical issue of slavery, he shows that racism became the rationale for the differential treatment of individuals based on their skin color, made possible by Europe's advantages in military and social technology in the 15th century.[94] Although the enslavement of one race by another is no longer socially acceptable, Whites still maintain their control of social, political, and economic resources, and racism remains a driving force behind white privilege in ideology and reality. Sociologists have developed various theories of racism and prejudice, which seek to explain how and why Whites have continued to preserve their power. Notable examples include the following: Joe Feagin's macrolevel conception of white privilege, systemic racism,[95] in which he incorporates Michael Omi and Howard Winant's theory of racial formation[96] and Stokely Carmichael and Charles Hamilton's concept of institutional racism or colonialism;[97] Donald Kinder and David Sears' explanation of symbolic racism;[98] Lawrence Bobo, James Kluegel, and Ryan Smith's concept of laissez-faire racism,[99] derived from Herbet Blumer's group position theory of prejudice;[100] and Eduardo Bonilla Silva's theory of color-blind racism,[101] which also encompasses such emerging theories as Tyrone Forman's notion of racial apathy that asserts that ignoring racism is racist.[102] These works have helped to explain the shift from old-fashioned, overt, Jim Crow era biological explanations of racial inferiority to modern, covert, justifications for Blacks' subservient group position. In addition, they have contributed to developing a better understanding of contemporary racist ideology.

Previous research has highlighted the challenges people of color face because of both historical and contemporary racial discrimination in major social institutions, including education, housing, the criminal justice system, and the labor market.[103] Furthermore, sociologists and critical race theorists have documented how white privilege and white supremacy serve to maintain existing social arrangements that preserve the power, status, and wealth of Whites, while simultaneously disadvantaging people of color.[104]

As a social institution, sport has served to reflect and reproduce dominant ideology and outcomes of the existing racial hierarchy, and studies have continued to show the existence of racial discrimination in sports contexts.[105] As discussed in the introduction, sports contexts have been historically characterized by racial exclusion and discrimination, and notions of racial groups' athletic superiority and inferiority have changed over time to privilege Whites and disadvantage racial minorities. Gary Sailes debunks biological notions of the racial superiority of Blacks, first citing their exclusion through widespread racial segregation and the perceived notion of Blacks as inferior, and thus unable to challenge Whites in athletic contexts. He uses empirical support to refute such contemporary theories of Blacks' athletic superiority as the matriarchy theory (that black athletes are more likely to come from single-mother households, so without fathers, seek bonds with male coaches and are hostile and unfocused, channeling this aggressiveness into sports), Mandingo theory (that slave owners intentionally bred slaves requiring physically large, muscular men), survival of the fittest theory (Blacks who survived the middle passage were more physically adept than those who did not), and psychological and dumb jock theories

(Blacks are not fit for leadership or pressure positions within and outside of sports contexts). To dispel these myths, Sailes discusses how genetic outcomes during slavery cannot possibly account for the 45 million African Americans currently living in the United States, because slave women were raped, free Blacks as well as the majority of slaves were able to choose their mates, African Americans often mated with Native Americans, and the gene pool from slave breeding, even if it did occur, would have been lost before the 20th century. Furthermore, he cites examples of Blacks who excel at intellectual, leadership, and pressure positions within sports and points to studies that show that black athletes are more untrusting of coaches, ultimately explaining disparities associated with Blacks' recent success in sports and entertainment using social variables in the economic opportunity structure.[106] Despite the fact that for decades, sociologists have provided such rational social justifications for black athletic dominance as racial segregation, discrimination, lack of social opportunity, economic limitations, and lack of access to domains apart from sports and entertainment,[107] racist essentialist ideology explaining black athletic success still prevails and serves to uphold the racist social structure.

David Leonard argues that with the success and adoration of such athletes as Shaquille O'Neal, Tiger Woods, and LeBron James, Whites are able through sports contexts to erase the many institutions and occurrences of racial politics and rework the reality of racial inequality in the United States to legitimize notions of colorblindness, freedom, equality, and democracy. He points out that "Black athletes not only elucidate the fulfillment of the American Dream, but also America's imagined racial progress . . . [which] overshadows the realities of segregated schools, police brutality, unemployment, and the White supremacist criminal justice system."[108]

Much of the adulation for black athletes is still related to the obsession with black athletic bodies where black athletes are celebrated more than their white counterparts with regard to brute physicality and athleticism. For example, Nancy Spencer demonstrates how the success of Venus and Serena Williams has consistently been attributed more often to their muscular bodies rather than to their intelligence or work ethic.[109] In fact, *The New York Times* recently asked Serena's white competitors to compare their bodies to hers,[110] drawing much criticism surrounding racism and sexism.[111]

In her content analysis of sports advertisements, Mikaela Dufur found that black athletes are more likely to be portrayed as succeeding because of innate physical abilities and as angry, violent, or hypersexual, whereas white athletes are more often portrayed as succeeding because of hard work, intelligence, or leadership qualities. In their study on the media portrayal of soccer players, David McCarthy, Robyn Jones, and Paul Potrac found that not only was the physicality of black players and cognitive ability of Whites emphasized but also black focus group participants viewed this distinction as a problematic reliance on stereotypes and white focus group participants were unsure that it was a true misrepresentation.[112]

Another example of the stereotypical portrayal of black bodies is photographer Annie Leibovitz's 2008 *Vogue* cover that juxtaposed model Giselle Buncheon in a green evening gown and high heels next to LeBron James who was wearing basketball clothes and sneakers, yelling and bouncing a ball.[113] The photo closely resembles the U.S. army recruitment poster image of "the mad brute," an ape-like, dark, muscular creature, holding a club in one hand and a white women wearing a green dress in the other.[114] After American Gabriel Douglas became the first black woman to win the all-around gold medal in gymnastics during the 2012 Olympic Games, commentator Bob Costa's summary of her success on National Broadcasting Company (NBC) was immediately followed by a commercial depicting a monkey performing a gymnastics routine dressed in U.S. (red, white, and blue) colors.[115] The timing of the commercial cannot be merely attributed to coincidence or purchased broadcast time, because the airing of the competition was delayed to occur during U.S. primetime, six hours after it originally happened in London and the commercial was for an NBC sitcom, giving network producers plenty of opportunity to change the selection.

Through role modeling and stereotyping, Blacks face income inequality in sport where their prominent presence in football, basketball, and baseball has not equated with their encouraged entrance into such high-revenue sports as golf, tennis, soccer, hockey, and horse and auto racing.[116] Lori Martin uses the example of Blacks' historic legacy in golf along with the racist treatment of Tiger Woods to illustrate that notions of "black sports" and "white sports" exist ideologically and serve to reinforce the reality.[117] These ideas of biological racial difference and natural proclivity to physicality and particular sports are comparable to the dominant ideology surrounding the existence of two distinct, separate sexes, female physical inferiority, and the distinction of "female sports" and "male sports." The way in which false essentialist racial and sexist ideology has resulted in historic and contemporary unequal treatment demonstrates the necessity for dismantling all notions of biological difference to achieve equality.

Sport as a Social Construction: Rationale for Changing Dominant Ideology Surrounding Physical Aptitude

As previously mentioned, even if inherent biological differences between sex and race groups existed, those differences would not necessarily result in differences in sports outcomes because sports are social inventions and, therefore, no group can be naturally disposed to success and failure. Not only do different sports require different skill sets but also within sports, different positions require different skill sets and the rules of sports are consistently changing, demonstrating the inappropriateness of the notion of natural athletic ability. It is commonly assumed that certain aspects of physicality result in success or failure in sports, but a sociological perspective suggests otherwise. For instance, in answering the question of why tall individuals are good at basketball, conventional wisdom relies on common constructions of knowledge rather than empirical evidence to justify the position, perhaps arguing that tall individuals are better because they are closer to the basket or have longer arms, without considering whether these qualities actually make someone better at basketball.

In the 2005 film, *Thank You for Smoking*, the protagonist's child is given a homework assignment to answer the question, "Why is American government the best government in the world?"[118] When the child asks the protagonist, a lobbyist for the tobacco industry, to help him write the essay, rather than relying on dominant ethnocentric notions of U.S. superiority to answer the question, he instead discusses why the question is unanswerable. He explains to his child that the question is flawed because, first, it makes the assumption that the U.S. government is the best, and second, that "best" is not a clear measure, which in this case could be defined by crime, poverty, literacy, and so on. The protagonist states that even if the United States had the best government, there would be no way to prove it; rather what matters in answering the question is how the argument is presented and if it will be accepted as correct. Similar to how asking children to explain why something is true rather than questioning whether it is true results in the social reproduction of dominant knowledge, values, and ideals, a sociological perspective proposes that the dominant ideology suggesting that tall individuals are good at basketball makes the notion a reality. Tall players are more likely to be scouted out and given additional attention by parents and basketball authorities to cultivate their game. Tall people may experience a positive self-fulfilling prophecy regarding how their height affects their ability and may have more self-confidence on the court, positively affecting their performance as well as furthering subsequent opportunities to make teams and impress coaches and achieve even greater success. In addition, tall people may work harder at basketball than other activities because they feel as though they already have a "natural" advantage and should thus focus their time and resources to development in this area.

Are tall people better at basketball? One could make the argument that they are by comparing the heights on competitive basketball rosters to the general population, but this does not prove causality. A better approach lies in questioning aspects of the question; for instance, what does it mean to be better? Does the tallest team always win the championship? Of course not. And what does "tall" even mean? Tall is a socially constructed category similar to sex and race where what is considered tall changes across time and space. Most people probably know a tall person who is terrible at basketball, as well as others who are unsuccessful at sports, even though stereotypes based on physiology would suggest otherwise. For instance, there are many Jamaicans who are slow runners and short people who are bad at gymnastics, but dominant ideology suggests that these groups have a natural disposition to these physical feats. Logically, living in a human-designated republic does not naturally result in a genetic disposition to running; rather the economic climate of the country and its cultural emphasis on track and field as a feasible and desirable avenue for national success and pride cultivate motivation, access, role modeling, knowledge, and socialization into running among Jamaican people. Similarly, the dominant notion that short people are naturally better at gymnastics is easily disproven. It is obvious that those who have never come into contact with such inventions as the pommel horse or vault would not be able to perform a routine, no matter how small they were; what matters is if they are socialized into using the equipment and their bodies, either by watching others or by being taught, in the socially constructed way in which the sport is defined. Similar to the existence of individuals who do not achieve athletic success in accordance with social stereotypes, successful athletes who do not fit stereotypical performance expectations can be pointed to dismantle dominant ideology surrounding natural physical athletic disposition. For example, Steph Curry, who is 6'3, 185 pounds (lbs), and lacks the muscle development typically seen in NBA players, received the league's Most Valuable Player (MVP) award in 2015.[119] Jordan Kilganon, who is white, recently set the world running box jumping record, clearing a box 75 inches tall.[120] David Fangupo, at 6'2, and 348 lbs—more than 100 lbs heavier than most running backs in the NFL—rushed for 538 yards and 10 touchdowns on 74 carries in his senior year of high school, leading his team to their third consecutive Big Island Interscholastic Federation title in 2013.[121] Conversely, running back Jay Carter, 4'9 and 140 lbs. made the Rice University football team as a walk on in 2011.[122] Despite these examples, a sociological perspective demonstrates that people believe stereotypes, because dominant ideology encourages their validation as well as the dismissal of contradictory evidence as exceptions; thus the rule proves the rule.

As sociologists, it is not our objective to look at individual examples that prove or disprove dominant ideology, but rather to examine empirical evi-

dence nullifying dominant sexist and racist ideals. Once essentialist ideology is changed, then policies that reflect and justify the ideology may also
be altered to achieve a greater standard of social justice. In the case of sexist
ideology suggesting women's inferior athletic ability, research suggests that
one of the, if not the most important, factors in current athletic disparities
is how gender role socialization perpetuates this ideology. Gender role
socialization begins before birth, where parents often learn the sex of their
offspring and begin treating their fetuses differently in terms of how they
speak to and about them, their expectations for them, what clothes and
toys they buy, how they decorate their nurseries, and so on. The fact that
parents even care to know the sex (and sometimes hope for a certain-sexed
child) illustrates how early gender role socialization begins. Gender role
socialization affects all aspects of life in modern society, and in sports contexts it has important links to motivation, self-esteem, self-efficacy, and
self-concept, diet, exercise patterns, perceived opportunities for success and
personal and financial rewards, and expectations. Furthermore, gender role
socialization does not just affect those participating in sports but it also
shapes the beliefs and behaviors of parents, peers, coaches, team owners,
educators and administrators, sports media personnel, and political actors
who influence sports' regulation and policy. Dominant cultural notions of
women's inferior abilities and interests result in their inferior treatment and
subsequent inferiority.

Once born, children are continually socialized into sex-specific environments and behaviors, the research of which shows, along with their other
such characteristics as race and SES, results in different interests, participation in activities, self-perceptions, and outcomes in sports contexts,[123]
and other social realms.[124] Thus, if the starting point of individuals' athletic
ability was represented by a neutral entity, "0," gender role socialization
results not only in the disadvantaging of women, represented as a negative,
"–," but also in the advantaging of men, represented as a positive "+." The
mathematical addition of the countless ways in which each sex group is
either negatively or positively socialized into and away from sports results
in their greater distance from the starting point in opposite directions as well
as from one another. Moreover, gender role socialization of sport disadvantages and advantages is manifest at both the micro- and macrolevels and is
reflected across all social institutions, including the family, education, workforce, government, and media, further reinforcing notions of females' inferiority and males' superiority.

Often, athletes themselves are not aware of their own socialization into
sports, believing that they are naturally skilled or athletically inclined. However, on further reflection, often at the end of their sports careers, athletes

realize that they have worked quite hard to achieve their success, frequently devoting countless hours to practicing and learning the game, whereas once they cease practicing, their "natural" skills deteriorate. So if it isn't biology, what makes people better or worse at sports? We believe that the opportunity for success is the most important factor affecting sports outcomes. If individuals do not have the opportunity to learn and play sports, they will not achieve any measure of success at them. Without the opportunity to achieve at the highest levels of competition, girls and women will not be successful. In these contexts, current Title IX policies promoting sex segregation limit women's potential for realizing athletic success and must be transformed to provide females with the same opportunity as their male counterparts.

CHAPTER FIVE

The Politics of Opportunity

Intentions, Aftermath, and the Necessity for Change

What we are trying to do is provide equal access for women and men students to the educational process and the extracurricular activities in a school, where there is not a unique facet such as football involved. We are not requiring that intercollegiate football be desegregated, nor that the men's locker room be desegregated.
—Statement of Senator Birch Bayh during Title IX hearings.[1]

Even as the legislation was being debated on the Senate floor, supporters of Title IX found themselves imposing constraints on the law, as it pertained to sports, especially contact sports. It can be argued that measures to exclude women[2] were and continue to be implemented because the social institution of sport is regarded as a masculine domain,[3] where ideology concerning perceived biological sex differences is reproduced[4] and the elite white patriarchy is maintained.[5] The emergence and expansion of organized varsity sports for high school boys were, in part, rooted in the notion that athletic participation could contribute to young male's physical and mental preparation for service in another adult masculine domain—the military.[6] According to Donald Sabo, a major function of mainstream sports is to socialize athletes to conform to traditional sex expectations of a patriarchal society—where young boys overtly assert their masculinity through aggression and competition.[7] In addition, Jay Coakley suggests that sexist ideology and practices in sport are detrimental to both male and female athletes, where everyone's opportunities for participation are limited by social expectations of which sports are deemed sex appropriate and inappropriate.[8]

Stereotypical conceptualizations of masculinity and femininity have been both reproduced and contested within the realm of sport. For social science researchers, a traditionally "masculine sport" is a social construct, defined by competiveness, aggression, and a high frequency of physical contact in contrast to a traditionally "feminine sport," which places more emphasis on spatial barriers, less physical contact, and body movements that are "aesthetically pleasing."[9] Sex and gender stereotypes have shaped not only individuals' socialization into and out of certain sports but also the attitudinal and behavioral expectations of athletes within those sports. Researchers have found that such sports that emphasize beauty and grace as gymnastics, dance, and figure skating are often regarded as "feminine," even though these sports also require strength and endurance, whereas such sports that include elements of violence, aggression, and physical contact as football, boxing, and combat sports are considered "masculine,"[10] even though these sports often require elements of homoeroticism, characterized by close contact for long periods of time.

These constructions of sex appropriateness encourage most youth to engage in only sports that are assumed to be "appropriate" for themselves, as boys or girls, where these traditional gender norms socialize boys to be aggressive and competitive, and girls to be graceful and docile. In this manner, perceived innate differences between boys and girls are "translated into the 'natural' supremacy of males in the larger social order."[11] Thus, girls and boys are encouraged to play particular sports that maintain sex differences, and sex-appropriate gendered expectations within sports are perpetuated, reproducing traditional gender views.[12]

For both ideological and structural reasons, women have had few opportunities to play professional sports. Until recently, few people would pay to watch women play anything but "ladylike" sports in which they competed alone (e.g., figure skating and golf) or competed with nets or dividers separating opponents and preventing physical contact (e.g., tennis and volleyball). Although more people today are willing to pay to watch women play sports, the most popular "female" spectator sports continue to be tennis, figure skating, gymnastics, and golf—all of which are consistent with traditional notions of femininity.[13] Although ideology and practices surrounding the sex typing of sports still exist, women's incorporation into sport has also given rise to the notion of some sports as more gender neutral and, thus, appropriate for both females and males to participate in, such as golf and swimming.[14] The social construction evident in sports sex typing is apparent in what constitutes sex-appropriateness changes across time and space. For instance, in the United States, men's professional soccer is not as popular as men's football and basketball, whereas in other countries, soccer (or football, as the sport is known to the rest of the world) often is the most popular sport and therefore is thought to evoke hypermasculinity.

Consequently, in the United States, soccer is viewed as an appropriate sport for females to play, whereas outside the United States, soccer is not often considered an acceptable activity for girls and women.[15]

In general, sport is most often associated with stereotypically masculine attitudes and behaviors, and sporting experiences in this framework have been linked to the reproduction of sex inequalities.[16] Through qualitative in-depth interviews of youth sport coaches, Michael Messner observed that coaches tend to frame playing sports as an option for girls and an assumed activity for boys. The language of choice for girls extends to most societal realms since the women's rights movement, which, for example, promoted a woman's right to choose to participate in the labor force in addition to rearing children. Messner posits that playing sports is framed as another "choice" that women can exercise. In contrast, the absence of the language of choice for boys indicates an assumption that boys' activities are driven by a predisposition to be active in sports. The absence of choice language for boys highlights the taken-for-granted view that boys, regardless of choice, will play sports. This different way of talking about girls' and boys' involvement in sport assumes innate differences between them, which Messner terms "soft essentialism."[17]

A recent discourse analysis of several court decisions about boys' petitions to be allowed to play on girls teams also revealed essentialist assumptions about girls' "innate fragility and athletic inferiority" and the inappropriate-ness for boys and girls to play together.[18] There is reason to believe that Title IX strategies that are put into place to ensure equality of opportunity may continue to essentialize biological differences between men and women because sex-segregated sports teams are the norm in both high school and college.[19] Women are ensured legal protection from discrimination and equitable opportunity to play sports in schools, yet messages of sex inequality are still communicated when girls are channeled into separate sports that are often given less resources and less media attention. Unequal distribution of monetary resources and media attention to men's teams also reinforce the idea that women's sports compared to men's sports are not as valued.

Sport is also a site for the reproduction of hegemonic masculinity.[20] In a case study of a small town football community, Douglas Foley found that the social interactions and rituals surrounding the high school football team reproduced class, race, and sex inequalities.[21] Football, in particular, was shown to be ". . . deeply implicated in the reproduction of the local ruling class of white males, hence, class, patriarchal and racial forms of domi-nance."[22] The main function of sport according to Sabo is to predispose athletes to conform to traditional sex expectations of a patriarchal society, which affirm male superiority to females, both on and off the field.[23] In particular, males who play sports theoretically will be exposed to a hegemonic masculine ideology, "which becomes a part of their gender identity and conception of women and society."[24] Ben Clayton and Barbara Humberstone describe how a group of male collegiate athletes engaged in a reproduction of their collective masculine identity as a team to "(re)affirm" their separation from women and gay men, while "inferiorizing" women through biological and sexual objectification.[25]

The sex stereotypes that children learn through sport affect their sports participation choices to the extent that their choices reflect sex divisions in society and the higher value placed on men's sports. Dorothy Schmalz and Deborah Kerstetter analyzed the sports participation choices of a sample of 8–10-year-old boys and girls and found that they were aware of the stereotypes certain sports carried.[26] Specifically, they observed that a higher proportion of girls played boys' sports (e.g., football and wrestling) than the proportion of boys playing girls' sports (e.g., cheerleading and ballet). Boys in this sample were conscious that their masculinity would be questioned if they were to play girls' sports. In their interviews, Sohaila Shakib and Michele Dunbar found that athletes who play basketball engage in maintenance of a hegemonic masculinity, when basketball is understood as a male-dominated sport. They also report that both male and female basketball players interpreted their sports participation in a framework that consistently subordinated female basketball players below males.[27]

Despite the significant advances that females have made, there is also continuing evidence of the pervasiveness and power of traditional ideologies asserting male superiority in sports.[28] Investigations into the relationship between sports participation and sex ideology have been relatively limited to small qualitative studies' content analysis of text and media publications, and localized, small-sample empirical studies. However, they have consistently provided compelling evidence that female athletes are structurally and ideologically disadvantaged compared to men in sports, despite their increasing rates of sports participation.[29] Nevertheless, if females are able to make visible their rejection of gendered norms by participating in male-dominated sports at a young age, then encouraging sports participation in young girls has the potential, over time, to dismantle commonly held notions of what are "appropriate" sports for girls.

High School Female's Participation in Men's Contact Sports

The Title IX contact sports exemption allows educational institutions to segregate contact sports teams solely on the basis of sex, even though in doing so, it is at odds with the Equal Protection Clause of the Fourteenth Amendment, which requires that individuals be allowed to try out for an athletic team based on their skill—regardless of their sex.[30] Although the specific activities designated as contact sports vary, the category typically includes such sports that involve bodily contact as combat sports, rugby, ice hockey, football, and basketball. Traditionally, all contact sports—especially hyper-aggressive sports like football—have played a role in shaping masculine norms in Western cultures.[31] In the United States, however, football has become "king sport" and perceived to be the most masculine and violent team sport in the United States for much of the past century.[32] Due to improvements in training regimen, diet, and so on, athletes have increased their physical prowess, and thus, the level of violence has escalated.[33] Thus, the prototypical image of the U.S. football player (e.g., muscular, or "ripped," and prone to violence) has resulted in the elevation of football as a sport, and football players as athletes, to the top of the hierarchy of masculinity in the United States.[34] Young boys, many who aspire to be, or at least be like, elite football players, are significantly influenced by masculine norms associated with football.[35] Because football plays such a central role in defining masculinity, dominant sex-appropriate gender norms in society frame and aggressively defend the boundaries of this sport as "male turf." In this regard, the contrast in public perceptions of the Women's Football League and Legends (formerly Lingerie) Football League might provide insight into the threat presented by women playing football. Both leagues play tackle (not flag) football, and both leagues have athletically talented female athletes. However, in the women's professional football leagues, players wear regulation football uniform and compete in games governed by traditional football rules, but in the Lingerie League, players wear highly sexualized nontraditional outfits. Simply comparing the Facebook likes for the two contrasting forms of women's professional football illustrates the relative low popularity and acceptance of women playing football under similar conditions as men (Women's Football Alliance—7,230 likes) versus the much greater popularity and acceptance of women playing football in sexualized ways that reaffirm rather than threaten masculine identity (Legends Football League—475,599 likes). Thus, compared to other sports, most males and females alike believe that playing football is not appropriate for girls and women. Nevertheless, the record shows that some females are interested in and can and do play football.[36]

Pre-Title IX Football

In recent years, most people likely have seen periodic media coverage of "exceptional" cases of females trying out for, or playing on, male contact sports teams. One recent example that received national media coverage involves Shelby Osborne, a high school girl who played football for Jefferson High School in Lafayette, Indiana. She recently made history in becoming college football's first female defensive back after being recruited by Campbellsville University in Kentucky.[37] Numerous other recent stories highlight female high school quarterbacks, women receiving tryouts for NFL teams, and the like. However, what most Americans do not know is that there have been instances of females playing football (and other contact sports) before Title IX. In 1939, Luverne Wise kicked six extra points for the Escambia County High School football team in Alabama,[38] and Agnes Risner kicked for the New Castle High School football team in Indiana.[39] Frankie Groves was the first girl known to have played football in the post-World War II era (1947) at Stinnett High School in Texas. These early exceptions clearly did not represent breakthrough moments that opened opportunities for other females to play football. Indeed, soon after Frankie Groves played in the football game, the state's ruling sports authority formally barred girls from playing high school football, and this ban remained until 1993.[40] In many ways, this type of response to sex integration is not unlike racial segregation in professional sports. Early on, black males participated in football and baseball, for example, but were subsequently officially banned, or blackballed, from those sports until reintegration was allowed many years later.

Post-Title IX Football

In the early years immediately following Title IX's passage, there were several instances of girls playing high school football. In 1973, for example, Dugan Wiess won a spot as a backup placekicker for Walton High School in Defuniak Springs, FL. The same year, a law was passed in California that gave girls the opportunity to play on boys' high school athletic teams. As a result, two 14-year-old girls tried out and made junior varsity football teams: Diane Thompson was a split end for Live Oak High School and Toni Ihler lettered as an offensive and defensive lineman at Portola High School.[41] Brenda Hand also played on her school's football team in 1975 in Sarasota, FL.[42] Alternatively, some states were less open to girls' participation in such sports as football. The Washington Interscholastic Activities Association barred Grays Harbor County's offensive guards Carol and Delores Darrin and running back Kathy Tosland from playing in any games, even though they had tried out and made the Wishkah Valley High School football team. The Darrins sought but, unfortunately, did not immediately receive a court order allowing them to play football. After two years of court battles, the rule that barred the Darrins from playing high school football was finally overturned, although they never got to play a regular season football game.[43] Sally Gutierrez became the first girl to play high school football in New Mexico as a backup guard for Quemado High School. Similarly to the Darrins' case, The New Mexico Activities Association initially barred Ms. Gutierrez from playing; however, unlike the Darrins, the timing of Ms. Gutierrez suit enabled her to play in some remaining season games after Santa Fe District Court Judge Thomas Donnelly issued an order overturning the regulation.[44] In 1977, the Maryland Department of Education permitted girls to try out for traditionally boys-only sports, and Karen Duke was one of the first girls to take advantage of the new legislation, participating in football tryouts at High Point High School with the hopes of playing as a defensive back or placekicker.[45] Other examples[46] include the following:

- Anne Babson is the first known girl to play on a football team in the state of Massachusetts. As an eighth-grader at Ipswich Junior High School, she played on both the offensive and defensive lines.
- Ida Fox won a spot on the junior varsity football team at Poolesville High School (Washington, DC) during her sophomore year as a second-string safety and a backup tailback.
- Mia Frederick played football for Fort Pierce Central High School (FL) in 1978 as a third-string defensive back who made four solo tackles in the four games she played.
- Tammy Lee Mercer played youth football for the McManus Vikings in Amherst (MA) and defensive tackle for the freshman football team at Amherst Regional High School.
- Lisa Mims, a punter at Louisville (AL) High School, averaged 40 yards per punt for the football squad during her sophomore year.
- Jackie Morgan won a starting tackle position on her junior high school's football team in Danville, Iowa, when she was in the eighth grade.
- Donna Wilborn was the first girl to play for a high school team in the state of Wisconsin at Mount Horeb High School.

Clearly, for quite some time, females have possessed both the interest and capability to compete in football (as well as other contact sports). Because coed youth sports competition has become relatively commonplace and girls are able to excel at sports at an early age, they may continue to seek similar opportunities in high school sports. That interest has grown since Title IX was enacted. According to Stuart Miller, in 1993–1994, 783 girls wrestled (compared with 0 a decade before), 353 girls played baseball (compared with 137 a decade before), and 334 girls played football on high school teams (compared with 13 a decade before).[47] As we show in the following charts, overtime trends demonstrate that increasing number of girls are taking advantage of football (and other contact sports) participation opportunities made available in more and more high schools across the country. Despite the pervasiveness of the dominant male paradigm in sports participation, girls increasingly engage in such hypermasculine sports as football.

During the 1971–1972 school year, before the passage of Title IX, no girls participated in high school contact sports. Importantly, Figure 5.1 reveals little change in access to participate in school-based contact sports in the first two decades following the passage of Title IX. Between 1972 and 1992, data from the NFHS show that only about 50 or fewer schools reported female participation in contact sports (football, baseball, ice hockey, and wrestling). However, in the years following the 1995 *Cohen v. Brown University* ruling—which pushed schools to employ the "proportionality test" in measuring Title IX compliance[48]—both high schools and colleges began to make more serious efforts to increase sport participation opportunities for females. As a result, the data show that beginning with the 1996–1997 school year, there were significant upward trends in the

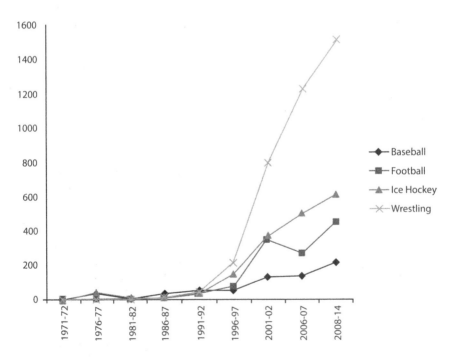

Figure 5.1   Number of Schools Allowing Girls to Participate in High School Male-Dominated Contact Sports: 1971–1972 to 2013–2014.[49]

number of high schools reporting that girls participated in football, base-ball, ice hockey, and wrestling. Since that point, Figure 5.2 reveals slow but fairly steady gains in the number of schools reporting girls' participation in baseball: from roughly 50 schools in 1996–1997 to more than 200 schools in 2013–2014. For football, the growth has been somewhat greater, although inconsistent: from about 70 schools in 1996–1997 to nearly 450 schools in 2013–2014. The gains in ice hockey have been larger and steady: from about 150 schools in 1996–1997 to more than 600 schools in 2013–2014. Likewise, gains in wrestling have been both substantial and steady: from a little more than 200 schools in 1996–1997 to more than 1,500 schools in 2013–2014. However, it should be noted that the rapid gains in ice hockey are due in large measure to high schools (especially in the North-east and Midwest regions) adding women's ice hockey as a growth sport to comply with Title IX. Nevertheless, at least some of this growth may also reflect increased opportunities for female participation on boys' ice hockey teams. The most significant point, however, is the growing sex integra-tion in such traditional hypermasculine contact sports as football, baseball, and wrestling. These trends not only show that sex integration in sports, including contact sports, is possible but also that it is indeed already hap-pening and at an increasing pace.

Figure 5.2 shows the number of girls participating in football, baseball, wrestling, and ice hockey. Because the number of females participating in contact sports is obviously dependent on the number of schools in which such participation is allowed, the trends reported here mirror those shown in Figure 5.1. Thus, Figure 5.2 also shows little change in the actual num-ber of girls who participated in high school contact sports for the first two decades after Title IX was passed. Between 1972 and 1992, NFHS data show that very few females participated in contact sports (football, base-ball, ice hockey, and wrestling).

However, after the 1995 *Cohen v. Brown University* ruling, we see that, with the exception of baseball, there was significant growth in girls' par-ticipation in high school contact sports. Specifically, since that point, the NFHS data in Figure 5.2 show a slight decline in the number of girls par-ticipating in baseball: from 1,126 female baseball players in 1996–1997 to 1,066 players in the 2013–2014 school year. For football, the growth in the number of females participating has been somewhat greater, although slower and less consistent: from just 74 female football players in 1996–1997 to 1,715 participants in 2013–2014. In contrast, the gains in the num-ber of females participating in ice hockey have been larger and steady: from 2,586 female ice hockey players in the 1996–1997 school year to 9,150 participants in the 2013–2014 school year. Likewise, gains in the

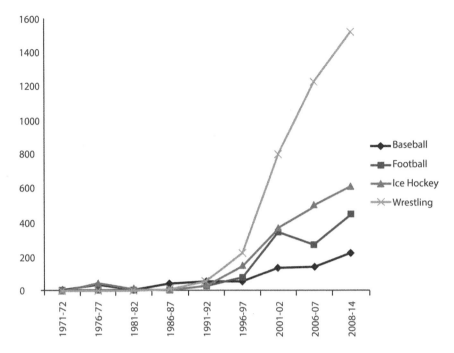

Figure 5.2   Number of Girls Participating in High School Male-Dominated Contact Sports: 1971–1972 to 2013–2014.

number of females participating in wrestling have been both substantial and steady: from 1,629 female wrestlers in the 1996–1997 school year to nearly a thousand (9,904) in the 2013–2014 school year.

As was shown for high school contact sports, females also possess both the interest and capability to compete in football and other contact sports at higher (college and professional) levels. However, female's opportunities to compete in contact sports tend to decline as the level of competition increases—from youth leagues, through high schools, on to colleges, and to the professional leagues. Since the actual number of female contact sports participants beyond the high school level is too small to present statistical data, we are limited to describing specific exemplary instances of women participants in intercollegiate men's contact sports.

Females in College Football[50]

- Liz Heaston became the first female to compete in a college game in 1997, kicking two extra points for Willamette University that competed in the National Association of Intercollegiate Athletics (NAIA).

- Ashley Martin became the first woman to play in a Division I football game in 2001, kicking 3/3 extra points for Jacksonville State University following her solid high school performance record (2/4 field goals; 79/92 extra points).
- Tanya Butler was a kicker throughout high school, at Middle Georgia Junior College, and at the University of West Alabama.
- Brittany Ryan broke Butler's record to become the highest scoring female kicker in NCAA history during her time playing at Lebanon Valley College, which competes in the NCAA Division III.
- Ashley Baker kicked 11 points for Framingham State (MA) this season, making her the NCAAs Division III all-time leading female scorer.
- KaLena "Beanie" Barnes, a punter at the University of Nebraska, was the first woman to play on a top-10 ranked Division I-A team.
- Katharine Anne "Katie" Hnida became the first woman to score in an NCAA Division I-A football game in 2003 as placekicker for the University of New Mexico. Previously in 1999, Hnida became the second woman to dress for a Division I-A game and the first to do so for a bowl game for the University of Colorado.
- Shelby Osborne in 2015 became the first woman to play a nonkicking position (cornerback) at a four-year college for Campbellsville University, which competes in the NAIA.
- Heather Sue Mercer, an all-state kicker at Yorktown Heights High School (NY), attempted to break the Division I sex barrier as a walk-on kicker for Duke University, but was cut from the team in both 1995 and 1996. After filing a discrimination law suit against Duke, Mercer was awarded $2 million (the school appealed the amount of the judgment but not the verdict).

Females in College Baseball

Although not as violent as football, baseball is also viewed as hypermasculine and has always been a heavily male-dominated sport. Indeed, as the NFHS data reported earlier regarding high school contact sports show, compared to football, ice hockey, and wrestling, baseball had fewer schools (Figure 5.1) offering the sport to girls and the lowest number of female participants (Figure 5.2). Softball, especially, fast-pitch softball, is often considered to be the "female counterpart" to baseball. However, it is important to point out that baseball was offered at some northeastern women's colleges as early as the mid-19th century.[51] Nevertheless, women have been traditionally excluded from participation on men's baseball teams. And although sex exclusion remains a significant obstacle at all levels in contemporary baseball, girls and women continue to pursue opportunities to play. For example, Sarah Hudek is a 5'10", left-handed pitcher who says she always knew that softball was not her true passion. She decided as early as 10 years of age that she was an exceptionally good baseball player. The fact that she recently earned a scholarship from Bossier Parish Community

College, a junior college in Louisiana in the fall of 2015, affirms her self-assessment. However, she is one of the very few females to receive an opportunity to play baseball at the collegiate level. According to her father, a former major league pitcher himself:

> The way she is with her command, changing speeds, pitching in and out, that's what pitchers should do regardless, . . . If you throw 95 [mph], if you throw 85, if you throw 80, you can do it. If you look at guys in the big leagues that don't throw hard, they do know how to pitch. They do move the ball. That's what I see her do, and that's when I saw there was a great opportunity for her to go play.[52]

Availability of Sex-Integrated Sports in High Schools

Next, we further explore the extent to which U.S. public high schools have adopted sex integration policies in their varsity sports programs using data from the U.S. Department of Education's *Educational Longitudinal Study* (ELS).[53] ELS is a nationally representative survey of high schools, students, teachers, and school administrators. Principals were asked what sports were offered to boys, and to girls, at their schools. Figure 5.3 shows the percentage of school administrators who indicated that girls were offered opportunities to play any of the following traditionally male contact sports—football, baseball, or wrestling. Not surprisingly, given the long history of sex segregation, the data show that the vast majority of U.S. high schools

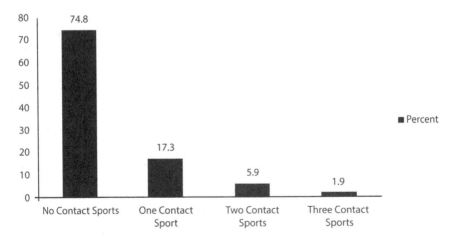

Figure 5.3 Percentage of High Schools Offering Girls Opportunities to Participate in Boys' Contact Sports.

(74.8 percent) do not provide females opportunities to participate in any of the three most popular male high school sports (football, baseball, and wrestling). However, girls were allowed to participate in one contact sport at 17.3 percent of high schools, two contact sports at 5.9 percent of high schools, and three contact sports at 1.9 percent of high schools. On one hand, these numbers clearly reflect continuing constraints on high school girl's athletic opportunities even though Title IX was passed more than 40 years ago. On the other hand, the same numbers also illustrate that, perhaps to a greater degree than most Americans might think, some high schools, at least, are beginning to accommodate females' growing interest in competing in boys' contact sports.

Opposition to Female Participation in Men's Contact

Opposition to sex integration in sports generally, and contact sports specifically, lacks a *credible* and *consistent* rationale. This fact represents a major challenge for proponents of female participation in traditionally "male" sports. The credibility problem exists because historically (as well as today) much of the resistance to sex integration is rooted in commonly held assumptions and beliefs—among many males and females—regarding what girls and women either cannot do (because of physical limitations) or should not do (because of potential harms to themselves). With regard to physical limitations, to be sure, there are average differences in specific sports-related physical traits (e.g., speed, strength, and weight). To some extent, these average differences may be biologically determined. Conversely, performance on tasks requiring speed and strength can to a great degree be shaped by such environmental factors as conditioning and training. Male football players, for example, have traditionally improved their speed and strength as they move from high school to college, and the NFL, through rigorous conditioning and training regimens. Thus, speed and strength are developmental, not solely biologically determined. The same relationship between biological determinism and environment factors operates for females as well. In many high schools and colleges, these strength and conditioning programs are primarily available to athletes who participate in contact sports, which, in effect, limits their accessibility to females. Yet, it is even more problematic when policy makers or courts use average group traits—male vs. female 40-yard dash times, for example—to determine policies about whether girls should be allowed to compete against boys in track events or even in football because it ignores the possibility that an individual girl may be quite capable of being competitive in, or even win, a particular boy's track event. Such a practice—restricting individual opportunities based on average group traits—amounts to statistical discrim- ination,[54] and in certain circumstances, may violate the law. When the oppo- sition's arguments focus on the issue of physical risks or harms, rather than physical limitations, many of their concerns are either outdated (risks to females' reproductive capacity) or they fail to fully consider existing evidence (risk of injury, e.g., concussion risk in women's soccer, and cheerleading are comparable to football).

With regard to the matter of consistency, it becomes difficult to under- stand the arguments of opponents to sex integration when one looks at the big picture (normative and regulatory constraints on male and female par- ticipation across different sports or even across different levels within the same sport). For example, as we have noted, U.S. football represents the ultimate sport context for displaying and protecting boundaries of mascu- linity. Yet, as the data in Figures 5.1 and 5.2 show, females appear to be making faster inroads in football than they have in baseball. In describing female access to intercollegiate men's contact sports, we found many more examples of females gaining opportunities in football than in baseball. Although baseball is also considered a masculine sport, one might expect that female penetration in that sport to have moved faster than in football. However, the slower penetration of females in baseball may solely be a consequence of gender-based structural barriers or cultural resistance, it may also, in part, be a result of females having access to softball (a similar although sex-segregated sport), whereas there are no school-based sports available to females that are similar to football. These data also showed that females have made faster inroads in wrestling than they have in baseball. Within the sport of baseball, females have had some very limited success in penetrating the lower levels (Little League and high school), but very little to no progress at the college level. The lack of consistency across com- petitive levels of a given sport can also be seen in competitive shooting. For example, even though NCAA rules declare rifle to be a men's sport, in prac- tice, it operated as a coed sport for more than three decades. Yet, at the Olympic level, the sport is officially sex-segregated, even though many of the international competitors are the same male and female athletes who competed together in sex-integrated settings in college. In effect, Olympic competition rules disregard the simple and obvious fact that, in this sport, females can and do compete successfully against male opponents.

Perhaps one reason that female participation in men's intercollegiate contact sports has not exhibited the type of gains observed in high school sports is that as part of their Title IX compliance strategies, many colleges have begun to establish an increasing number of such sex-segregated women's contact sports teams as rugby, ice hockey, and lacrosse. For example, in 2013–2014, lacrosse was the sport most added (+29). The number of institutions offering women's rugby has more than tripled, from 105 colleges in 1981–1981 to 443 colleges in 2013–2014. Similarly, the number of institutions offering women's ice hockey has more than quadrupled, from 17 schools in 1981–1981 to 90 colleges in 2013–2014. Women's rugby is also growing but remains well below the number of sponsored teams required to move beyond its current classification as an "emerging sport" to a "championship sport," where it would be necessary that approximately three times as many colleges and universities offered rugby than they currently offer. However, the number of rugby teams currently offered (14) has more than doubled since 2012 when only six schools offered women's varsity rugby.[55] This strategy for growing women's sports and allowing colleges to comply with Title IX provides expanded opportunities for women to play contact sports while at the same time maintaining sex segregation. And, as noted in Chapter 2, adding these sports does little to promote race–ethnic diversity in women's college athletics.

Dees has suggested that the original motivation behind Title IX was to increase women's participation in sports to expand their opportunities in the labor market and, in particular, provide them with the competitive edge that men already possessed.[56] Although increased athletic participation has resulted in economic returns for women in nonathletic job arenas,[57] women are still unable to reap the same opportunities and rewards as men within sports contexts. Empirical research has documented persisting sex discrepancies in pay differentials in male and female athletics, and a general lack of job opportunities for women,[58] in all levels of sport. Sex integration in sports would ensure that women have the opportunity to develop the same earning potential as men employed as professional athletes, and as coaches, referees, trainers, and so on at all levels of sport. Eliminating separate arenas of sport may also shatter the glass ceiling for women working in more peripheral roles in athletics and enhance opportunities for women in such occupations as sports lawyers, sports agents, sports reporters, and those working in advertising, public relations, and academic services.

The counterargument to sex integration from those who believe that sports should be kept "separate but equal" is also located within the framework of opportunity. Regardless of whether sex differences in physical ability are rooted in biological, social, psychological, or economic factors or some combination of these, the fact is that differences in average size, speed, and strength currently exist. As a result, there is an understandable fear that applying the integration principle advanced in *Brown* to athletics would diminish, if not eliminate, significant participation opportunities for women. Resolutions to the dichotomy of disagreement about whether sex integration in sport would result in more or less opportunity for women can be established in the original motivation of the *Brown* decision. In addition, the way in which sex integration is implemented has the possibility of satisfying those advocating "separate but equal," if efforts are specifically concentrated on achieving maximum opportunity for women.

A central argument of this book is that sex equity in sports requires a complete commitment to the principle of equality of opportunity. Such a commitment demands equal *chances*, not equal *results*. In sports, competition not only exists between different teams but there is also competition for a place on the team. What Title IX should mean in athletics is that female athletes should be allowed *opportunities* to compete in the same sports, at the same time, as their male counterparts. This argument parallels the point made by Thurgood Marshall in his oral argument before the Supreme Court in *Brown v. Board of Education*. As the NAACP attorney for the plaintiff, Marshall asserted that black students must be given the opportunity to learn in the same classrooms, at the same time, as white students.[59] Despite the challenges that integration in athletic contexts presents, sex integration—which provides women the same opportunities at the same time as men—is the only means of achieving the ultimate promise of Title IX—full sex equity.

CHAPTER SIX

The Elimination of Sex Categories in Sport

Benefits in Athletics and Beyond

On July 5, 2015, an estimated 24.5 million viewers watched the FIFA Women's World Cup final match between the United States and Japan, making it the most-watched soccer event in U.S. television history, easily beating the 2014 FIFA Men's World Cup match between the United States and Portugal (18.2 million viewers), the 2015 Stanley Cup Finals (7.6 million viewers), and even the 2015 NBA Finals (average overnight rating of 13.9 million and the most watched NBA Finals since Michael Jordan's last championship in 1998).[1] However, although the U.S. women's team received $2 million in prize money for their victory, the 2014 FIFA World Cup male victors of Germany received $35 million; even the U.S. men's team who lost in the first round of the knockout stage was awarded $8 million.[2] Although one could make the argument that these disparities reflect the differential worldwide popularity of men's vs. women's soccer, within the United States, the National Women's Soccer League (NWSL) teams have a salary cap of $265,000 whereas Major League Soccer (MLS) teams have a $3.49 million salary cap. This difference results in NWSL salaries between only $6,843 and $37,800 and men's minimum salaries starting well above the peak of the women's, with MLS players receiving anywhere between $60,000 and $7.17 million in 2015. Because of the near poverty-level wages in the NWSL, as grown adults, soccer players often select to live with host families to financially survive the season.[3]

Not only is the soccer sex disparity financial but it is also evident in differential media coverage and visibility, and is damaging to women both inside and outside of the game. Notions of inferiority are promoted through invisibility, suggesting that female athletes and women's accomplishments do not matter.[4] Although feminists and other academics have generally not focused on sport as a serious site for promoting social change, scholar Cheryl Cooky, who recently interviewed in an *Atlantic* article, stated that feminists need to focus on the institution of sport because it is an area endemic of such "serious" issues as sexual violence, pay inequality, and a lack of women in leadership.[5] We also feel that the structure of sport can serve as a catalyst for promoting positive large-scale social change in such areas as intimate partner and domestic violence, safety, injury, health, and sex verification testing and discrimination against LGBT and nongender-conforming athletes.

Challenges to Sex Integration in Sport

Although research has highlighted the positive returns of sport participation in such areas as academic achievement,[6] self-esteem and efficacy,[7] and psychological health and well-being,[8] we are careful not to oversell the benefits of sport and those associated with sex integration. Many athletic contexts are currently integrated in terms of race and SES, yet racism and classism permeate the institution of sport and continue to result in disparities in treatment[9] and participation.[10] Likewise, even in sex-integrated sports contexts, sexist attitudes and practices often give rise to differential gender outcomes.[11]

Even when formerly all-white schools became desegregated, their classrooms remained largely racially segregated. Most black students were excluded from the most desirable learning opportunities in high-track classes, honors courses, and gifted programs. Instead, black students were typically assigned to lower-level, racially segregated, classrooms in erstwhile desegregated schools.[12] Similarly, following Title IX's passage, most schools and colleges have relegated female athletes to lower-status, sex-segregated, sports. In effect, implementation of policies like the contact sports exclusion under Title IX has created a two-tier system that sorts girls into sex-segregated, and lower-status, sports in erstwhile "Title IX-compliant" high schools and colleges. However, there are aspects of the two-tier system that often go unnoticed. For example, the 2013–2014 NCAA Sports Sponsorship and Participation Rates Report data list the following as coed sport teams: (a) cross country, (b) equestrian, (c) fencing, (d) golf, (e) rifle,

(f) sailing, (g) skiing, (h) swimming and diving, (i) indoor track and field, and (j) outdoor track and field.[13] However, the vast majority of these "coed sports" do not involve sex-integrated competition. With the exception of some equestrian and sailing events, most of these sports—track and field, cross country, swimming and diving, and golf—only provide females opportunities to compete against other females. As such, the label of coed sports may be misleading. Even in the context of sex-integrated, or true coed, sports, several issues must be addressed. Some aspects of the dominant sex ideology present in sports (and society) generally will carry over into coed sports contexts, where it must be acknowledged and confronted. In addition, sex-integrated sport contexts will need to adapt and accommodate new and different participants.

As we remain firmly convinced of the potential of integration to combat social problems, we are cognizant of the challenges that athletic sex integration presents, especially in terms of the possible elimination of opportunities for women, and the hostility that has historically characterized new spaces of integration. We have previously addressed the concern that integration will result in women's exclusion because of the false ideology that women are not physically capable of competing at the same levels as men by refuting the essentialist ideology on which segregation depends, providing recent data on contact sports that suggest otherwise and offering a legal argument documenting the social justice goals surrounding equal opportunity rather than equal representation. In addition, with consideration of the successes and failures of previous integration policy and the examples of HBCUs and women's-only colleges as effective models, Chapter 7 proposes specific recommendations for implementing policy measures that prevent the elimination of women's opportunities.

More difficult to combat than women's exclusion from sport is the resistance to sex integration, often in the form of harassment and violence, which was also characteristic of the process of inclusion in formerly racially segregated schools and sex-segregated employment contexts. Racial violence, along with the physical and verbal abuse experienced by The Little Rock Nine and countless other black students attending formerly all-white schools, as well as the sexual harassment and assault previously and continuously endured by women in such male-dominated occupational contexts as the military, is used as an intimidation tactic born from fear surrounding changes to the dominant social order. Nooses as symbolically violent representations of the systemic lynching of African Americans from the Reconstruction era to the mid-20th century are still hung in workplaces and schools to denote the historical dehumanization of Blacks and the affirmation of white superiority as well as to evoke terror in those whose actions challenge this ideology.

In the context of women's sports, one example of resistance to sex integration specifically is that of Katie Hnida, who in 2003, as a placekicker at the University of New Mexico, became the first woman to score in an NCAA Division 1-A game. Hnida had transferred to New Mexico from the University of Colorado Boulder and has publicly disclosed that she was raped by one of her Colorado teammates in 2000 and sexually harassed by other teammates on multiple occasions.[14] Kapano Ratele states: "Men's violence against women and girls can be seen not only as an attempt to reassert heteropatriarchal domination over women and girls but perhaps always an attempt to discursively and bodily invalidate these gains."[15] The threat of resistance as an argument against integration demonstrates the necessity of dismantling the sexist hierarchy evident in the segregated structure of sport; it is a reason for systematic institutional change and the implementation of policies that thwart sexist ideology and practices permeating sports contexts. Specifically, it is necessary to demolish the existence of sport as a cultural site that encourages men to separate themselves from women, resulting in women's oppression and men's repression.[16] In addition, as evidenced by women's continued recent success in sex-neutral and men's sports settings, integration is happening, although slowly and unequally, and a policy aimed toward reducing exposure to discrimination and abuse is warranted. To address these issues and objectives, Chapter 7 outlines a bottom-up framework for the integration process that normalizes women's presence in sports and socializes children into sex-integrated athletic settings to reduce resistance.

Although there are obstacles associated with sex integration in athletics, these obstacles are often overemphasized in public discourse because they serve to preserve the existing ideology and social structure. As discussed in Chapter 4, due to socialization and the process of knowledge and value reproduction, rationalization of the dominant social order becomes effortless and routine, whereas invalidating it takes critical thought in accessing and evaluating alternative evidence. In the case of sex segregation in sports, justifications, no matter how irrational (e.g., women and men cannot play together because then they would have to share locker rooms and that would result in utter chaos!), dominate the conversation, and potential strategies that address the underlying concerns (e.g., athletes still may use separate locker rooms, change in bathroom stalls already found in most locker rooms, or wear undergarments to their desired level of comfort) are seldom considered. Using a socio-legal perspective, George refutes such arguments against sex integration as girls will get hurt, it will change the nature of the sport, there will be fewer playing and scholarship opportunities, and attendance and revenues would suffer; however, his proposal for integration relies on sexed rules reifying the sex binary.[17] Larena Hoeber found that although female and male administrators, coaches, and athletes understood the meaning of sex equity in a variety of ways, none of their respondents' definitions of sex equity disrupted traditional assumptions surrounding male privilege and superiority in athletics.[18] Furthermore, because the potential benefits of sex integration contradict prevailing gender ideology and practices, they are rarely contemplated or discussed, highlighting the importance of considering the possible advantages of integration presented in this chapter. Although dominant sexist ideology focuses on negative outcomes for women in coed sports contexts, studies have shown that in mixed-sex settings, women still achieve positive returns in such areas as motivation, social support and connectedness, and competence.[19] Throughout this chapter, it is our intention to frame the explanation of potential benefits of sex desegregation in sport not as one of women's gains and men's losses, but rather as positive and beneficial to society overall.[20] In addition, it can be argued that women's gains are also men's gains. Bob Pease discusses how sex equality results in men's improved physical and emotional well-being as well as the benefits for men to function in a social world that is not ridden with human-caused problems.[21]

The focus on social benefits of sex integration as an avenue for collective progress provides a compelling state interest argument for promoting policy changes. For instance, Dr. Milner recently attended a talk given by Congresswoman Eddie Bernice Johnson, where the Congresswoman discussed that the U.S. government will create opportunities for women and racial minorities in STEM fields not simply because it is morally correct, but rather because if they do not, we as a country, and especially once Whites become the U.S. numerical minority, will continue to fall behind China, Russia, and other nations that continue to promote the success of all individuals rather than only the powerful.[22] Likewise, sexism in the military does not simply hurt female servicemembers, it hurts our entire military; classism in our education system does not merely hurt the poor, it results in crime and a less-educated, less-productive and, therefore, more vulnerable population; denying gay people the right to adopt or serve as foster parents does not just hurt gay people, it hurts children who currently do not have stable homes. By focusing on broad societal gains and mutually beneficial outcomes, we hope to reduce opposition and hostility to the controversial policy of sex integration in athletic contexts.

Sex Integration and the Reduction of Violence Against Women

Violence and, specifically, violence against women come with a large social cost. For instance, it is estimated that intimate partner violence against women alone carried a price tag of roughly $8 billion dollars in direct health costs and indirect costs through lost productivity in a single year in the United States[23] The recent high-profile cases of NFL players Ray Rice and Adrian Peterson have resulted in public attention devoted to linking male athletic participation and domestic violence, whereas a rape allegation against 2015 NFL first overall draft pick and Heisman Trophy recipient, Jameis Winston, has drawn attention to the association between athletics and sexual assault and, specifically, sexual assault of women on U.S. college campuses.[24] Although there are mixed empirical findings about whether male athletes are more violent toward women than nonathletes, sports and "the need to win" have been associated with antisocial behaviors as sexual assault and domestic violence.[25] Not only does the culture of hypermasculine sports promote aggression and dominance,[26] but the culture surrounding sex-segregated male groups—including fraternities—has also been connected with sexual assault and aggression.[27] It is plausible that the presence of women in sex-integrated sports teams could help neutralize all-male, hypermasculine sport cultures. Furthermore, sex integration in sport might also reduce violence by modifying hypermasculine peer networks and social ties that have been connected to violent behavior in athletes and nonathletes as well as to the objectification of women.[28]

It is also possible that a newfound respect for women could develop as a consequence of their participation in sex-integrated athletics at the highest levels, which changes the current landscape of sex relations and diminishes the occurrence of violence against them.[29] For example, in 1993, the United Nations (UN) documented that violence against women manifests from unequal sexed power relations.[30] The UN has since recognized sport as a tool to promote sex equity and women's empowerment goals.[31] In addition, Amanda Roth and Susan Basow suggest that increasing women's displays of physical power could result in an improvement in women's confidence, power, respect, wealth, enjoyment of physicality as well as reduce their experience of rape and the fear of rape.[32]

Even in sex-segregated sports contexts, studies have shown that for women, athletic participation has a protective effect. For instance, Tonya Dodge and James Jaccard found that athletes exhibit lower levels of sexual risk behavior and were significantly less likely to become pregnant than nonathletes.[33] Miller et al. found that female athletes exhibit lower-frequency levels of sexual intercourse, fewer sex partners, and higher age of coital onset.[34] In terms of violence specifically, Jorunn Sundgot-Borgen et al. found that sports participants' experience of sexual harassment and abuse was slightly less common for elite athletes than for nonathletes,[35] and Dr. Milner and her colleague, Elizabeth Baker, found that sports participation was associated with lower prevalence of experiencing intimate partner violence victimization for women. Because similarly to Miller et al., the researchers attributed findings linking positive sports outcomes for women to their rejection of traditional gender norms, it is possible that reducing sex disparities and gendered culture in sport may have positive returns for all athletes. In fact, Milner and Baker found that although sport participation reduced female athletes' likelihood of victimization, this result did not hold for male athletes, suggesting that the notion of athletes as perpetrators of violence may prevent male victims from comprehending, leaving, or seeking help in situations of abuse.[36]

Decreasing the association between sports and hypermasculinity may also reduce female athletes' likelihood of perpetration of violence. Although males are the overwhelming offenders in situations of domestic violence and sexual assault, recent high-profile cases of female athletes participating in traditionally masculine sports committing domestic violence (e. g., Olympic soccer gold-medalist Hope Solo and Women's National Basketball Association [WNBA] players Brittany Griner and Glory Johnson)[37] highlight the potential for diminishing the socialization and perception of sports spaces as masculine sites of aggression and dominance. Sex integration in sports may serve to decrease aggressive behavior and perceptions of athletic contexts as hypermasculine domains, where instead, such other ideological values associated with sports as cooperation, fair play, teamwork, and common goals may take precedence in popular culture. George suggests that sex-integrated college sports settings may enable them to be viewed in terms of their benefit to education rather than training grounds for professional teams.[38] Not only might a new focus on communal objectives serve to empower women,[39] a shift away from a cultural emphasis on masculinity may also improve men's health, where men may become more likely to adopt such healthy behaviors as seeking medical care and eating healthy foods that defy conventional notions of what it means to "be manly."[40] There is also evidence to suggest that sex integration in sport, through the mechanisms of broadening friendships beyond same-sex peer networks, promoting cross-sexed friendships, and decreasing stress associated with masculine gender identity and performance, may reduce levels of marijuana and alcohol use among males.[41] Furthermore, sex integration in sport may result in increased personal satisfaction and commitment for all participants through the reduction of hypermasculine athletic ideals. In fact, Isabel

Castillo et al. found that among both adolescent boys and girls, greater satisfaction was found in sports and classroom settings when achievement was measured through personal improvement and hard work, whereas achievement related to the hypermasculine demonstration of superiority over others was associated with boredom and low interest in the activity.[42]

Sex Integration and Violence Within Sport: Addressing Concerns of Safety and Injury

Similarly to how the link among sports, hypermasculinity, and violence is becoming an increasing social concern, so too is the connection between exposure to violence during athletic competition and serious injury, and even premature death. Recent research found that 76 out of 79 deceased NFL players had degenerative brain disease and that almost 80 percent of former professional, semiprofessional, and college football players tested positive for chronic traumatic encephalopathy (CTE).[43] Because of the increasing evidence linking participation in football to brain damage and degenerative mental conditions, President Obama stated that if he had a son he would not allow him to play professional football,[44] while writer Malcom Gladwell called the sport "a moral abomination."[45] In fact, San Francisco 49ers linebacker, Chris Borland, at 24 years old, recently retired from professional football because of safety concerns, forfeiting the $540,000 he was contracted to make during the 2015–2016 season.[46]

President Obama's comments about safety concerns in football are particularly interesting because he speaks about a hypothetical son but does not discuss his two actual daughters.[47] His statement relies on sexist ideology and suggests that a dialogue about his daughters' potential participation in professional football is not necessary because it is obvious that neither he nor any other parent would want their daughters playing football or being exposed to physical trauma in sports. Traditional understandings of sex suggesting that women and girls need to be protected while boys and men are more aptly to be able to handle injury and abuse still persist, although the existence of sex differences in this area has been empirically disproven.[48]

A recent case that highlights how sexist ideology may have negatively affected player safety and well-being is that of the Grambling State University football team. In 2013, Grambling State football players complained of unsanitary and dangerous conditions, including mold and mildew on equipment and facilities, improper cleaning of uniforms resulting in staph infections, and bus rides of more than 600 miles, eventually leading to players' boycott of travel and competition.[49] It can be argued that traditional conceptions of masculinity may have been a contributing factor to players' continued mistreatment, suggesting that as men participating in a hyper-masculine sport, they were expected to "tough it out," where the game should take precedence over their physical and mental well-being. However, it is also important to note that as a historically underfunded public HBCU, without meaningful media revenue streams, Grambling, despite its remarkable achievements in football (e.g., head coach Eddie Robinson once had more victories than any coach in college football history; Doug Williams was the first Black quarterback to win a Super Bowl), lacked adequate resources to support its football program.

Another example of how sexist ideology may result in unsafe playing conditions can be seen in FIFA's decision to use artificial turf rather than real grass at the 2015 Women's World Cup. Because artificial turf has never been used in a FIFA Men's World Cup match and because it results in players' heightened exposure to such injuries as burns, abrasions, concussions, and joint stress, women soccer players took legal action, ultimately withdrawing their suit once FIFA agreed never to use artificial turf at a Women's World Cup again. Artificial turf not only leads to increased risk of injury but also essentially changes the rhythm and nature of the game of soccer;[50] therefore, it is reasonable to suggest that the unprecedented judgment to use turf occurred because of perceptions of the women's tournament as fundamentally inferior to or less important than the men's World Cup.

In athletic contexts, in particular, such sexist ideological principles, rules, and behaviors as the idea that sex integration is undesirable because girls and women will get hurt[51] serve to effectively exclude women from participating as players and in the long run limit their postretirement opportunities in coaching, and other areas, especially in such contact sports as baseball, football, boxing, and wrestling. Furthermore, sexist beliefs regarding male physical superiority, resilience, and natural athletic inclination result in a lack of emphasis on injury prevention measures in men's sports, putting boys and men at risk of physical harm. Perhaps sex integration and the widespread incorporation of women into such male-dominated, high-impact contact sports as football would result in a reexamination of safety measures and regulations that would ultimately benefit all participants. In addition, safety levels in sport may improve as a result of sex integration because male athletes self-report more such instances of poor sportsmanship that have the potential to result in injury as fighting and cheating than their female counterparts.[52] Furthermore, parents, coaches, referees, and fans may be more diligent in policing their own and others' behavior in sex-neutral rather than sex-segregated sports settings, where dominant gender ideology associated with perceptions of women's need for protection perhaps would result in the protection of all players.

The potential of sex integration for increased attention devoted to safety issues in sports has implications beyond those participating. Similarly to violence against women, sports injuries result in great social and financial costs and have also been linked to prescription drug abuse, depression, and obesity, which consequently result in even greater societal costs in such areas as health care and worker productivity.[53] Thus, reducing the occurrence and severity of sports injuries should result in societal benefits. Because the sex desegregation process would force the reassessment of current sports practices and development of new policy targeting uniforms, equipment, facilities, and rules, sex integration provides an opportunity ripe for changing existing procedures to improve a variety of safety measures for the benefit of all.

Sex Integration and Improved Physical and Mental Health

Aside from injury prevention, sex integration in sport has other potential positive mental and physical health consequences. For instance, integration may result in the reduction of rigid constructions of sex-appropriate gender performance, which may give way to more diverse opportunities for self-expression and self-acceptance. Because aptitude and desirability are socially constructed and change throughout time and space, modifications in what constitutes talent and appeal in sports contexts are translatable to the larger social structure. One area, in particular, in which we see prospects for health gains is that of body image and, specifically, in the reduction of unhealthy behaviors used to achieve socially prescribed measures of physical ability and attractiveness.

Amy Slater and Marika Tiggemann found that girls may not be participating in sports at the same rates as boys partly because of body image concerns in addition to perceptions that participation is not cool or feminine.[54] This is important because, in a later study, Slater and Tiggemann found that for girls, sport participation not only served as a protective mechanism against self-objectification over time but also self-objectification increased over time for girls who did not participate in sports. Furthermore, the researchers found that self-objectification was related to disordered eating.[55] Therefore, it is plausible that an expansion in the perception of which specific sports are deemed to be sex-appropriate for girls may not only increase their participation but also lessen self-objectification and eating disorders among women over time. In addition, improvements in girls' and women's body image may positively affect public health. Jean Lamont found that among women, not only does body shame relate to psychological health it also relates to physical health, where body shame was linked with poor health outcomes in terms of infections, self-rated health, and symptoms of physical illness.[56]

Sex integration in sport may not only serve to increase participation through diminishing cultural barriers associated with social appropriateness it may also provide rewards that extend beyond those of conforming to traditional notions of sex-appropriate behavior. For example, a tall and heavy girl may currently feel compelled to manipulate her body with food reduction or excessive levels of exercise to conform to current standards of beauty for women, which often revolve around thinness. However, if she had the opportunity to make millions of dollars in the NFL as an offensive lineperson, she may embrace and cultivate her physicality rather than battle it (just as heavy males currently do).[57] Similarly, a short, thin boy who is given the chance to earn a college scholarship as a "flyer" on a cheerleading squad may be more accepting of his frame and less likely to try to alter it with steroids or other unhealthy means.

Sharon Wheeler's research suggests that sporting cultures are transmitted through families, and parents are presently investing earlier and more heavily in their children's sports participation than did their own parents.[58] It is plausible that opportunities for women to gain financial and personal sports rewards similar to those of men may result in even greater levels of investment of parents in their daughters. This, in turn, could lead to more sex-neutral expectations and socialization practices in the home, perhaps resulting in higher levels of self-acceptance among all children. Furthermore, a greater investment by parents in their daughters' sporting success may promote women's participation and opportunities for achievement in athletics, and this cycle could continue across generations as parents continue to offer more substantial sport support than did their own parents.

Sex Integration as a Means to Combat Pay Inequality

In her blog, social psychologist, Nadira Faber (2012), discusses various arguments for and against sex segregation in sport, and ultimately poses the question, "but how can opportunities be created that are *really equal* (also in terms of popularity and payment) in the case of men and women?[59] Although women's athletic participation is associated with several positive career outcomes in the mainstream labor market, ironically, within athletic contexts, women have not closed the sex rewards gap[60] as disparities persist in men's and women's compensation and opportunities, as both players and coaches.[61] In the area of rewards for participation, sex segregation makes sport a rich area for studying sex disparities; however, it does not provide much room to reduce them. That is to say, much of the argument for unequal pay outcomes revolves around a dominant gender ideology that women's sports are less valuable, and therefore, female athletes should not be compensated at rates similar to men. Sex segregation not only supports the ideological rationale for this financial disparity (i.e., women are physically inferior to men and, therefore, so too are women's competitions) but also perpetuates inequality because this disparity limits financial incentives for women to pursue athletic competition at the highest levels. It is currently much more lucrative for women, even elite athletes who compete at the top levels, to focus on careers outside of sports than attempt to become professional athletes because the overwhelming majority of female professional athletes make much less money than their male counterparts. In addition, disparities in pay cannot presently be measured accurately in sex-segregated sports contexts because of the perception that male and female athletes are not essentially doing the same job. Current justifications for such unequal earnings as those surrounding quality of the respective nature of the game, fan bases, and level of player skills are difficult to quantify as well as socially reproduced through media and other social structures. For instance, although soccer is the most watched and most lucrative sport in the world,[62] Americans frequently describe the game as boring or slow. This is not, however, an objective description because soccer only has one pause in play at the half, whereas most such popular team sports contests in the United States as football and basketball are characterized by time outs, some of which are media scheduled and as such can disrupt the flow and continuity of the games. Most Americans view sports very parochially, U.S. sports as better simply because Americans do them, not because they are objectively superior in any quantifiable way.

Likewise, differences in the value of men's and women's sports, and male and female athletes, are unquantifiable. For example, Collin Flake, Dufur, and Erin Moore document differential payouts for women and men in professional tennis; however, dominant gender ideology would justify these differences in financial returns with the notion that male players "work harder" because they play the best out of five rather than three sets, and men's matches are more highly attended. However, the researchers refute these arguments by showing that in less prestigious tournaments, men also play three sets, players are not paid less if they dominate their opponent in straight sets resulting in shorter matches, and often when spectators purchase a tournament ticket, they can access both women's and men's matches, thus making popularity undeterminable.[63] Although researchers are able to document inequities in pay, there are many other intangible and unspec-ifiable variables in differentially sexed sports contexts to directly refute the dominant gender ideology rationalizing disparities. Sex integration would provide a means to measure, track, and reduce inequities, where salaries of men and women on the same teams and in the same leagues would offer quantifiable points of comparison.

Unequal financial returns in sports participation do not just affect pro-fessional athletes. Matthew Linford found that former high school male ath-letes, regardless of sport played, reported significantly higher income six years after high school graduation than their peers who did not play sports. Although this relationship was stronger for athletes who played a cultur-ally popular sport, only female athletes who played basketball reported a significantly higher income six years after high school graduation.[64] In addi-tion to differential returns on income for participation, several studies by Warren Whisenant and colleagues highlight how men have reinforced their power and leadership roles in sports employment contexts. In their study of collegiate athletic directors, Whisenant, Paul Pererson, and Bill Oben-sour confirmed institutionalized hegemonic masculine control, resulting in women's lack of representation at the most esteemed and powerful levels of sport, which consequently results in a reproduction of the lack of repre-sentation of women in decision-making processes and in such other ath-letic positions as coaches.[65] In the case of high school athletic director positions, Whisenant, John Miller, and Paul Pederson found that 17 percent of jobs advertised in Texas mandated that the athletic directors also serve as the head football coach, which led the researchers to conclude that these schools were partaking in unfair employment practices that serve as a sys-tematic barrier to women's hiring.[66] Also, at the high school level, Whisenant found a significant underrepresentation of women in leadership positions associated with sexed administrative hierarchies, in which men dominated both principal (76 percent) and athletic director (85 percent) positions, and evidence of homologous reproduction was apparent at the coaching level.[67]

In a related study, Laura Burton et al. found that even though sports man-agement students deemed feminine traits as important for the role of ath-letic director, they deemed masculine traits to be more strongly associated with the position, suggesting that women may be evaluated as less capable leaders, even if they possess qualities that would make them successful in leadership roles.[68] Newman Wadesango et al. also found that the absence of women in such decision-making positions in sport organizations as in the 2010 FIFA World Cup administrative structure resulted in not only a lack of opportunity for women but also the creation and reification of stereotypes surrounding women's incompetence and men's superiority in sports.[69] Research suggests that the incorporation of women into decision-making processes in athletics will not just benefit women, but rather administrative systems as a whole. Pamela Wicker, Christoph Breuer, and Tassilo von Hanau found that the incorporation of women into leadership positions benefits sports organizations, where in their study of sports clubs, they observed a significant inverse relationship between women's representation as board and regular members and sports organizations confronting severe organizational problems.[70] This confirms recent studies in business contexts that suggest that companies benefit from greater representation of women in decision-making positions because women's leadership styles, perception of potential difficulties, and problem-solving skills ultimately benefit the overall well-being of organizations.[71]

Not only would sex desegregation in sports benefit organizations but it would also provide women the opportunity to procure the same earning potential as men in athletic contexts. In addition, integration may also result in a modeling effect where women become more respected as coaches, referees, trainers, sports lawyers, sports agents, sports reporters, and so on across all levels of sport. Currently, many women are often excluded from these positions simply because they never played certain types of such sports as football or played at the top levels and therefore are not perceived to have either the interest or the ability to serve in such capacities (even though many men who currently work in these areas never played certain sports, and if they did, they did not excel).

Sex integration could also prove financially lucrative for traditional male-dominated sports teams as a way to expand their fan bases to women, a strategy that the NFL has attempted to use as a means to increase profits. This is evident by their sale of slim-fit jerseys marketed to women and the league's attempt to minimize such fallout from players' mistreatment of women as in the case of the two rape allegations levied against Ben Rothesburger.[72] Manase Chiweshe's research on women's experiences in Zimbabwe soccer stadiums demonstrates that in male-dominated sports spaces, female fans use various coping mechanisms to endure misogynic tendencies.[73] Similarly, Garry Crawford and Victoria Gosling show that female ice hockey consumers in the United Kingdom are often not considered "real fans" interested in the game, but instead are merely lusting after the players.[74] Sex-integrated sports contexts may reduce misogyny in stadiums as well as support the idea that if women can be "real players," they can also be "real fans," improving the overall spectator experience and generating greater value in game attendance and team support, in turn resulting in a supply and demand increase in ticket and merchandise sales and prices.

Sex Integration and Improved Media Coverage

Similar to the difficulty of combatting pay disparities in sex-segregated sports contexts because of justifications centered around women's athletic inferiority, it is difficult to address the underpresentation of women's sports in mainstream media because interest and demand are socially constructed and reproduced in accordance with dominant ideology. In their study of audience building through differential verbal and visual presentations of the NCAA women's and men's basketball tournaments, Messner, Margaret Dunca, and Faye Wachs demonstrated how media does not simply comply with demand, rather media creates the demand.[75] Knowledge about sports in terms of rules, players, and leagues generates anticipation and enjoyment for consumption and also shapes feelings of satisfaction once the competition is complete; however, access to sports knowledge is unequally produced. For example, in 2014, the media generated excitement leading up to Super Bowl XLVIII, and at the time the game aired, the broadcast broke the record for the most-watched program in U.S. history.[76] However, the game was one sided and uneventful because the Seatle Seahhawks built a 22-0 lead over the Denver Broncos by halftime and won 43-8.[77]

One factor that may have shaped the enjoyment of this and other games despite their one sidedness is a vested interest in a certain team winning or losing, whether it is through personal identification with one team or another, support or opposition for various reasons, or such personal gain as in the case of a wager on the result. However, the media also fosters interest and indifference, and ideas surrounding which sports, games, and players are important are then reproduced through such other agents of socialization as family, peers, and schools. For instance, Dr. Milner was socialized by her parents to oppose combat sports; however, the UFC has become popular among her age cohort, so for her peers to convince her to watch certain fights, she asks them for information on why she may find them exciting, whether there is a rivalry, the possibility of a record being set, or even such a personal reason to root for an athlete as they are from her hometown or also advocate for equity in sport. The important component of this example is that the media is not only responsible for dissemination (or concealment) of this sort of information surrounding rivalries, records, and athletes' backgrounds but also how the information is framed. As a social institution, the media represents the interests of the powerful, and media content is not presented arbitrarily or coincidently; conversely, decisions are made that serve to preserve the status quo with regard to sex, race, and class stratification. The absence or gross underrepresentation of women, along with racial minorities, lower-SES, and LGBT individuals in the upper-levels of media management and ownership serves to continuously silence the social, economic, and political interests and significance of these groups in the institution of sport and in other social structures.

In terms of sex disparities in media coverage of athletics, many studies have documented how men's sports and male athletes are portrayed in conformity with the ideological framework suggesting importance, excitement, dominance, and superiority, whereas women's sports and female athletes are simultaneously trivialized, ignored, inferiorized, or sexualized, thus reifying existing power dynamics and ideology in the social structure of sport.[78] Although Cooky, Messner, and Michela Musto found some qualitative changes evident in media coverage in the past five years, these disparities have persisted despite increases in women's rates of sport participation and the popularity of women's sports.[79] Because of their distorted presentation of both the quantity and quality of female athletes, Kane argues that not only is the media disregarding sportswomen but also the media actively constructs a *false* narrative that women are uninterested and unskilled in sport, which in effect serves to preserve male power and dominance in sport.[80]

Sex-integrated sport contexts force the presentation of female athletes in the media where televised competition and coverage of games, rosters, stats, and so on, if nothing else, will include female participants. Although biases may still persist in coverage of female athletes as is the case in media representations of racial minorities and LGBT athletes, at least there will be an account of their interests and skills. In addition, there is evidence that opportunities are emerging for female athletes to transcend historical mainstream representations through social media and alternative coverage that may serve as important sites for more accurate portrayals and inclusion.[81] Furthermore, sex integration and obligatory media coverage may promote knowledge, support, and role modeling of female athletes.[82] WNBA, NCAA, and Olympic champion, Maya Moore, recently wrote an article citing visibility as the key to her own and other women's athletic success, where growing up she said the following of her favorite players: "I saw myself in them and them in me."[83]

In addition, a diversification and increase in female sports role models may increase women's sports participation as well as women's status worldwide. For example, Merrill Melnick and Steven Jackson found that New Zealand youth not only expressed simple admiration for U.S. celebrities they idolized but also that these cultural icons actually influenced beliefs, values, self-appraisals, and behaviors.[84] The opportunity for U.S. women to inspire youth across the globe is beneficial for the country in terms of improving the United States' international reputation and relations, and it has implications for the universal goal of sex equality, which may reduce such broad social problems as the sexual trafficking of women and girls and sex disparities in access to education. In fact, Sumaya Samie et al. show how the United States championed women's access to sports participation in its "Empowering Women and Girls through Sports" initiative to achieve such goals surrounding the status of women in the "developing world" as promoting cross-cultural understanding, personal and professional development, critical thinking about sex equality, inclusion and human rights, and women as active agents of positive change.[85] The ideology of The Olympic Games also includes values of equality, respect, and friendship and we along with other scholars argue that sex segregation is counterproductive to achieving these goals.[86] Furthermore, modeling sex integration in U.S. sports may serve to promote female athletes globally. In her study on European women's and men's access to sports, Clotilde Talleu argues that sex disparities are a genuine problem in the continent and Cheryl Roberts even refers to the way in which the South African government systematically provides unequal financial allocation to women's and men's sports as a human rights abuse, hindering the progress of South African sportswomen.[87]

Sex Integration as Sex Inclusion: Benefits for LGBT, Nongender-Conforming Athletes, and Everyone Else

The broad issue of sex integration as a means to promote equality is a topic that is receiving increasing public and scholarly attention. With the rise in awareness about the experiences of transgender people, there have been new efforts to desegregate such previously sex-segregated spaces as bathrooms and college campuses. For example, in 2014, Laverne Cox was the first openly transgender person to be nominated for an Emmy,[88] 128 U.S. universities and colleges currently offer gender-neutral housing,[89] and such women's colleges as Barnard, Bryn Mar, Mount Holyoke, Mills, Scripps, and Simmons have changed their policies to admit trans women.[90] In July 2015, Ash Carter, the United States' Secretary of Defense, issued two initiatives to allow transgender individuals to serve openly in the military,[91] whereas the state of Hawaii ratified legislation granting transgender individuals the right to change the sex listed on their birth certificates.[92] In terms of sports specifically, such athletes as South African runner, Caster Semenya, and Indian sprinter, Dutee Chand, have drawn public awareness and scholarly attention to issues surrounding sex verification and eligibility,[93] and former Olympic decathlon men's event champion, born Bruce Jenner, recently came out as a trans women, Caitlyn Jenner, and was presented the Excellence in Sports Performance Yearly Award (ESPY), Arthur Ashe Courage Award in 2015.[94] Other current cases involve Yvette Cormier who was banned from Planet Fitness for complaining about a trans woman using the women's locker room,[95] and Cholie Jonsson, a personal trainer and transgender woman, who is currently suing Crossfit for $2.5 million in damages for prohibiting her from participating in a Crossfit competition for women.[96]

Eliminating sex categories in sport would benefit intersexed and transgender athletes so they would no longer be subjected to discrimination, outing, and other violations of privacy commonly experienced under current policy and in the absence of official policy.[97] In fact, it seems that sex integration in athletics could have a positive impact on the LGBT community in general. Scholars have exposed the negative consequences of homophobia in sports contexts,[98] and studies on sportswomen specifically have demonstrated that lesbians participating in sports have been silenced, sensationalized, and constructed as deviant while all female athletes are still socialized to fear and reject the lesbian label through sex-appropriate gender performance.[99] If athletics became integrated, there would be less association among certain sports, body types, and behaviors with masculinity and femininity, which may reduce stereotypes surrounding individuals who participate or are interested in certain sports. Since the concepts of sex, gender, and sexuality are intrinsically tied, breaking down sex and gender barriers may also result in the disassociation of gay males with femininity and gay females with masculinity, which would limit stereotyping of sexual minorities as well as heterosexual athletes who participate in nongender-conforming sports. Furthermore, sex integration in sports would benefit all individuals, including those who identify as cisgender and/or heterosexual, because diminishing these rigid associations among sex, gender, sexuality, and sports could serve to promote freedom of identity, interest, and behavior for all. Throughout the past decade, sports studies have demonstrated the need for both improvement and opportunity for continued positive change in the area of sex, gender, sexuality, and athletics.[100]

Judith Owen Blakemore and Renee Centers show that sex-neutral toys were more likely than gender-typed toys to develop children's physical, cognitive, artistic, and other skills, whereas gender-typed toys were less supportive of optimal development.[101] In fact, on August 7, 2015, the popular retailer, Target, recently announced that it will phase out gender-based signage and colors in its stores in such product areas as toys and bedding.[102] We also believe that in sports, dissociation with sex-, gender-, and sexuality-specific categories will benefit both participants and nonparticipants. In addition, Geoff Nichols, Richard Tacon, and Alison Muir suggest that a common love of sport through collective identity fostered by shared values, norms, and understanding may bridge demographic divisions and serve as a source of bonding.[103] Perhaps sex integration in sports could also lead to the destruction of arbitrary sex distinctions in other institutional contexts because sports play such a central part in sex role socialization in U.S. society. For instance, the Academy Awards (or Oscars) currently relies on separate sex categories for such best performances in films as best actress/best actor; the notion that women can compete with men in sports may inspire desegregation in additional cultural areas of entertainment with the possibility of a snowball effect in reducing sex disparities in other social intuitions.

Can Sex Integration in Sports Really Influence Gender Ideology?: A Case Example

Following a similar logic of the distinguished social and behavioral science researchers who signed the social science statement submitted to the Supreme Court in *Brown v. Board of Education*, we suggest that changing the structural conditions under which male and female students participate in school sports—from sex-segregated to sex-integrated—will likely lead to more favorable attitudes and support for sex and gender equity. For example, when *Brown* was passed in 1954, most white Americans strongly opposed school integration, especially in the South. Opponents of the Court ruling adamantly argued that the nation was not ready for such a dramatic change in schools. They contended that efforts to integrate schools should wait until some unspecified future time when racial attitudes become more favorable. However, social science theory and empirical evidence strongly suggested that the more effective way of promoting more favorable racial attitudes in society would be through creating favorable conditions for greater intergroup contact in schools. This intergroup contact hypothesis has been borne out. In the years following *Brown*, white Americans' support for racial integration grew stronger, especially among those who experienced school integration directly (as students), or indirectly (as parents of students attending integrated schools). To apply this logic to sex segregation in sports, we present an analysis illustrating how sex ideology in sports might be changed through providing opportunities for girls and boys to compete in sex-integrated contexts.

Developing academic skills is only one of many functions of public education. Schools also socialize young people for responsible adult social roles. Especially at the elementary and secondary levels, schools play an important role as socializing institutions in transmitting society's culture and values to its young as well as preparing them with appropriate knowledge and skills for leading productive and fulfilling adult lives. Cultural social-ization in schools plays a very important part in shaping sex roles and attitudes. Through their personal and vicarious experiences in school activ-ities, as well as through their exposure to the formal school curriculum, U.S. youth learn, among other things, socially constructed sex-appropriate gender roles and behaviors. In this context, the role of school sports is quite influential. The ways in which schools structure and allocate sport participation opportunities can influence boys' and girls' views regarding acceptable sports for each sex.

Data, in Figure 6.1, from the ELS reveal that students who attend schools where girls are allowed to participate in contact sports (i.e., football, base-ball, ice hockey, and wrestling) are more likely to support the idea of coed sports.[104] In Figure 6.1, we see that overall 59 percent of students in high schools where contact sports are not available to girls agree with the state-ment: "For most sports, girls should have the opportunity to be on the same team with boys."

In contrast, among students attending high schools where one contact sport is offered to girls, 63 percent agree with the statement. In high schools where two contact sports are available to girls, 68 percent agree with the statement; where three contact sports are available to girls, 74 percent of students agree with the statement. We also see similar patterns for sex sub-groups. Fifty-one percent of boys and 66 percent of girls in high schools

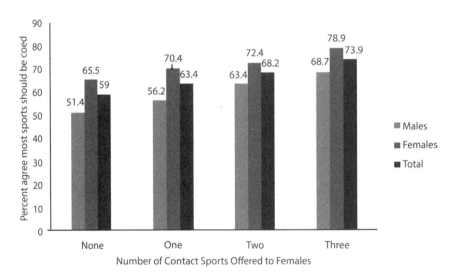

Figure 6.1   High School Context and Male's and Female's Support for Coed Sports.

where contact sports are not available to girls agree with the statement: "For most sports, girls should have the opportunity to be on the same team with boys." In contrast, among students attending high schools where one contact sport is available to girls, 56 percent of boys and 70 percent of girls agree with the statement. In high schools where two contact sports are available to girls, 63 percent of boys and 72 percent of girls agree with the statement; where three contact sports are available to girls, 69 percent of boys and 80 percent of girls agree with the statement.

Although it is not surprising that girls are more supportive of coed sports than boys, the relatively high level of support among both groups is encouraging. While these are not causal analyses, the patterns shown here strongly suggest that students' exposure to females' participation in contact sports is associated with increased acceptance of coed sports. This should encourage a broad range of interest groups—educators, administrators, parents, and the courts—to rethink the Title IX contact sports exclusion. Other researchers have also noted that exposure plays a role in promoting acceptance of sex equity in sports. Male athletes are significantly more likely to support sex equality and Title IX than male nonathletes.[105]

Ultimately, however, it is important for both Title IX supporters and opponents to recognize that because the contact exclusion clause excludes individual female athletes from participating in male contact sports based on, either objective or stereotypical, average traits of females—as a group— *this policy ignores the abilities and interests of individual female athletes.* Thus, the contact exclusion clause operates as a form of "sex profiling," which like "racial profiling" creates an uneven playing field. And like racial profiling, sex profiling in any truly democratic society should be viewed as problematic, if not illegal. Criminal justice researchers have begun to document the deleterious effects of racial profiling, on Black and Latino males in particular, resulting from "stop and frisk" policies.[106] In research on gender and race discrimination in employment, economists and sociologists often examine the exclusion of either female or minority employees or job applicants based on their groups' attributes as evidence of statistical discrimination. Whether it is deemed legal, or not, statistical discrimination in any context is harmful to particular members of any group who are denied opportunities without having their individual merits taken into account because their groups' traits are used as proxies to judge their worthiness. This is more than an abstract legal or scientific argument. To illustrate what this means in practice, consider the following scenario. Among males and females, the distribution of athletic abilities (size, strength, speed, and the like) falls under a bell-shaped curve. On average, males would rank higher on each of these abilities than females. However, half of males fall below their groups' average, whereas half of females fall above their groups' average. If the female talent distribution is superimposed on the male talent distribution, it is clear that the athletic abilities of well above average females would rank higher than the athletic abilities of average males. Yet, because of the contact sports exclusion clause, well above average females are denied opportunities to play boys contact sports—even on junior varsity high school teams, or NCAA Division III, NAIA, or junior college teams—whereas average (or even below average) boys are not excluded.

In their examination of U.S. legal cases of boys pursuing the right to play on girls' high schools teams, Adam Love and Kimberly Kelly conclude that building a critical mass of integrated sports may result in the end of sex as a legal form of discrimination.[107] To maximize the potential benefits of sex integration in sports, specific policy recommendations and evaluation procedures must be defined.

CHAPTER SEVEN

How Sex Integration Is Possible

Recommendations for Dismantling Ideological and Structural Barriers to Desegregation in Sports

The "Student-Athletes Bill of Rights," a law that financially protects college athletes at four Pacific-12 Conference schools was ratified in California in 2012,[1] and in 2014, Northwestern University football players were granted the right to unionize.[2] Although these cases were considered victories for student-athletes and to have the potential to transform college athletics through their conversion from amateur to professional status, progress has halted and players are still not compensated by the NCAA. Although there is an ongoing debate about whether college-athletes should be paid, many pundits, who feel that change is necessary, are unsure of how such policies should be implemented. The mandatory compensation of student-athletes would result in many questions regarding how type of sport, division level, attendance rates, winning percentage, and so on should affect pay, if at all, and also presents issues surrounding salary caps, health insurance, scholarship allocation, tax consequences, and so on.[3] It can be argued that reform is yet to happen because addressing these concerns is immensely complicated, articulated by *Forbes* contributor Victor Lipman in his description of the transformation of college athletes to professional athletes as "Pandora's box."[4] Complexity, however, does not negate necessity, and the question about how to implement change should not precede the question of whether or not it should occur. In the case of sex integration in sports, critics may point to the complexity, challenges, and unknowns surrounding the process to diminish the need for sex integration. Throughout this book, we have presented both social theories and empirical evidence supporting our arguments that sex integration in sports is socially, legally, and morally necessary; this chapter draws on wisdom gained from *Brown*, Title IX, and previous sports policy research to provide specific and tangible policy recommendations for how to both implement and evaluate sex integration in sports, thus reducing difficulties and uncertainties associated with the sex-integration process.

Implementing Sex Integration in Sport

Talleu's report to the Council of Europe[5] and the UN's guide[6] for improving women's access to and experiences within sport serve as a general starting point for implementing athletic sex equity policy. Specific recommendations given, which should be applied to the process of desegregating sports, include adequately training educators, coaches, and staff on issues of sex inequality, involving women in decision-making processes, coordinating and disseminating an exchange of information, developing proper role models, prohibiting sexed language, establishing antiharassment and abuse policies, cataloguing instances of prejudice, reinforcing policies with appropriate regulation, legislation, and funding, and ensuring media promotion of successes and good practices, and condemnation of discrimination.[7] We also value other sports scholars' calls for transparency in government criteria for decision-making positions in athletics,[8] internal coordinators within schools and sports organizations that conduct regular policy compliance self-evaluations,[9] a clear and common definition of sex equity,[10] and sports contexts that encourage identification of oppressive systems and formation of partnerships with feminist organizations[11] in the development and execution of the desegregation process. We feel that sex-integrated sports will specifically benefit from the support and legitimation of key actors (prominent male and female athletes) and institutions (media). In addition, because of the way in which white females and females of color have differentially benefited from Title IX, we are adamant that women of color must be included in all decision-making processes concerning sex integration, and that policy assessments pay particular attention to intersectional outcomes associated with sex and race. In terms of the implementation of the sex-integration process, we have three specific recommendations: (1) establishment and enactment of universal rules in sex-segregated athletic contexts, (2) a bottom-up approach to inclusion over time, and (3) preservation of women-only sport spaces.

Establishment and Enactment of Universal Rules
in Sex-Segregated Athletic Contexts

Rule changes, and even drastic changes, are common in sport. For instance, in 2015, NCAA women's basketball adopted a four-quarter format among other game modifications as well as relaxed regulations on amplified music,[12] whereas NCAA men's basketball confirmed modifications associated with the shot clock, time outs, fouls, dunking, and officiating.[13] The NFL also approved rule changes associated with extra points and two-point conversions in 2015.[14]

Before sex integration can commence, it is necessary to establish one set of universal rules for each sport offered in the United States although these regulations and procedures may differ at the youth, middle school, high school, club (e.g., travel team and Amateur Athletic Union [AAU] competitions), college, and professional levels to accommodate differences in size and skill. Currently, there are discrepancies between men's and women's sports, including ball size (e.g., basketball), length of competition (e.g., tennis), event characteristics (e.g., gymnastics), equipment (e.g., lacrosse), sanctions for contact (e.g., ice hockey), and uniforms (e.g., volleyball). Both men's and women's competitions in each sport should be required by law to adhere to mandated rule changes. Because of dominant patriarchal ideology, it is assumed that most sports will implement current men's regulations; women should start training accordingly and begin to use new rules in organized competition and practice as soon as the rule changes are released. Even though dominant ideology asserts the superiority of men's contests, some such women's sports that are currently more popular than men's as gymnastics may experience universal adoption of women's rules. In addition, some such sports with similar rules that are typically viewed as either women's or men's games as in the case of softball and baseball should retain their autonomy as separate sports to increase total opportunity for participation. Josh Tinley argues that girls play softball because they have been excluded from baseball,[15] and if this is the case, maintaining both sports may increase opportunities for both females in baseball and males in softball.

In addition, such sexed sports rules in contexts that are currently coed as those typical of college intramurals must be standardized according to the newly adopted rules. Even assuming that sexed rules were created with the intention to promote women's active participation, Zacharias Wood explains the importance of eliminating sex modifications (such as higher point values for touchdowns in football or goals in soccer scored by female players) in coed sports. He argues that not only do sexed rules rely on and reify dominant sexist ideology maintaining women's athletic inferiority but they also diminish the integrity of the game.[16] One example of well-meaning objectives for sex equity that instead depend on and result in the reproduction of sexist ideology and outcomes is the newly formed professional Mixed Gender Basketball Association (MGBA). Although MGBA creator John Howard emphasizes collaboration rather than antagonism as well as such women's contributions to the game as greater commitment to discipline and fundamentals, he relies on such sexed rules as a given number of male and female players allowed on the court at a time and the existence of a four-point shot for women.[17] In addition, George presents a compelling argument for the elimination of sex segregation in sports; however, he believes in requiring that team makeup consists of 50 percent females and 50 percent males and that playing time be divided equally among women and men.[18] This logic evident in sexed rules not only reifies the sex binary and women's perceived inability to compete with men under the same set of rules but it also enables discrimination against transgender and other nongender-conforming athletes.

It may be helpful to consult with international federations in choosing which style of play sports will maintain in the United States so that the country will not lose competitive advantage in the Olympics and other global events. However, research suggests that this should not be a central area for concern. Ivo van Hilvoorde, Agnes Elling, and Ruud Stokvis find that contrary to popular belief and justifications for increasing national sport funding, the stories of Olympic athletes, rather than Olympic medal counts, create a sense of national belonging and pride.[19] In addition, international competition may also be changing to reflect more egalitarian principles. In their report on sex equality in the London 2012 Olympics, Peter and Michelle Donnelly show that despite women's participation gains in percentage, sport type, and national representation, sex inequality was evident in funding, sponsorship, publicity, media representation, sex testing, and structural rule differences. The researchers specifically focused on rule discrepancy, where they found that only 35.8 percent of the events were equal for men and women and thus call for equalization in the number of events and medals as well as expert examinations of the rules of competition to establish consistency within and between sports.[20] As mentioned in Chapter 6, investigation into sport rules may result in increased safety benefits, and rule changes that result in benefits should not be dismissed simply because they deviate from those used in international competition. For instance, although the Fédération Internationale de Hockey (FIH) does not permit protective eyewear without medical reason, USA Field Hockey sanctions approved face protection without medical reason, and "cage style" goggles are favored in U.S. high schools, although they are not permitted by either USA Field Hockey or FIH.[21]

To assess sports' rules and regulations, Donnelly and Donnelly suggest the creation of expert panels consisting of agents from sports governing bodies, relevant members of the sports medicine and sports science community, and athletes and former athletes.[22] U.S. national and state sports organizations should work together to form panels responsible for initiating rule changes in U.S. sports. To promote equity in decision making during this first step of the sex-integration process, we recommend that panel quotas are established. Johanna Adriaanse and Toni Schofield found that to achieve goals associated with sex equity in Australian sports governance bodies, a minimum of at least three women were necessary on each National Sport Organization board. Other important dimensions for progress evident in this research included board members' understanding of the value of sex equity, appointment of women to decision-making positions, and sex solidarity expressed through corporation, collaboration, and influential male board members' active support and endorsement of female board members.[23] Because U.S. panels assessing sports rules may differ in their number of members according to sports popularity and prestige, we recommend a minimum representation of 50 percent women, because women currently account for 50.8 percent of the U.S. population.[24]

For panel formation, we also suggest the incorporation of experts on social justice as well as a diverse set of committee members who fit the criteria described by Donnelly and Donnelly,[25] where a wide range of individuals and issues associated with historically disadvantaged groups are represented. For example, scholars have discussed how current regulations in sports dress codes may serve to exclude Muslim women.[26] At the same time, sex integration may reduce Muslim[27] and such other religious groups as Hasidic Jews opportunities for participation; it is important that these concerns are appropriately expressed and addressed during discussions of best rules and practices for each sport.

In addition to how the opportunity to evaluate current sports regulations may result in increased safety, assessment of other sports practices may serve to benefit the greater good rather than powerful entities and organizations that currently profit disproportionately from contemporary sports procedures. For instance, Dufur and Seth Feinberg discuss how the present monopoly structure of the NFL Combine and Draft that regulates entrance into the league serves to increase owners' and coaches' power while undermining players' dignity[28]; a review panel consisting of former and current NFL players as well as individuals who specialize in issues of discrimination and inequitable treatment may be able to suggest alternatives to the way in which players are recruited into the league, thus reducing their exposure to exploitation. Rule differences in practices for drafting players into U.S. professional leagues currently differ both by sport type (e.g., basketball and baseball) and sex, even within the same sport (e.g., basketball) in terms of requirements associated with age, college attendance, and so on. Whereas panels may still establish rules for entrance into professional leagues that differ by sport type, there should be uniform eligibility rules established between corresponding men's and women's sports teams. This reexamination of eligibility requirements for professional teams may also result in positive social outcomes. For instance, if the NBA changed its age minimum (currently 19) to that of the WNBA (currently 22),[29] NCAA men's basketball players' graduation rates may improve.

Bottom-up Approach to Inclusion Over Time

Once sports rules are determined, required, and legally reinforced in competition, sex integration should be implemented with a bottom-up approach. A bottom-up approach to integration is recommended not only to socialize children into integrated contexts but also to ensure women's continued participation through exposure at a young age and sustained opportunity as they mature. Jeroen Schreeder et al. highlight the importance of early socialization into sport, where they found that adolescent sport participation is a better predictor of adult sport participation than SES.[30] In addition, early socialization is important not only for those participating in sports but also to accommodate possible changes in ideology associated with the evaluation of what is deemed socially acceptable and sex-appropriate behavior in sport. The contact hypothesis and ELS data presented in Chapter 6 demonstrate that officially supported exposure to nontraditional sports experiences results in the acceptance of sex integration in sports. Although our analysis of the ELS data focuses on peer evaluation of sport participation, similar gains in social approval of sex integration would be expected to occur from the exposure of parents, coaches, administrators, and others involved in sports decision-making processes to sex-integrated sports over time.

A bottom-up approach to sex integration is logical because the younger the child, the less time they are exposed and affected by dominant sex and gender ideology. Within the arena of sport, it is especially important that individuals beginning to play in integrated contexts are not damaged by an ideology that defines men as physically superior to women and deems certain sports as either being more or less appropriate for females. A similar logic also applies to perceived biological aspects of sex where there are less pronounced differences in children than adults.[31] Many youth sports in the United States are currently coed and, in addition, young children are less affected by changes in sports legislation, whereas those participating in sport at the professional and collegiate levels have vested personal and monetary interests in their participation and success. Bottom-up integration will afford female athletes the ability to maintain long-term involvement in sports while also giving them time to learn new skills associated with rule changes, if necessary. By creating a common set of rules between male and female sports and starting integration at the lowest levels, athletes will be socialized into playing by the same rules and playing together, therefore maximizing women's involvement at subsequent levels.

Recently, the United Kingdom successfully implemented one-year increases in the age at which girls and boys may play on the same soccer teams. In the 2010–2011 season, only children under 11 could play together, whereas in the 2014–2015 season, female and male players under 16 had the opportunity to compete on the same teams.[32] This example should serve as a model for bottom-up integration in the United States, where the first cohort experiencing mandatory sex integration would always compete in coed contexts. Both club and nonschool-based teams should implement age guidelines for yearly integration, whereas school districts may use multiyear models, depending on the structure of competition in their current league. For instance, a large school district league with 7th and 8th grade middle school teams and freshman, junior varsity, and varsity high school teams might use yearly integration. A smaller school district with few teams, for example, only one middle school and one high school team per sport might integrate the middle school competition first and then the high school, four years later, once those children who have always competed in integrated contexts were moving into high school. For example, integration at the high school level would begin once the first cohort of 5th graders who always experienced middle school-integrated play would be in 9th grade, and the 6th, 7th, and 8th graders who played in integrated sports in middle school (now in 10th, 11th, and 12th grade) would have had previous experience playing in integrated contexts.

After 11 years (when the fifth graders from the previous example have completed their senior year of college and high schools have been fully integrated for seven years), the NCAA may proceed with the process because those attending college would have played in integrated contexts in middle and high school and those currently both seeking to begin to participate and those seeking to continue to participate in college athletics would have had ample time to prepare. In addition, the vast majority of students who played in integrated contexts in high school would have graduated college at this point in time, so this would not place students who were socialized into sex segregation or who are currently playing sex-segregated college sports at a disadvantage.

During the time that sex integration is being implemented in schools, professional teams should be allowed to draft any woman or man according to the new rules established by the national sport organization panels. After 4 years of integrated NCAA play, 15 years after the implementation of the sex-integration process begins in schools, all professional teams should integrate. Formally, sex-segregated teams would not have to fold or merge into one team; it is plausible that there will be a demand for multiple professional teams per sport. Professional organizations should look to minor league baseball as an example, where especially in smaller cities that lack other professional sports teams to support and games to attend, minor league baseball continues to be a large draw.

Preservation of Women-Only Sport Spaces

Simultaneously encouraging sex-integrated sports while maintaining women's sport spaces is consistent with some other scholars' recommendations for best achieving equity in athletics.[33] In our proposed model, schools and sport organizations would not reduce the number of sports they offer. For instance, if a high school currently offers four basketball teams (girls junior varsity, boys junior varsity, girls varsity, and boys varsity), they may still offer four teams after integration so that neither men's nor women's opportunities are diminished, similarly to how college sports are divided into three divisions with different levels of competitiveness. Even if in certain sports women or men become disproportionately concentrated at higher or lower levels, everyone still has access to opportunities to both participate and achieve success. Although schools that currently offer a certain number of sex-segregated boys and men's teams (such as football or wrestling) may choose to add teams to meet new demand, to preserve opportunities for girls and women, schools will be prohibited from reducing the number of teams that were formerly offered solely to girls and women. This mandatory nonelimination requirement applies to both teams that formerly offered such separate females' and males' teams as often in the case of basketball, lacrosse, track, and soccer, as well as such girls and women-only teams as often the case in softball, field hockey, and volleyball.

Although research assessing whether or not single-sex education is beneficial has been inconclusive, sex-segregated schooling is becoming increasingly popular in the United States.[34] To preserve girls' opportunities in these contexts, all-girls schools should retain all-girls teams, whereas legislation should also require that school-aged girls have the opportunity to play on any teams in both school- and nonschool-based leagues. In the case of all-boys middle and high schools, girls attending nearby schools or who are homeschooled should have access to team participation and all-boys middle and high school teams should be required to play coed teams and all-girls teams who wish to compete against them. Transgender and other nongender-conforming girls and women should be afforded the opportunity to play on either coed or girls-only teams. Similarly to how HBCUs provide additional opportunities for higher education and do not diminish opportunities or "steal" success from racially integrated colleges, opportunities for women to play sports should be preserved at the college level in the case of women's-only colleges. Where there are currently many active women's colleges, there are few nonreligious, four-year men's-only institutions in the United States, providing ample prospects for sportswomen to play at the college level. Although HBCUs are not exclusively open to black students (e.g., white students are often recruited to play such low-impact, high-revenue sports at HBCUs as golf and tennis), women's-only colleges and sports teams should remain as such, only open to women, including trans women. The justification for this difference in sports policy between HBCUs and women's colleges is that whereas Blacks are not currently perceived to be inferior to Whites in sports, women are still perceived to be athletically inferior to men, and therefore, women's-only sports spaces must be preserved.

Ann Travers explains that single-sex opportunities in sports for girls and women are necessary as long as their minority status continues.[35] In fact, one of Lauren Rauscher and Cooky's criticisms of current girl-centered sports programs is that they mask large-scale issues of sexism and male privilege.[36] The existence of women's-only colleges and sports teams is necessary in the current sex-stratified system to ensure equitable opportunities as well as to draw attention to structural inequality. Unlike women's-only teams under total segregation, women's-only teams in a sex-integrated sports system do not necessarily denote women's inferiority; rather, similarly to HBCUs and women's colleges, they promote the success of a historically and continually disadvantaged group. In addition, the countless individuals thriving in women's-only colleges and HBCUs and those who are successful after graduation serve as exemplars for changing dominant sex and racial ideologies by demonstrating that for these groups, opportunity, not differential ability, is the key to academic success. Women's-only sports contexts within an integrated sport structure also have the ability to promote women's status and success.

Recognizing the value of resistance when marginalized groups segregate themselves, Love and Kelly argue for the maintenance of women's-only sport spaces within integrated contexts; however they question whether complete equality can be achieved without complete integration.[37] We are optimistic that initiating sex integration in school sports will not only lead to complete athletic integration but also that sex integration in sports will reduce macrolevel societal sexist practices that results in the current necessity to maintain such women's-only sport spaces in the United States as those associated with unequal pay, domestic and sexual violence, lack of political representation, unequal housework and childcare responsibilities, and the absence of guaranteed maternity leave. To effectively assess the short-term and potential long-term outcomes for sex integration in sports both within athletic contexts and the larger social structure, it is crucial that the sex-integration process and its' consequences are appropriately and consistently evaluated.

Evaluating Sex Integration in Sport

The *Brown* decision deemed separate educational facilities to be inherently unequal, yet did not provide clear-cut procedures for achieving integration in schools, resulting in continued segregation and inequality for Blacks in education, housing, and the labor market.[38] When reflecting on the large body of research on racial desegregation, we believe that social research may have been more harmful than beneficial to Blacks because of the manner in which researchers sought to assess whether *Brown* was "working." Specifically, as discussed in Chapter 3, researchers assessed outcomes associated with educational achievement tests, rather than those examining the extent and quality of educational access provided to Black and Latino students. Scholars who assessed Title IX, however, presumably learning from racial desegregation research, defined the effectiveness of the law in terms of equitable opportunities, where Title IX was undoubtedly deemed successful because it "worked" to drastically increase women's participation in sports. Because achievement outcomes were closely linked with the way in which desegregation was implemented, we posit that if the proper questions regarding fair access in *Brown* similarly to those evident in the assessment of Title IX were examined instead, then today, the nation may have been in a much better place with regard to both race relations and equality of educational opportunity. This is partially because before racial desegregation had time to "work" in terms of racial progress evidenced by such achievement outcomes as test scores, subsequent educational policy after *Brown* resulted in implementation of ability grouping and "tracking" in schools, in turn resulting in resegregation in those very buildings the law was intended to integrate. Thus, evaluating the "right thing" is essential to achieving the goals associated with the original justifications for policy implementation; assessment has the potential to affect the success or failure of such educational policies as in the case of *Brown* and Title IX.

Similarly to the way in which success was defined in the evaluation of Title IX and arguably should have been in *Brown*, sex integration in sports should first be measured in terms of equitable opportunity. Although public discourse asserts that Title IX has resulted in equity in access and, sometimes, even disproportional access for women in the case of supposed eliminated men's opportunities, Sabo and Philip Veliz show that in U.S. high schools, boys are still participating in sports at higher rates than girls and are consistently provided with more opportunities for participation.[39] Research evaluating sex integration should examine how policy affects the extent and quality of women's equitable access to sports participation and the potential for continued improvement in access over time. That is to say that policy studies should primarily use sex integration as the dependent rather than the independent variable. In this model, predictor variables of interest should focus on macro- and microlevel catalysts and barriers to desegregation, and both quantitative and qualitative studies should be used to examine such possible compounding social factors related to achieving sex integration as those associated with race, SES, region, urbanity, and sexuality as well as organizational, political, and economic forces that exacerbate inequality.[40] In addition, empirical research should assess sex integration as an outcome measure not only in terms of access for athletic participation but also for equitable opportunities for women in sports as coaches, referees, administrators, broadcasters, lawyers, physicians, agents, and other positions resulting in women's prospects for employment and decision-making power in athletic contexts.

Although policy should above all be evaluated in terms of access, we do not deny the importance of assessing the consequences of sex desegregation in sports. Researchers should be especially concerned with demonstrating how sex-conscious sport policy offers collective, societal benefits that extend beyond individuals. Specifically, research in this area should focus on providing evidence of why sport desegregation represents a compelling state interest in terms of national stability, social cohesion, and public health. Throughout this book, we have presented an abundance of information concerning how sexist ideology and discriminatory practices are embedded in sports contexts; it is crucial for sex-integration researchers to be self-aware of how their own biases may affect their evaluation of the integration process and corresponding outcomes. For instance, Dr. Braddock recently attended his granddaughter's junior Olympics swimming competition in Maryland, and although he noticed the scoreboards were color-coded pink for girls and blue for boys, other family members, the competitors, coaches, officials, and event organizers did not seem to be aware nor take issue with the sexed message. Although this example may seem arbitrary, in this context, girls—and everyone else—were reminded, perhaps subconsciously, by the final ranking sheets that they were girls, reinforcing their perceived athletic inferiority, whereas boys were simultaneously reminded of their maleness and presumed superiority. This type of subtle gender priming could potentially affect boys' and girls' future performances as well as subsequent self-evaluation and ability. This seemingly innocuous "gendered scoresheet" color distinction could potentially invoke stereotype threat, where girls' minority status and socially presupposed physical inferiority are highlighted, resulting in impaired future performances.[41]

When considering the overwhelming inequities in sports contexts, it is also important that researchers and policy makers retain a sense of optimism and patience for the possibility for improvement over time. Núria Puig and Alan Ingham urge scholars to consider that sports space is a social construction that not only merits examination but can also be changed,[42] whereas Janet Fink encourages reflection on collective empirical evidence that points to social progress in sports, even though there is still much work to be done.[43] Finally, it is imperative that during implementation and evaluation of the sex-integration process, the social, legal, and moral justifications for integration are continuously and consistently articulated and respected. Similarly to the *Brown* decision, integration is ultimately the only means to ensure equitable access to the resources, experiences, and connections that facilitate full and equal participation in mainstream U.S. society. Sex integration in sports is essential for providing females the opportunity to compete and achieve at the highest levels and receive maximum rewards; it is the only way that women will be able to fully realize their potential as athletes, as individuals, and as a class of people.

Notes

Chapter One

1. Associated Press, "Girl Wrestler Not Bitter About Default Win," *ESPN*, last modified February 18, 2011, http://sports.espn.go.com/ncaa/highschool/news/story?id=6135272.

2. Title IX of the Education Amendments of 1972, 20 U.S.C. §1681–1688.

3. *Brown v. Board of Education of Topeka*, Shawnee County, Kan., 347 U.S. 483 (1954).

4. *Plessy v. Ferguson*, 163 U.S. 537 (1896).

5. Combahee River Collective Staff, *The Combahee River Collective Statement: Black Feminist Organizing in the Seventies and Eighties* (Brooklyn: Kitchen Table/Women of Color Press, 1986); Patricia Hill Collins, *Black Feminist Thought: Knowledge, Consciousness and the Politics of Empowerment* (New York: Routledge, 1991); bell hooks, *Feminist Theory: From Margin to Center* (Boston, MA: South End Press, 1984).

6. Stephen Steinberg, *The Ethnic Myth* (New York: Plenum Press, 1981).

7. Arnold K. Ho et al., "Evidence for Hypodescent and Racial Hierarchy in the Categorization and Perception of Biracial Individuals," *Journal of Personality and Social Psychology* 100 (2011): 492–506.

8. Jo B. Paoletti, *Pink and Blue: Telling the Boys from the Girls in America* (Bloomington, IN: Indiana University Press, 2012).

9. Matthew Mitten et al., *Sports Law and Regulation: Cases, Materials, and Problems*, 2nd ed. (New York: Aspen Publishers, 2009), 765–66.

10. Ibid., 766.

11. Ibid., 767–68.

12. Title VI of the Civil Rights Act of 1964, 42 U.S.C. § 2000d.

13. Mitten et al., *Sports Law*, 768.

14. Roger Saylor, "Black College Football," *College Football Historical Society Newsletter* 13 (2000): 4–7.

15. Ronald E Hall, "The Ball Curve: Calculated Racism and the Stereotype of African American Men," *Journal of Black Studies* 32 (2002): 104–19; Herbert D. Simons, "Race and Penalized Sports Behaviors," *International Review for the Sociology of Sport* 38 (2003): 5–22; Nancy E. Spencer, "Sister Act IV: Venus and Serena Williams at Indian Wells: Sincere Fictions and White Racism," *Journal of Sport and Social Issues* 28 (2004): 115–35.

16. Gary A. Sailes, "An Investigation of Campus Stereotypes: The Myth of Black Athletic Superiority and the Dumb Jock Stereotype," *Sociology of Sport Journal* 10 (1993): 88–97.

17. Jill Brown and Gordon Bear, "Minorities in Major League Baseball 1952–1987," *International Review for the Sociology of Sport* 34 (1999): 411–22; David Tokiharu Mayeda, "From Model Minority to Economic Threat: Media Portrayals of Major League Baseball Pitchers Hideo Nomo and Hideki Irabu," *Journal of Sport and Social Issues* 23 (1999): 203–17; Gary A. Sailes, "The African American Athlete: Social Myths and Stereotypes," in *African Americans in Sport: Contemporary Themes*, ed. Gary A. Sailes (New Brunswick, NJ: Transaction Publishers, 1998), 183–98.

18. Mikaela Dufur, "Race Logic and 'Being Like Mike': Representations of Athletes in Advertising, 1985–1994," *Sociological Focus* 30 (1997): 345–56; David McCarthy and Robyn Lloyd Jones, "Speed, Aggression, Strength, and Tactical Naivete: The Portrayal of the Black Soccer Player on Television," *Journal of Sport and Social Issues* 21 (1997): 348–62; David McCarthy, Robyn Lloyd Jones, and Paul Potrac, "Constructing Images and Interpreting Realities: The Case of the Black Soccer Player on Television," *International Review for the Sociology of Sport* 38 (2003): 217–38.

19. Claire F. Sullivan, "Gender Verification and Gender Policies in Elite Sport: Eligibility and 'Fair Play'," *Journal of Sport and Social Issues* 35 (2011): 400–19.

20. See for example a work that does suggest integration, Eileen McDonagh and Laura Pappano, *Playing with the Boys: Why Separate Is Not Equal in Sports* (New York: Oxford University Press, 2008).

21. Deborah L. Brake, *Getting in the Game: Title IX and the Women's Sports Revolution* (New York: New York University Press, 2010); Wendy Parker, *Beyond Title IX: The Cultural Laments of Women's Sports*, accessed June 20, 2012, http://www .amazon.com/Beyond-Title-IX-Wendy-Parker-ebook/dp/B008DFZV9E; Welch Suggs, *A Place on the Team: The Triumph and Tragedy of Title IX* (Princeton, NJ: Princeton University Press, 2006).

22. Tom Vanden Brook, "Pentagon Opening Front-Line Combat Roles to Women," *USA Today*, last modified June 18, 2013, http://www.usatoday.com/story /news/politics/2013/06/18/women-expected-on-front-lines-by-2016/2434911/; C. J. Lin, "One Year Later, Military Criticized Over Rate of Progress for Women in Combat," *Stars and Stripes*, last modified January 30, 2014, http://www.stripes .com/news/one-year-later-military-criticized-over-rate-of-progress-for-women-in -combat-1.264805.

23. Abigail Tracy, "Nobel Laureate Tim Hunt Under Fire for Sexist Comments," *Forbes*, last modified June 10, 2015, http://www.forbes.com/sites/abigailtracy/2015 /06/10/nobel-laureate-tim-hunt-sexist-comments-apology/.

24. Cyd Zeigler, "With the Drafting of Shane Ray, NFL Confirms Michael Sam Is Target of Homophobia," *SB Nation*, last modified April 30, 2015, http://www.outsports.com/2015/4/30/8265615/shane-ray-michael-sam-draft.

25. Cyd Zeigler, "One Year Later, Has Michael Sam Been Frozen Out of the NFL?," *SB Nation*, last modified February 8, 2015, http://www.outsports.com/2015/2/8/8000303/michael-sam-nfl-teams-gay-roster.

26. Zeigler, "With the Drafting of Shane Ray."

27. Mary Loftus, "Diana Nyad Completes Record Swim from Cuba to Key West," *Emory Magazine*, last modified September 18, 2013, http://news.emory.edu/stories/2013/09/emag_diana_nyad/campus.html.

28. Ibid.

29. For a full list of countries, see Jeffery Clair, Jason Wasserman, and Adrienne N. Milner, Forthcoming, "Sport and Social Theory," in *Wiley-Blackwell Encyclopedia of Sociology*, 2nd ed., ed. George Ritzer (Malden, MA: Wiley Blackwell).

30. "NASCAR Condemns Indiana's 'Religious Freedom' Law," *The Huffington Post*, last modified March 31, 2015, http://www.huffingtonpost.com/2015/03/31/nascar-indiana-law_n_6978922.html.

31. Erik Brady, Jim Corbett, and Tom Pelissero, "If Arizona Bill Becomes Law, Will NFL Move Super Bowl?," *USA Today*, last modified February 25, 2014, http://www.usatoday.com/story/sports/nfl/2014/02/25/arizona-anti-gay-legislation-super-bowl-national-football-league/5821799/.

32. Bill Chappell, "Year of the Woman at the London Games? For Americans, It's True," *NPR*, last modified August 10, 2012, http://www.npr.org/sections/thetorch/2012/08/10/158570021/year-of-the-woman-at-the-london-games-for-americans-its-true.

33. Erin Gloria Ryan, "First Woman to Complete the American Ninja Warrior Course Is So Badass," *Jezebel*, last modified July 16, 2014, http://jezebel.com/first-woman-to-complete-the-american-ninja-warrior-cour-1605907801.

34. Scooby Axson, "Mo'ne Davis on This Week's National *Sports Illustrated* Cover," *Sports Illustrated*, last modified August 20, 2014, http://www.si.com/more-sports/2014/08/19/mone-davis-little-league-world-series-sports-illustrated-cover.

35. Liam Boylan-Pett, "Meet Becky Hammon, the Spurs Coach Who Made History in Summer League," *SB Nation*, last modified July 12, 2015, http://www.sbnation.com/nba/2015/7/12/8937181/becky-hammon-spurs-coach-nba-first-woman-summer-league.

36. "Coaching the Big Leagues: Natalie Nakase Makes NBA History," *NPR*, last modified August 2, 2014, http://www.npr.org/2014/08/02/337359843/coaching-the-big-leagues-natalie-nakase-makes-nba-history.

37. Gary Estwick, "Jen Welter Hired by Arizona Cardinals, Becomes NFL's First Female Coach," *AL.com*, last modified July 27, 2015, http://www.al.com/sports/index.ssf/2015/07/jen_welter_hired_by_arizona_ca.html.

38. Andrew Keh and Harvey Araton, "Establishing Her Position in the Post: Michele Roberts, New N.B.A. Union Leader, Isn't Afraid to Throw Elbows," *The*

New York Times, last modified November 26, 2014, http://www.nytimes.com/2014
/11/27/sports/basketball/michele-roberts-new-nba-players-union-leader-isnt
-afraid-to-throw-elbows.html?ref=sports&_r=0.

39. Dan McQuade, "This Trailblazing Woman Just Made Hockey History in Fin-
land," *Mic*, last modified September 22, 2014, http://mic.com/articles/99486/this
-trailblazing-woman-just-made-hockey-history-in-finland.

40. Lindsay Gibbs, "Anything You Can Do, Women Can Do Better: The Race
for Equality in Bobsledding," *VICE Sports*, last modified December 18, 2014,
https://sports.vice.com/article/anything-you-can-do-women-can-do-better-the
-race-for-equality-in-bobsledding.

41. "UConn Women's Coach Says Men's College Basketball 'A Joke'," *The Seattle
Times*, last modified April 1, 2015, http://www.seattletimes.com/sports/uw-husky
-basketball/uconn-womens-coach-says-mens-college-basketball-a-joke/.

42. Rodger Sherman, "Portland's Cassandra Brown Drills 9 Straight to College
3-Point Shootout Over Gonzaga's Kevin Pangos: The Girls Outshot the Boys This
Year," *SB Nation*, last modified April 2, 2015, http://www.sbnation.com/2015/4/2
/8338159/college-3-point-shootout-cassandra-brown-portland-kevin-pangos
-gonzaga.

43. D'Arcy Maine, "Phenom Sam Gordon Set to Star in First Girls Tackle Football League," *ESPN*, last modified May 22, 2015, http://espn.go.com/espnw/athletes
-life/the-buzz/article/12932083/phenom-sam-gordon-set-star-first-girls-tackle
-football-league.

44. "Pat Summitt Fast Facts," *CNN*, last modified June 2, 2015, http://www.cnn
.com/2015/01/06/us/pat-summitt-fast-facts/.

Chapter Two

1. B. Glenn George, "Fifty/Fifty: Ending Sex Segregation in School Sports," *Ohio
State Law Journal* 63 (2002): 1107.

2. H. R. 12344—93rd Congress: Women's Educational Equity Act of 1974.

3. Elaine M. Blinde and Diane E. Taub, "Women Athletes as Falsely Accused
Deviants: Managing the Lesbian Stigma," *Sociological Quarterly* 33 (1992): 521–
33; Bernice R. Sandler, "'Too Strong for a Woman'—The Five Words That Created
Title IX," *Equity and Excellence in Education* 33 (2000): 9–13; Andrew Fishel and
Janice Pottker, *National Politics and Sex Discrimination in Education* (Lexington, MA:
Lexington Books, 1977).

4. Lindsay Brewer Roskovensky, Douglas Grbic, and David Matthew, "The
Changing Gender Composition of U.S. Medical School Applicants and Matricu-
lants," *Association of American Medical Colleges Analysis in Brief* 12 (2012): 1–2.

5. Sara Frueh, "Is the Gender Gap Narrowing? New Data on Female Faculty in
Science and Engineering," *National Academics in Focus* 9 (2009): 1.

6. "Title IX Athletics Polices: Issues and Data for Education Decision Makers,"
National Coalition for Women and Girls in Education, accessed December 1, 2002,
http://ncwge.org/PDF/Title_IX_Coalition_Report_Final.pdf.

7. "Title IX Still Applies: The Battle for Gender Equity in Athletics During Difficult Economic Times," National Women's Law Center, last modified May 15, 2011, http://www.nwlc.org/resource/title-ix-still-applies-gender-equity-athletics-during-difficult-economic-times.

8. Michael A. Messner, *Taking the Field: Women, Men, and Sports* (Minneapolis, MN: University of Minnesota Press, 2002).

9. Jay Coakley, "The Good Father: Parental Expectations and Youth Sports," *Leisure Studies* 25 (2006): 153–63; Raewyn Connell, "Masculinity Construction and Sports in Boys' Education: A Framework for Thinking About the Issue," *Sport, Education and Society* 13 (2008): 131–45.

10. Michael A. Messner, "Still a Man's World? Studying Masculinities and Sport," in *Handbook of Studies on Men and Masculinities*, ed. Michael S. Kimmel, Jeff Hearn, and R. W. Connell (Thousand Oaks, CA: Sage, 2005), 313–25.

11. 118 CONG. REC. 5804, 5808 (Feb. 28, 1972), statement of Sen. Bayh.

12. Sex Discrimination Regulations, Hearings before the House Subcommittee on Postsecondary Education of the Committee on Education and Labor, 94th Cong. 1st Sess. 438 (1975).

13. Crista D. Leahy, "The Title Bout: A Critical Review of the Regulation and Enforcement of Title IX in Intercollegiate Athletics," *Journal of College and University Law* 24 (1998): 489, 493–94.

14. Vivian R. Acosta and Linda Jean Carpenter, "Women in Sport," in *Sport and Higher Education*, ed. Donald Chu, Jeffrey O. Segrave, and Beverly J. Becker (Champaign, IL: Human Kinetics, 1985), 313–25; Deborah L. Brake, *Getting in the Game: Title IX and the Women's Sports Revolution* (New York: New York University Press, 2010).

15. Education Amendments of 1974, Pub. L. No. 93–380, § 884, 1974 U.S.C.C. A.N. 695.

16. 34 C.F.R. § 106.41 (2002).

17. "Title IX Legislative Chronology," Women's Sports Foundation, accessed September 14, 2015, http://www.womenssportsfoundation.org/home/advocate/title-ix-and-issues/history-of-title-ix/history-of-title-ix.

18. Ibid.

19. Welch Suggs, *A Place on the Team: The Triumph and Tragedy of Title IX* (Princeton, NJ: Princeton University Press, 2006); Renee Forseth, Jennifer Karam, and Eric J. Sobocinski, "Progress in Gender Equity: An Overview of the History and Future of Title IX of the Education Amendments Act of 1972," *Villanova Sports and Entertainment Law Forum* 2 (1995): 51–98.

20. Jomills Henry Braddock II et al., "Uneven Playing Fields: State Variations in Boy's and Girl's Access to and Participation in High School Interscholastic Sports," *Sociological Spectrum* 25 (2005): 231–50.

21. *Grove City College v. Bell*, 465 U.S. 555 (1984).

22. "Title IX Legislative Chronology."

23. Matthew Mitten et al., *Sports Law and Regulation: Cases, Materials, and Problems*, 2nd ed. (New York: Aspen Publishers, 2009), 828.

24. Braddock II et al., "Uneven Playing Fields."

25. Deborah J. Anderson, John J. Cheslock, and Ronald G. Ehrenberg, "Gender Equity in Intercollegiate Athletics: Determinants of Title IX Compliance," *Journal of Higher Education* 77 (2006): 225–50; Angela J. Hattery, Earl Smith, and Ellen Staurowsky, "They Play Like Girls: Gender Equity in NCAA Sports," *Journal for the Study of Sports and Athletes in Education* 1 (2007): 249–72; Judith Taylor, "Who Manages Feminist-Inspired Reform? An In-Depth Look at Title IX Coordinators in the United States," *Gender and Society* 19 (2005): 358–75.

26. Gary Orfield and Erica Frankenberg, "Brown at 60: Great Progress, a Long Retreat and an Uncertain Future," The Civil Rights Project, last modified May 15, 2014, http://civilrightsproject.ucla.edu/research/k-12-education/integration-and -diversity/brown-at-60-great-progress-a-long-retreat-and-an-uncertain-future/Brown -at-60-051814.pdf, 4–9.

27. Civil Rights Act of 1964, Pub. L. No. 88-352, § 78, Stat. 241 (1964).

28. *Riddick v. School Board of the City of Norfolk*, 784 F.2d 521, 527 (4th Cir. 1986).

29. *Biediger v. Quinnipiac University*, 616 F. Supp. 2d 277 (D. Conn. 2009).

30. "Fort Valley State University Reinstates Women's Volleyball Team to Avoid Title IX Suit," *Public Justice*, last modified August 13, 2012, http://publicjustice.net /content/fort-valley-state-university-reinstates-womens-volleyball-team-avoid -title-ix-suit-1.

31. "1969–2014 High School Athletics Participation Survey," National Federation of State High School Associations, accessed June 8, 2015, http://www.nfhs.org /ParticipationStatics/PDF/Participation%20Survey%20History%20Book.pdf.

32. Moneque Walker Pickett, Marvin P. Dawkins, and Jomills Henry Braddock II, "The Effect of Title IX on Participation of Black and White Females in High School Sports: Evidence from National Longitudinal Surveys," *Journal of Race and Policy* 5 (2009): 79–90.

33. Donald Sabo et al., "Her Life Depends on It: Sport, Physical Activity and the Health and Well-Being of American Girls," Women's Sports Foundation, last modified December 8, 2004, http://celticfl.net/wp-content/uploads/2012/09/Her -life-depends-on-it.pdf; Lynn Phillips, *The Girls Report: What We Know and Need to Know About Growing Up Female* (New York: National Council for Research, 1998).

34. Tracy K. Richmond et al., "Can School Income and Racial/Ethnic Composition Explain the Racial/Ethnic Disparity in Adolescent Physical Activity Participation?," *Pediatrics* 117 (2006): 2164.

35. Donna Lopiano, "Gender Equity and the Black Female in Sport," Women's Sports Foundation, last modified 2001, http://www.womenssportsfoundation.org /en/home/research/articles-and-reports/athletes-of-color/gender-equity-and-the -black-female-athlete.

36. Naomi Fejgin, "Participation in High School Competitive Sports: A Subversion of School Mission or Contribution to Academic Goals?," *Sociology of Sport Journal* 11 (1994): 211–30; Suzanne Bouffard et al., "Demographic Differences in Patterns of Youth Out-of-School Time Activity Participation," *Journal of Youth Development* 1 (2006): 24–39.

37. Ralph B. McNeal, Jr., "Participation in High School Extracurricular Activities: Investigating School Effects," *Social Science Quarterly* 80 (1999): 291–309.

38. Pat António Goldsmith, "Race Relations and Racial Patterns in School Sports Participation," *Sociology of Sport Journal* 20 (2003): 147–71; See Ary Spatig-Amerikaner, "Unequal Education: Federal Loophole Enables Lower Spending on Students of Color," Center for American Progress, last modified August 2012, https://cdn.americanprogress.org/wp-content/uploads/2012/08/UnequalEduation-1.pdf.

39. Fejgin, "Participation in High School Competitive Sports"; Tami M. Videon, "Who Plays and Who Benefits: Gender, Interscholastic Athletics, and Academic Outcomes," *Sociological Perspectives* 45(4): 415–44.

40. Terris Ross et al., "Higher Education: Gaps in Access and Persistence Study Statistical Analysis Report," U.S. Department of Education Institute of Education Sciences National Center for Education Statistics, last modified August 2012, http://files.eric.ed.gov/fulltext/ED534691.pdf, 81.

41. Braddock II et al., "Uneven Playing Fields"; Pickett, Dawkins, and Braddock, "Effect of Title IX"; Moneque Walker Pickett, Marvin P. Dawkins, and Jomills Henry Braddock II, "Race and Gender Equity in Sports: Have White and African American Females Benefited Equally from Title IX?," *American Behavioral Scientist* 56 (2012): 1581–60.

42. Mira Grieser et al., "Black, Hispanic, and White Girls' Perceptions of Environmental and Social Support and Enjoyment of Physical Activity," *Journal of School Health* 78 (2008): 314–20.

43. See Gary Orfield, John Kucsera, Genevieve Siegel-Hawley, "E Pluribus . . . Separation: Deepening Double Segregation for More Students," The Civil Rights Project, last modified September 19, 2012, http://civilrightsproject.ucla.edu/research/k-12-education/integration-and-diversity/mlk-national/e-pluribus . . . separation-deepening-double-segregation-for-more-students/orfield_epluribus_revised_omplete_2012.pdf.

44. Donald Sabo and Philip Veliz, "Go Out and Play: Youth Sports in America," Women's Sports Foundation, last modified October 8, 2008, http://www.womenssportsfoundation.org/home/research/articles-and-reports/mental-and-physical-health/go-out-and-play.

45. Fatima Goss Graves et al., "Finishing Last: Girls of Color and School Sports Opportunities," National Women's Law Center and Poverty and Race Research Action Council, last modified April 2015, http://www.nwlc.org/sites/default/files/pdfs/final_nwlc_girlsfinishinglast_report.pdf; Title IX of the Education Amendments of 1972, 20 U.S.C. §1681–1688; Title VI of the Civil Rights Act of 1964, 42 U.S.C. § 2000d.

46. Richmond et al., "School Income and Racial/Ethnic Composition," 2160.

47. Ibid., 2163.

48. Pickett, Dawkins, and Braddock II, "Race and Gender Equity."

49. "1981–1982—2012–2013 National Collegiate Athletic Association (NCAA) Sports Sponsorship and Participation Rates Report," NCAA, last modified October 2014, http://www.ncaapublications.com/productdownloads/PR2014.pdf.

50. "Criteria for Emerging Sports," NCAA, accessed August 23, 2015, http://www.ncaa.org/sites/default/files/Criteria%2Bfor%2BEmerging%2BSports.pdf.

51. "Sports Sponsorship and Participation Rates Report, 1981–1982—2014–2015," forthcoming, NCAA, Indianapolis, IN.

52. Walker Pickett, Dawkins, and Braddock II, "Race and Gender Equity."

53. NCAA, "1981–2013 Sponsorship and Participation Report."

54. Ibid.

55. NCAA, "Sports Sponsorship 1981–2015."

56. NCAA, "1981–2013 Sponsorship and Participation Report."

57. NCAA, "Sports Sponsorship 1981–2015."

58. Ibid.

59. Walker Pickett, Dawkins, and Braddock II, "Race and Gender Equity."

60. NCAA, "1981–2013 Sponsorship and Participation Report."

61. NCAA, "Sport Sponsorship, Participation and Demographics Search," accessed September 14, 2015, http://web1.ncaa.org/rgdSearch/exec/main.

62. See "1999-00—2005-06 NCAA Student-Athlete Race and Ethnicity Report," NCAA, last modified April 2006, http://www.ncaapublications.com/productdownloads/ETHN06.pdf; "1981–1982—2007–2008 NCAA Sports Sponsorship and Participation Report," NCAA, last modified April 2009, http://www.ncaapublications.com/productdownloads/PR2009.pdf; Leticia Smith-Evans et al., "Unlocking Opportunity for African American Girls: A Call to Educational Equity," NAACP Legal Defense Fund and the National Women's Law Center, last modified September 19, 2014, http://www.nwlc.org/sites/default/files/pdfs/unlocking_opportunity_for_african_american_girls_report.pdf.

63. NCAA, "Sponsorship, Participation, Demographics."

64. Ibid.

65. Moneque Walker Pickett, "The Invisible Black Woman in the Title IX Shuffle: An Empirical Analysis and Critical Examination of Gender Equity Policy in Assessing Access and Participation of Black and White High School Girls in Interscholastic Sports" (PhD diss., University of Miami, 2009).

66. For a review of females' experiences and the benefits of sport, see Karen M. Appleby and Elaine Foster, "Gender and Sports Participation," in *Gender Relations in Sport*, ed. Emily A. Roper (The Netherlands: Sense Publishers), 1–20.

67. Lynn Barnett and John J. Weber, "Perceived Benefits to Children from Participating in Different Types of Recreational Activities," *Journal of Park and Recreation Administration* 26 (2008): 1–20.

68. James S. Coleman et al., *Equality of Educational Opportunity* (Washington, DC: U.S. Government Printing Office, 1966); Donna Eder and David A. Kinney, "The Effect of Middle School Extra Curricular Activities on Adolescents' Popularity and Peer Status," *Youth and Society* 26 (1995): 298–324; Sohalia Shakib et al., "Athletics as a Source for Social Status Among Youth: Examining Variation by Gender, Race/Ethnicity, and SES," *Sociology of Sport Journal* 28 (2011): 303–28.

69. Shakib et al., "Athletics as a Source for Social Status."

70. Casey A. Knifsend and Sandra Graham, "Too Much of a Good Thing? How Breadth of Extracurricular Participation Relates to School-Related Affect and Academic Outcomes During Adolescence," *Journal of Youth and Adolescence* 41 (2012a): 379–89; Casey A. Knifsend and Sandra Graham, "Unique Challenges Facing Female Athletes in Urban High Schools," *Sex Roles* 67 (2012b): 236–46.

71. Jeroen Schreeder et al., "Sports Participation Among Females from Adolescence to Adulthood," *International Review for the Sociology of Sport* 41 (2006): 413–30; "U.S. Anti-Doping Agency 2012 Annual Report," U.S. Anti-Doping Agency, accessed June 4, 2015, http://www.usada.org/wp-content/uploads/2012_annual _report.pdf.

72. Betsey Stevenson, "Title IX and the Evolution of High School Sports," *Contemporary Economic Policy* 25 (2007): 486–505; Betsy Stevenson, "Beyond the Classroom: Using Title IX to Measure the Return to High School Sports," *The Review of Economics and Statistics* 92 (2010): 284–301.

73. For example, see "U.S. Anti-Doping Agency Report."

74. Amy Slater and Marika Tiggemann, "Time Since Menarche and Sport Participation as Predictors of Self-Objectification: A Longitudinal Study of Adolescent Girls," *Sex Roles* 67 (2012): 571–81; Marika Tiggemann, "Person x Situation Interactions in Body Dissatisfaction," *International Journal of Eating Disorders* 29 (2001): 65–70.

75. Kathleen Miller et al., "Athletic Participation and Sexual Behavior in Adolescents: The Different Worlds of Boys and Girls," *Journal of Health and Social Behavior* 39 (1998): 108–23; Donald Sabo et al., "Sport and Teen Pregnancy," Women's Sports Foundation, last modified October 5, 1998, http://www.womenssports foundation.org/home/research/articles-and-reports/mental-and-physical-health /sport-and-teen-pregnancy.

76. Beverly A. Browne and Sally K. Francis, "Participants in School-Sponsored and Independent Sports: Perceptions of Self and Family," *Adolescence* 28 (1993): 383–91; Brianne L. Burr, "Do Extracurricular Activities Help Adolescents Develop Academic Self-Efficacy? Evidence for How and Why" (MA thesis, Brigham Young University, 2012); Wendy Dei.aney and Christina Lee, "Self-Esteem and Sex Roles Among Male and Female High School Students: Their Relationship to Physical Activity," *Australian Psychologist* 30 (1995): 84–87; David R. Shaffer and Erin Wittes, "Women's Precollege Sports Participation, Enjoyment of Sports, and Self-Esteem," *Sex Roles* 55 (2006): 225–32.

77. Sarah J. Donaldson and Kevin R. Ronan, "The Effects of Sports Participation on Young Adolescents' Emotional Well-Being," *Adolescence* 41 (2006): 369–89; Jodi B. Dworkin, Reed Larson, and David Hansen, "Adolescents' Accounts of Growth Experiences in Youth Activities," *Journal of Youth and Adolescence* 32 (2003): 17–26; David M. Hansen, Reed W. Larson, and Jodi B. Dworkin, "What Adolescents Learn in Organized Youth Activities: A Survey of Self-Reported Developmental Experiences," *Journal of Research on Adolescence* 13 (2003): 25–55; Eva-Carin Lindgren, "The Impact of Sports on Young Women's Attitude to Physical Activity in Adult Life," *Women in Sport & Physical Activity Journal* 9 (2000): 65–86; Neely,

Kacey C. and Nick Holt, "Parents' Perspectives on the Benefits of Sport Participation for Young Children," *Sport Psychologist* 28 (2014): 255–68; Christopher E. Sanders, "Moderate Involvement in Sports Is Related to Lower Depression Levels Among Adolescents," *Adolescence* 35 (2000): 793–97.

78. "Psychological Benefits of Exercise," Association for Applied Sport Psychology, accessed August 23, 2015, http://www.appliedsportpsych.org/resource-center /health-fitness-resources/psychological-benefits-of-exercise/.

79. Lindsay Taliaferro et al., "High School Youth and Suicide Risk: Exploring Protection Afforded Through Physical Activity and Sport Participation," *Journal of School Health* 78 (2008): 545–53.

80. Virginia R. Chomitz et al., "Is There a Relationship Between Physical Fitness, and Academic Achievement? Positive Results from Public School Children in the Northeastern United States," *Journal of School Health* 79 (2009): 30–37; Amy F. Feldman and Jennifer L. Matjasko, "The Role of School-Based Extracurricular Activities in Adolescent Development: A Comprehensive Review and Future Directions," *Review of Educational Research* 75 (2005): 159–210; M. Kent Todd et al., "Comparison of Health and Academic Indices Between Campus Recreation Facility Users and Nonusers," *Recreational Sports Journal* 33 (2009): 43–53; Claudia K. Fox et al., "Physical Activity and Sports Team Participation: Associations with Academic Outcomes in Middle School and High School Students," *Journal of School Health* 80 (2010): 31–37.

81. Jacquelynne S. Eccles et al., "Extracurricular Activities and Adolescent Development," *Journal of Social Issues* 59 (2003): 865–89.

82. Will J. Jordan, "Black High School Students' Participation in School-Sponsored Sports Activities," *Journal of Negro Education* 68 (1999): 54–71; Ralph B. McNeal, Jr., "Extracurricular Activities and High School Dropouts," *Sociology of Education* 68 (1995): 62–81; Tamela McNulty Eitle, "Do Gender and Race Matter? Explaining the Relationship Between Sports Participation and Achievement," *Sociological Spectrum* 25 (2005): 177–95.

83. Sandra L. Hanson and Rebecca S. Kraus, "Women, Sports, and Science: Do Female Athletes Have an Advantage?," *Sociology of Education* 71 (1998): 93–110; Sandra L. Hanson and Rebecca S. Kraus, "Science Experiences Among Female Athletes: Race Makes a Difference," *Journal of Women and Minorities in Science and Engineering* 9 (2003): 287–323.

84. Patrick J. Rishe, "A Reexamination of How Athletic Success Impacts Graduation Rates: Comparing Student-Athletes to All Other Undergraduates," *American Journal of Economics and Sociology* 62 (2003): 407–27.

85. Michael A. Messner and Nancy M. Solomon, "Social Justice and Men's Interests: The Case of Title IX," *Journal of Sport and Social Issues* 31 (2007): 162–78.

86. Erin Zgonc, "NCAA Sports Sponsorship and Participation Rates Report: 1981–1982—2009–2010," NCAA, accessed July 24, 2015, http://www.nwcaonline .com/nwcawebsite/docs/downloads/PR2011.pdf?sfvrsn=0, 8–9.

87. Ibid.

88. NCAA, "Sponsorship, Participation, Demographics."

89. Peter Kaufman and Eli A. Wolff, "Playing and Protesting: Sport as a Vehicle for Social Change," *Journal of Sport and Social Issues* 34 (2010): 154–75.

90. Bruce Kidd, "A New Social Movement: Sport for Development and Peace," *Sport in Society* 11 (2008): 370–80.

91. Bruce Kidd and Peter Donnelly, "Human Rights in Sports," *International Review for the Sociology of Sport* 35 (2000): 131–48.

92. Title IX of the Education Amendments of 1972, 20 U.S.C. §1681–1688.

93. Kaufman and Wolff, "Playing and Protesting."

94. Cynthia Fabrizo Pelak, "Athletes as Agents of Change: An Examination of Shifting Race Relations Within Women's Netball in Post-Apartheid South Africa," *Sociology of Sport Journal* 21 (2005): 59–77.

95. Peter Kaufman, "Boos, Bans, and Backlash: The Consequences of Being an Activist Athlete," *Humanity and Society* 32 (2008): 215–37.

96. See "Female Executives Say Participation in Sport Helps Accelerate Leadership and Career Potential," EY Women Athletes Business Network, last modified October 10, 2014, http://www.ey.com/GL/en/Newsroom/News-releases/news-female-executives-say-participation-in-sport-helps-accelerate--leadership-and-career-potential.

97. Håvard Mokleiv Nygård and Scott Gates, "Soft Power at Home and Abroad: Sport Diplomacy, Politics and Peace-Building," *International Area Studies Review* 16 (2013): 235–43.

98. Ibid.

99. Gustavus T. Kirby, "Report of the Chef de Mission," in *Report of the United States Olympic Committee 1948 Games*, ed. Asa S. Bushnell (New York: United States Olympic Association), 247.

100. John Nauright, *Long Run to Freedom: Sport, Cultures and Identities in South Africa* (Morgantown, WV: Fitness Information Technology, 2010); Saskia Irene Welschen, "Making Sense of Being South African: The Analysis of National Identity Construction in Talk" (paper presented at the ISA World Congress of Sociology, Gothenburg, Sweden, July 11–17, 2010).

101. Bill Chappell, "Year of the Woman at the London Games? For Americans, It's True," *NPR*, last modified August 10, 2012, http://www.npr.org/sections/thetorch/2012/08/10/158570021/year-of-the-woman-at-the-london-games-for-americans-its-true.

102. "United States Olympic Committee 2012 Quadrennial Report," United States Olympic Committee, last modified June 1, 2013, https://www.google.com/url?sa=t&rct=j&q=&esrc=s&source=web&cd=1&cad=rja&uact=8&ved=0CCEQFjAAahUKEwj068ajpMLHAhXIlh4KHf8JAT4&url=http%3A%2F%2Fwww.teamusa.org%2F~%2Fmedia%2FTeamUSA%2FDocuments%2FLegal%2FQuadrennial%2520Congressional%2520Reports%2FUnited%2520States%2520Olympic%2520Committee%2520Report%2520to%2520the%2520President%2520and%2520Congress%2520for%2520the%2520Period%2520of%25202009-2012.pdf&ei=olnbVfSSBsitev-ThPAD&usg=AFQjCNGnXoGY7zWessd8dGaFZDi6Q60J0w, 10.

103. Jomills Henry Braddock, II et al., "Gender Diversity and U. S. Olympic Team Success at the 2012 London Games" (paper presented at the annual meetings for the Southern Sociological Society, Atlanta, GA, April 24–27, 2013).

Chapter Three

1. A. Jerome Dees, "Access or Interest: Why Brown Has Benefited African-American Women More Than Title IX," *University of Missouri Kansas City Law Review* 76 (2008): 625.

2. Evelyn Nakano Glenn, *Unequal Freedom: How Race and Gender Shaped American Citizenship and Labor* (Cambridge, MA: Harvard University Press, 2002).

3. Ibid.

4. James D. Anderson, *The Education of Blacks in the South 1860–1935* (Chapel Hill, NC: University of North Carolina Press, 1988).

5. Sawanobori Bunji, "Brown v. Board of Education: Its Continuing Significance," *Nanzan Review of American Studies* 26 (2004): 27–41.

6. Earl Warren, *Brown v. Board of Education of Topeka*, Shawnee County, Kan., 347 U.S. 483 (1954).

7. Ibid.

8. Amy Stuart Wells, "The 'Consequences' of School Desegregation: The Mismatch Between the Research and the Rationale," *Hastings Constitutional Law Quarterly* 28 (2002): 771–97.

9. Ibid.; Kenneth B. Clark, "Some Principles Related to the Problem of Desegregation," *Journal of Negro Education* 23 (1954): 339–47; Kenneth B. Clark, "The *Brown* Decision: Racism, Education, and Human Values," *Journal of Negro Education* 57 (1988): 125–32.

10. Thurgood Marshall, *Brown v. Board of Education.*

11. Joyce L. Epstein, "After the Bus Arrives: Desegregation in Desegregated Schools," *Journal of Social Issues* 41 (1985): 23–43; Jeannie Oakes, "Two Cities' Tracking and Within-School Segregation," *Teachers College Record* 96 (1996): 681–90; Jeannie Oakes, "Within-School Integration, Grouping Practices, and Educational Quality in Rockford Schools" (report prepared in conjunction with *People Who Care et al. v. Rockford, IL. Independent School District*, 2000).

12. Meyer Weinberg, *Minority Students: A Research Appraisal* (Washington, DC: National Institute of Education, 1978).

13. Anderson, *Education of Blacks.*

14. Harold B. Gerard, "School Desegregation: The Social Science Role," *American Psychologist* 38 (1983): 873.

15. Caroline Hoxby, "Peer Effects in the Classroom: Learning from Gender and Race Variation," National Bureau of Economic Research, accessed July 12, 2015, http://www.nber.org/papers/w7867.pdf.

16. Richard D. Khaleberg, "From All Walks of Life: New Hope for School Integration," *American Educator* 36 (2013): 2–7, 10–14.

17. Epstein, "After the Bus."

18. Amy Stuart Wells et al., "How Society Failed School Desegregation Policy: Looking Past the Schools to Understand Them," *Review of Research in Education* 28 (2004): 47–99.

19. James S. Coleman et al., *Equality of Educational Opportunity* (Washington, DC: U.S. Government Printing Office, 1966).

20. Dorothy Clement, Margaret Eisenhart, and John R. Wood, "School Desegregation and Educational Inequality: Trends in the Literature 1960–1975," in *The Desegregation Literature: A Critical Appraisal* (Washington, DC: National Institute of Education, 1976), 1–77.

21. Benjamin P. Carr, "Can Separate Be Equal? Single-Sex Classrooms, the Constitution, and Title IX," *Notre Dame Law Review* 83 (2007): 409–42.

22. Ashley English, "Restoring Equal Opportunity in Education: An Analysis of Arguments for and Against the Bush Administration Single-Sex Education Regulations," *Institute for Women's Policy Research*, last modified July 30, 2009, http://files.eric.ed.gov/fulltext/ED556716.pdf; Migdal et al., "The Need to Address Equal Educational Opportunities for Women and Girls," *Human Rights* 35 (2008): 16–25.

23. Welch Suggs, "Title IX at 30," *The Chronicle of Higher Education*, last modified June 21, 2012, http://chronicle.com/article/Title-IX-at-30/23200/.

24. Ibid.

25. Deborah J. Anderson, John J. Cheslock, and Ronald G. Ehrenberg, "Gender Equity in Intercollegiate Athletics: Determinants of Title IX Compliance," *Journal of Higher Education* 77 (2006): 225–50; Angela J. Hattery, Earl Smith, and Ellen Staurowsky, "They Play Like Girls: Gender Equity in NCAA Sports," *Journal for the Study of Sports and Athletes in Education* 1 (2007): 249–72; Judith Taylor, "Who Manages Feminist-Inspired Reform? An In-Depth Look at Title IX Coordinators in the United States," *Gender and Society* 19 (2005): 358–75.

26. Ibid.; Lexie Kuznick and Megan Ryan, "Changing Social Norms? Title IX and Legal Activism: Comments from the Spring 2007 *Harvard Journal of Law and Gender* Conference," *Harvard Journal of Law and Gender* 31 (2008): 367–406; Suggs, "Title IX at 30."

27. Warren, *Brown*.

28. Judith Lorber, *'Night to His Day': The Social Construction of Gender* (New Haven, CT: Yale University Press, 1994).

29. Eli Torild Braathen and Sven Svebak, "Motivational Differences Among Talented Teenage Athletes: The Significance of Gender, Type of Sport and Level of Excellence," *Scandinavian Journal of Medicine* 2 (2007): 153–59; Jacquelynne S. Eccles and Rena D. Harold, "Gender Differences in Sport Involvement: Applying the Eccles' Expectancy-Value Model," *Journal of Applied Sport Psychology* 3 (1991): 7–35.

30. Philip T. K. Daniel, "The Not So Strange Path of Desegregation in America's Public Schools," *Negro Educational Review* 56 (2005): 57–66; Vincene Verdun, "The Big Disconnect Between Segregation and Integration," *Journal of Negro Education* 56 (2005): 67–82.

31. Verdun, "Big Disconnect."

32. David J. Armor, "The Evidence on Busing," *Public Interest* 28 (1972): 90–126.

33. Epstein, "After the Bus"; Maureen T. Hallinan, "Ability Group Effects on High School Learning Outcomes" (paper presented at the annual meeting of the American Sociological Association, Washington, DC, August 12–15, 2000); Roslyn Arlin Mickelson, "Subverting Swann: First- and Second-Generation Segregation in the Charlotte-Mecklenburg Schools," *American Educational Research Journal* 38 (2001): 215–52; Oakes, "Two Cities"; Oakes, "Within-School Integration."

34. Carol H. Weiss, *Evaluation Research: Methods of Assessing Program Effectiveness* (Englewood Cliffs, NJ: Prentice-Hall, 1972).

35. Michael Scriven, "The Methodology of Evaluation," in *Perspectives of Curriculum Evaluation*, ed. Ralph W. Tyler, Robert M. Gagne, and Michael Scriven (Chicago, IL: Rand McNally and Co., 1967), 39–83.

36. Mickelson, "Subverting Swann"; Oakes, "Two Cities"; Oakes, "Within-School Integration."

Chapter Four

1. Marissa Payne, "Ronda Rousey Says She Could 'Beat 100 Percent' of Male UFC Fighters—In Theory," *The Washington Post*, last modified March 5, 2015, https://www.washingtonpost.com/news/early-lead/wp/2015/03/05/ronda-rousey-says-she-could-beat-100-percent-of-male-ufc-fighters-in-theory/.

2. Ibid.

3. Jon Werthiem, "The Unbreakable Ronda Rousey Is the World's Most Dominant Athlete," *Sports Illustrated*, last modified May 13, 2015, http://www.si.com/mma/2015/05/12/ronda-rousey-ufc-mma-fighter-armbar.

4. Payne, "Ronda Rousey Says."

5. Nick Schwartz, "Ronda Rousey Says She 'Could Beat 100 Percent' of Men in Her Weight Class," *USA Today*, last modified March 8, 2015, http://ftw.usatoday.com/2015/03/ufc-ronda-rousey-compete-against-men.

6. See Ashley Montagu, *The Natural Superiority of Women* (New York: Altamira Press, 1999).

7. Rosemarie Tong, "Feminist Perspectives on Empathy as an Epistemic Skill and Caring as a Moral Value," *Journal of Medical Humanities* 18 (1997): 153–58; Jean M. Twenge, "Status and Gender: The Paradox of Progress in an Age of Narcissism," *Sex Roles* 61 (2009): 338–40.

8. Will H. Courtenay, "Constructions of Masculinity and Their Influence on Men's Well Being: A Theory of Gender and Health," *Social Science and Medicine* 50 (2000): 1385–401.

9. For a recent example, see "Women Are, After All, Better Drivers Than Men," *The Telegraph*, last modified May 15, 2015, http://www.telegraph.co.uk/news/uknews/road-and-rail-transport/11605509/Women-are-after-all-better-drivers-than-men.html.

10. Michael Burke, "Women's Standpoints and Internalism in Sport," *Journal of the Philosophy of Sport* 41 (2013): 39–52.

11. Ernestine Friedl, "Society and Sex Roles," *Human Nature* 1 (1978): 8–75; Heather Pringle, "New Women of the Ice Age," *Discover*, last modified April 1, 1998, http://discovermagazine.com/1998/apr/newwomenoftheice1430#.UOMpq -Qj7gU.

12. Sheri A. Berenbaum, Judith E. Owen Blakemore, and Adriene M. Beltz, "A Role for Biology in Gender-Related Behavior," *Sex Roles* 64 (2011): 804–25; Deborah L. Best, "Another View of the Gender-Status Relation," *Sex Roles* 61 (2009): 341–51; Celia Roberts, "Biological Behavior? Hormones, Psychology, and Sex," *National Women's Studies Association Journal* 12 (2000): 1–20.

13. Edward Sapir, *Culture, Language and Personality* (Berkeley, CA: University of California Press, 1958); Benjamin Whorf, *Language, Thought, and Reality: Selected Writings of Benjamin Lee Whorf*, ed. John B. Carroll (Cambridge, MA: MIT Press, 1956).

14. Judith Butler, *Gender Trouble: Feminism and the Subversion of Identity* (New York: Routledge, 2006); Simone de Beauvoir, *The Second Sex* (New York: Vintage Books, 1973); Judith Lorber, *'Night to His Day': The Social Construction of Gender* (New Haven, CT: Yale University Press, 1994); Margaret Mooney Marini, "Sex and Gender: What Do We Know?," *Sociological Focus* 5 (1990): 95–120; John Stoltenberg, *Refusing to Be a Man: Essays on Sex and Justice* (New York: Routledge, 1999).

15. de Beauvoir, *Second Sex*, 301.

16. de Beauvoir, *Second Sex*.

17. Monique Wittig, "One Is Not Born a Woman," in *The Lesbian and Gay Studies Reader*, ed. Henry Abelove, Michele Aina Barale, and David M. Halperin (New York: Routledge, 1993), 103–109.

18. "The Etymology of 'Woman'," *This Wretched Hive // Of Words and Nerdery*, last modified May 24, 2011, http://thiswretchedhive.blogspot.com/2011/05/ety mology-of-woman.html?m=1.

19. "Women, Womyn, Wimyn, Womin, and Wimmin: Why the Alternatives Spellings?," *Womyn Creating Consciousness Collectively*, accessed June 7, 2015, https://www.msu.edu/~womyn/alternative.html.

20. de Beauvoir, *Second Sex*; Wittig, "One Is Not Born."

21. Kalia White, "New ASU English Class: 'The Problem of Whiteness,'" *AZ Central*, last modified January 24, 2015, http://www.azcentral.com/story/news /local/tempe/2015/01/23/asu-offers-class-race-theory-problem-of-whiteness /22229195/.

22. Tom Coyne, "Notre Dame's 'White Privilege' Seminar Draws Scrutiny," *WISH-TV*, last modified January 24, 2015, http://wishtv.com/2015/01/24/notre -dames-white-privilege-seminar-draws-scrutiny/.

23. Catherine MacKinnon, "Difference and Dominance: On Sex Discrimination," in *Feminist Legal Theory*, ed. Katharine Bartlett and Rosanne Kennedy (Boulder, CO: Westview Press, 1991), 81–94.

24. Ibid., 82–83.

25. Morgan Holmes, "Re-membering a Queer Body," *Undercurrents* 6 (1994): 11–13.

26. Nick Tate, "Why Heart Disease Kills 5 Times More Women Than Breast Cancer," *Newsmax*, last modified August 14, 2013, http://www.newsmax.com/Health/Health-News/heart-disease-women-death/2013/08/14/id/520313/.

27. "Male Breast Cancer," National Breast Cancer Foundation, accessed August 22, 2015, http://www.nationalbreastcancer.org/male-breast-cancer.

28. Stoltenberg, *Refusing to Be a Man*, 22–23.

29. Butler, *Gender Trouble*.

30. Anne Fausto-Sterling, "The Five Sexes: Why Male and Female Are Not Enough," *Sciences* 33 (1993): 20–24; Anne Fausto-Sterling, "The Five Sexes, Revisited," *Sciences* 40 (2000): 18–23.

31. Anne Fausto-Sterling, "Nature," in *Critical Terms for the Study of Gender*, ed. Catherine R. Stimpson and Gilbert Herdt (Chicago, IL: University of Chicago Press, 2014), 294–315; Anne Fausto-Sterling, *Sex/Gender: Biology in a Social World* (New York: Routledge, 2012).

32. "Blue Whale Penis," *Whale Facts*, accessed August 22, 2015, http://www.whalefacts.org/blue-whale-penis/.

33. See Carol Livoti and Elizabeth Topp, *Vaginas: An Owner's Manual* (New York: Thunder's Mouth Press, 2004).

34. Gloria Steinem, "If Men Could Menstruate," *Ms. Magazine* 7 (1978): 110.

35. Emily Martin, "The Egg and the Sperm: How Science Has Constructed a Romance Based on Stereotypical Male-Female Roles," *Signs* 16 (1991): 485–501.

36. "Your Bra May Be Killing You—Scientists Call for Boycott of Komen," *Inquisitr*, last modified April 6, 2014, http://www.inquisitr.com/1202191/your-bra-may-be-killing-you-scientists-call-for-boycott-of-komen/.

37. See Fatema Mernissi, "Size 6: The Western Women's Harem," in *Scheherazade Goes West: Different Cultures, Different Harems*, ed. Fatima Mernissi (New York: Washington Square Press, 2001): 208–20.

38. Catherine Palmer, "Drinking Like a Guy? Women and Sport-Related Drinking," *Journal of Gender Studies* 19 (2013): 1–13.

39. "Why Can't Women Ski Jump?," *Time*, accessed June 10, 2015, http://content.time.com/time/specials/packages/article/0,28804,1963484_1963490_1963447,00.html.

40. "Our Olympic Story," *Women's Ski Jumping USA*, accessed June 10, 2015, http://www.wsjusa.com/olympic-inclusion/.

41. Mika Hämäläinen, "A Sport with Untapped Potential to Empower Women," *Journal of the Philosophy of Sport* 41 (2014): 53–63.

42. Mark C.J. Stoddart, "Constructing Masculinized Sportscapes: Skiing, Gender and Nature in British Columbia, Canada," *International Review for the Sociology of Sport* 46 (2010): 108–24.

43. Nadav Goldschmied and Jason Kowalczyk, "Gender Performance in the NCAA Rifle Championships: Where Is the Gap?," *Sex Roles* 71 (2014): 1–13.

44. Anne Marie Bird, "Nonreactive Research: Applications for Sociological Analysis of Sport," *International Review for the Sociology of Sport* 11 (1976): 83–89;

Ann M. Hall, "How Should We Theorize Sport in a Capitalist Patriarchy?," *International Review for the Sociology of Sport* 20 (1985): 109–16; Jennifer A. Hargreaves, "Gender on the Sports Agenda," *International Review for the Sociology of Sport* 25 (1990): 287–307.

45. Vikki Krane, "A Feminist Perspective on Contemporary Sport Psychology Research," *Sport Psychologist* 8 (1994): 393–410.

46. Jack K. Nelson et al., "Gender Differences in Children's Throwing Performance: Biology and Environment," *Research Quarterly for Exercise and Sport* 57 (1986): 280–87.

47. Krane, "Feminist Perspective," 404.

48. Fontini Venetsanou and Antonia Kambas, "Environmental Factors Affecting Preschoolers' Motor Development," *Early Childhood Education Journal* 37 (2009): 319–27.

49. Andrew P. Smiler, "Thirty Years After the Discovery of Gender: Psychological Concepts and Measures of Masculinity," *Sex Roles* 50 (2004): 15–26.

50. Irwin W. Silverman, "Sex Differences in Simple Visual Reaction Time: A Historical Meta-Analysis," *Sex Roles* 54 (2006): 57–68.

51. Heinz Krombholz, "Physical Performance in Relation to Age, Sex, Birth Order, Social Class, and Sports Activities of Preschool Children," *Perceptual and Motor Skills* 102 (2006): 466–84.

52. Joe Torg and Jeff Ryan, "Risk Potential from Mixed Gender Athletics," *Goeata.org*, 2004, accessed June 16, 2015, http://goeata.org/protected/EATACD04/Downloads/PDF/packet-ryantorg.pdf.

53. Debra A. Lewis, Eliezer Kamon, and James L. Hodgson, "Physiological Differences Between Genders Implications for Sports Conditioning," *Sports Medicine* 3 (1986): 357–69.

54. Lynda Birke and Gail Vines, "A Sporting Chance: The Anatomy of Destiny?," *Women's Studies International Forum* 10 (1987): 337–58.

55. Gertrud Pfister, "Appropriation of the Environment, Motor Experiences and Sporting Activities of Girls and Women," *International Review for the Sociology of Sport* 28 (1993): 159–72.

56. Andrea Park, "9 Female Athletes Speak Candidly About Their Body Hang-Ups," *Women's Health*, last modified July 16, 2015, http://www.womenshealthmag.com/fitness/female-athlete-body-insecurity?cid=NL_WHDD_-_07242015_9FemaleAthletesSpeakCandidlyAboutTheirBodyHangUps.

57. Shari L. Dworkin, "'Holding Back': Negotiating a Glass Ceiling on Women's Muscular Strength," *Sociological Perspectives* 44 (2001): 333–50.

58. Mari Kristin Sisjord and Elsa Kristiansen, "Elite Women Wrestlers' Muscles: Physical Strength and a Social Burden," *International Review for the Sociology of Sport* 44 (2009): 231–46.

59. Anna Kavoura, Marja Kokkonen, and Tatiana Ryba, "The Female Fighter Phenomenon in Denmark and Greece: Exploring Gender Dynamics in Judo," in *Fighting: Intellectualising Combat Sports*, ed. Keith Gilbert (Champaign, IL: Common Ground Publishing, 2014), 87–96.

60. Jesse A. Steinfeldt et al., "Muscularity Beliefs of Female College Student-Athletes," *Sex Roles* 64 (2011): 543–54.

61. Anne Torhild Klomsten, Herb W. Marsh, and Einar M. Skaalvik, "Adolescents' Perceptions of Masculine and Feminine Values in Sport and Physical Education: A Study of Gender Differences," *Sex Roles* 52 (2005): 625–36.

62. Herbert W. Marsh and Susan A. Jackson, "Multidimensional Self-Concepts, Masculinity, and Femininity as a Function of Women's Involvement in Athletics," *Sex Roles* 15 (1986): 391–415.

63. Anna Dreber, Emma von Essen, and Eva Ranehill, "Outrunning the Gender Gap—Boys and Girls Compete Equally," *Experimental Economics* 14 (2011): 567–82.

64. Howard L. Nixon II, "The Relationship of Friendship Networks, Sport Experiences, and Gender to Expressed Pain Thresholds," *Sociology of Sport Journal* 13 (1996): 78–86.

65. Shelly A. McGrath and Ruth A. Chananie-Hill, "'Big Freaky-Looking Women': Normalizing Gender Transgression Through Bodybuilding," *Sociology of Sport Journal* 26 (2009): 239.

66. Alan Dundes, "Into the Endzone for a Touchdown: A Psychoanalytic Consideration of American Football," *Western Folklore* 37 (1978): 75–88.

67. Nick Trujillo, "Machines, Missiles, and Men: Images of the Male Body on ABC's *Monday Night Football*," *Sociology of Sport Journal* 12 (1995): 403–23.

68. See Susan Bordo, "Pills and Power Tools," *Men and Masculinities* 1 (1998): 87–90; Francesca M. Cancian, "The Feminization of Love," *Signs* 11 (1983): 692–709; Stoltenberg, *Refusing to Be a Man*.

69. Kathleen Miller et al., "Athletic Participation and Sexual Behavior in Adolescents: The Different Worlds of Boys and Girls," *Journal of Health and Social Behavior* 39 (1998): 108–123.

70. C. Lynn Carr, "Where Have All the Tomboys Gone? Women's Accounts of Gender in Adolescence," *Sex Roles* 56 (2007): 439–48.

71. Thalma E. Lobel, Michelle Slone, and Gil Winch, "Masculinity, Popularity, and Self-Esteem Among Israeli Preadolescent Girls," *Sex Roles* 36 (1997): 395–408.

72. Mary Jo Kane, "The Female Athletic Role as a Status Determinant Within the Social Systems of Adolescents," *Adolescence* 23 (1988): 253–64.

73. Donald R. McCreary, "The Male Role and Avoiding Femininity," *Sex Roles* 31 (1994): 517–31.

74. Eric Anderson, "Orthodox and Inclusive Masculinity: Competing Masculinities Among Heterosexual Men in a Feminized Terrain," *Sociological Perspectives* 48 (2005): 337–55; Eric Anderson, "'I Used to Think Women Were Weak': Orthodox Masculinity, Gender Segregation, and Sport," *Sociological Forum* 23 (2008): 257–80.

75. Elizabeth A. Daniels and Heidi Wartena, "Athlete or Sex Symbol: What Boys Think of Media Representations of Female Athletes," *Sex Roles* 65 (2011): 566–79.

76. Oliver Turnbull et al., "Reports of Intimate Touch: Erogenous Zones and Somatosensory Cortical Organization," *Cortex* 53 (2014): 146–54.

77. Ben Spencer, "Guess What Girls? Men Are from Venus Too! Expert Says Our Brains Are Not 'Hardwired' in Different Ways," *Daily Mail*, last modified September 5, 2014, http://www.dailymail.co.uk/sciencetech/article-2744358/Guess-girls-Men-Venus-Expert-says-brains-not-hardwired-different-ways.html.

78. Sarah Knapton, "Men and Women Do Not Have Different Brains, Claims Neuroscientist," *The Telegraph*, last modified March 8, 2014, http://www.telegraph.co.uk/news/science/science-news/10684179/Men-and-women-do-not-have-different-brains-claims-neuroscientist.html.

79. Cooper et al., "Prevalence of NIDDM Among Populations of the African Diaspora," *Diabetes Care* 20 (1997): 343–48.

80. Ichiro Kawachi, Norman Daniels, and Dean E. Robinson, "Health Disparities by Race and Class: Why Both Matter," *Health Affairs* 24 (2005): 343–52.

81. "The Unexamined Population," *Nature Genetics* 36 (2004): S3.

82. Jason Silverstein, "Genes Don't Cause Racial-Health Disparities, Society Does," *The Atlantic*, last modified April 13, 2015, http://www.theatlantic.com/health/archive/2015/04/genes-dont-cause-racial-health-disparities-society-does/389637/.

83. Jay S. Kaufman et al., "The Contribution of Genomic Research to Explaining Racial Disparities in Cardiovascular Disease: A Systematic Review," *American Journal of Epidemiology* 187 (2015): 464–72.

84. "Illuminating BiDil," *Nature Genetics* 8 (2005): 903; Silverstein, "Genes Don't Cause Racial-Health Disparities."

85. Bruce G. Link and Jo C. Phelan, "Social Conditions as Fundamental Causes of Disease," *Journal of Health and Social Behavior* extra issue (1995): 80–94.

86. See Elizabeth H. Baker, Michael S. Rendall, and Margaret M. Weden, "Epidemiological Paradox or Immigrant Vulnerability? Obesity Among Young Children of Immigrants," *Demography* 52 (2015): 1295–320; Henna Budhwani, Kristine Ria Hearld, and Daniel Chavez-Yenter, "Depression in Racial and Ethnic Minorities: The Impact of Nativity and Discrimination," *Journal of Racial and Ethnic Health Disparities* 2 (2015): 34–42; Cythnia Diefenbeck, Barret Michalec, and Robbi Alexander, "Lived Experiences of Racially and Ethnically Underrepresented Minority BSN Students: A Case Study Specifically Exploring Issues Related to Recruitment and Retention," *Nursing Education Perspectives* (2015), DOI: http://dx.doi.org/10.5480/13–1183; Maria Pisu et al., "Economic Hardship of Minority and Non-Minority Cancer Survivors One Year After Diagnosis: Another Long Term Effect of Cancer?" *Cancer* (2015), DOI: 10.1002/cncr.29206; Abigail A. Sewell, "Disaggregating Ethnoracial Disparities in Physician Trust," *Social Science Research* 54 (2015): 1–20; Mieke Beth Thomeer, Stipica Mudrazija, and Jacqueline L. Angel, "How Do Race and Hispanic Ethnicity Affect Nursing Home Admission? Evidence from the Health and Retirement Study," *Journals of Gerontology: Social Sciences* 70 (2015): 628–38.

87. David Chae et al., "Do Experiences of Racial Discrimination Predict Cardiovascular Disease Among African American Men? The Moderating Role of Internalized Negative Racial Group Attitudes," *Social Science & Medicine* 71 (2010): 1182–88; David Chae et al., "Discrimination, Racial Bias, and Telomere Length in

African-American Men," *American Journal of Preventive Medicine* 46 (2014): 103–11.

88. David Chae et al., "Association Between an Internet-Based Measure of Area Racism and Black Mortality," *PLoS One* 10 (2015), DOI: 10.1371/journal. pone.0122963.

89. Irena Stepanikova, "Racial and Ethnic Biases, Time Pressure, and Medical Decisions," *Journal of Health and Social Behavior* (2012): 329–43.

90. Matthew R. Anderson et al., "The Role of Race in the Clinical Presentation," *Family Medicine* 33 (2001): 430–34.

91. Stephen Steinberg, *The Ethnic Myth* (New York: Plenum Press, 1981).

92. See "Jane Elliot's Blue Eyes Brown Eyes Exercise," Jane Elliot, accessed August 22, 2015, http://www.janeelliott.com/.

93. Donald Spivey, *Fire from the Soul: A History of the African-American Struggle* (Durham, NC: Carolina Academy Press, 2003).

94. James Loewen, *Lies My Teacher Told Me: Everything Your American History Textbook Got Wrong* (New York: Touchstone, 1995), 142–46.

95. Joe R. Feagin, *Systemic Racism: A Theory of Oppression* (New York: Routledge, 2006).

96. Michael Omi and Howard Winant, *Racial Formation in the United States: From the 1960s to the 1990s*, 2nd ed. (New York: Routledge, 1994).

97. Stokely Carmichael and Charles V. Hamilton, *Black Power. The Politics of Liberation in America* (New York: Random House, 1967).

98. Donald R. Kinder and David O. Sears. "Prejudice and Politics: Symbolic Racism Versus Racial Threats to the Good Life," *Journal of Personality and Social Psychology* 40 (1981): 414–31.

99. Lawrence D. Bobo, James R. Kluegel, and Ryan A. Smith, "Laissez-Faire Racism: The Crystallization of a Kinder, Gentler Antiblack Ideology," in *Racial Attitudes in the 1990s: Continuity and Change*, ed. Steven A. Tuch and Jack K. Martin (Westport, CT: Praeger, 1997), 15–44.

100. Herber Blumer, "Race Prejudice as a Sense of Group Position," *Pacific Sociological Review* 1 (1958): 3–7.

101. Eduardo Bonilla-Silva, *Racism Without Racists: Color-Blind Racism and the Persistence of Racial Inequality in the United States* (New York: Rowman and Littlefield, 2003).

102. Tyrone A. Forman, "Color-Blind Racism and Racial Indifference: The Role of Racial Apathy in Facilitating Enduring Inequalities," in *The Changing Terrain of Race and Ethnicity*, ed. Maria Krysan and Amanda Lewis (New York: Russel Sage, 2004), 43–66.

103. See Herman D. Bloch, *The Circle of Discrimination: An Economic and Social Study of the Black Man in New York* (New York: New York University Press, 1969); Susan E. Howell, Huey L. Perry, and Matthew Vile, "Black Cities/White Cities: Evaluating the Police," *Political Behavior* 26 (2004): 45–68; Jonathan Kozol, *Savage Inequalities* (New York: Crown Press, 1991); Douglas Massey and Nancy Denton, *American Apartheid* (Chicago, IL: University of Chicago Press, 1993); Gary Orfield

and Chungmei Lee, "Why Segregation Matters: Poverty and Education Inequality," The Civil Rights Project, last modified January 13, 2005, http://civilrightsproject .ucla.edu/research/k-12-education/integration-and-diversity/why-segregation -matters-poverty-and-educational-inequality; Vincent J. Roscigno, *The Face of Discrimination: How Race and Gender Impact Work and Home Lives* (Lanham, MD: Rowman and Littlefield, 2007); Kevin Stainback, Corre L. Robinson, and Donald Tomaskovic-Devey, "Race and Workplace Integration: A Politically Mediated Process?," *American Behavioral Scientist* 48 (2005): 1200–28; Loïc Wacquant, "Deadly Symbiosis: Rethinking Race and Imprisonment in Twenty-First Century America," *Boston Review* 27 (2002): 21–31.

104. See Derrick Bell, *Faces at the Bottom of the Well: The Permanence of Racism* (New York: Basic Books, 1992); Eduardo Bonilla-Silva, *White Supremacy and Racism in the Post-Civil Rights Era* (Boulder, CO: Lynne Rienner Publishers, 2001); Michael K. Brown et al., *Whitewashing Race: The Myth of a Color-Blind Society* (Berkeley, CA: University of California Press, 2003); Kimberle Crenshaw et al. (eds), *Critical Race Theory: The Key Writings That Formed the Movement* (New York: New Press, 1988); bell hooks, *Talking Back: Thinking Feminist, Thinking Black* (Boston, MA: South End Press, 1989); Christopher Metzler, "Barack Obama's Faustian Bargain and the Fight for America's Racial Soul," *Journal of Black Studies* 40 (2010): 395–410; Melvin L. Oliver and Thomas M. Shapiro, *Black/Wealth/White Wealth: A New Perspective on Racial Inequality* (New York: Routledge, 1995).

105. See Lisa Doris Alexander, "Race on First, Class on Second, Gender on Third, and Sexuality up to Bat: Intersectionality and Power in Major League Baseball, 1995–2005" (PhD diss., Bowling Green State University, 2006); George B. Cunningham and Michael R. Regan, "Political Activism, Racial Identity and the Commercial Endorsement of Athletes: Athlete Activism," *International Review for the Sociology of Sport* 47 (2011): 657–69; George B. Cunningham, Kathi Miner, and Jennifer McDonald, "Being Different and Suffering the Consequences: The Influence of Head Coach–Player Racial Dissimilarity on Experienced Incivility," *International Review for the Sociology of Sport* 48 (2013): 689–705; Fabrice Delsahut and Thierry Terret, "First Nations Women, Games, and Sport in Pre-and Post-Colonial North America," *Women's History Review* 23 (2014): 976–95; C. Richard King and Charles Fruehling Springwood, "Fighting Spirits: The Racial Politics of Sports Mascots," *Journal of Sport and Social Issues* 24 (2000): 282–304; Janice Fanning Madden, "Differences in the Success of NFL Coaches by Race, 1990–2002 Evidence of Last Hire, First Fire," *Journal of Sports Economics* 5 (2004): 6–19; Bo Shen et al., "Urban African-American Girls' Participation and Future Intentions Toward Physical Education," *Sex Roles* 67 (2012): 323–33.

106. Gary A. Sailes, "The African American Athlete: Social Myths and Stereotypes," in *African Americans in Sport: Contemporary Themes*, ed. Gary A. Sails (New Brunswick, NJ: Transaction Publishers, 1998), 183–98.

107. Sandra C. Castine and Glyn C. Roberts, "Modeling in the Socialization Process of the Black Athlete," *International Review for the Sociology of Sport* 9 (1974): 59–74; Harry Edwards, *The Revolt of the Black Athlete* (New York: Free Press, 1969);

Ralph H. Hines, "Social Expectations and Cultural Deprivation," *Journal of Negro Education* 33 (1964): 136–42; Jack Olsen, *The Black Athlete: A Shameful Story: The Myth of Integration in American Sport* (New York: Time-Life Books, 1968); David A. Schulz, *Coming up Black: Patterns of Ghetto Socialization* (Upper Saddle River, NJ: Prentice-Hall, 1969).

108. David J. Leonard, "The Next M. J. or the Next O. J.? Kobe Bryant, Race, and the Absurdity of Colorblind Rhetoric," *Journal of Sport and Social Issues* 28 (2004): 288–89.

109. Nancy E. Spencer, "Sister Act IV: Venus and Serena Williams at Indian Wells: Sincere Fictions and White Racism," *Journal of Sport and Social Issues* 28 (2004): 115–35.

110. Ben Rothenberg, "Tennis's Top Women Balance Body Image with Ambition," *The New York Times*, last modified July 10, 2015, http://mobile.nytimes.com /2015/07/11/sports/tennis/tenniss-top-women-balance-body-image-with-quest -for-success.html?smid=tw-nytimesand_r=3andreferrer=.

111. Zeba Blay, "When We Attack Serena Williams' Body, It's Really About Her Blackness," *The Huffington Post*, last modified July 13, 2015, http://www.huffington post.com/entry/serena-williams-policing-of-black-bodies_55a3bef4e4b0a4 7ac15ccc00?ir=Womenandncid=fcbklnkushpmg00000046; Amelia Mc-Donell-Parry, "The NY Times Asked a Bunch of White Female Tennis Players About Serena Williams' Body," *The Frisky*, last modified July 10, 2015, http://www.thefrisky.com /2015-07-10/the-ny-times-asked-a-bunch-of-white-female-tennis-players-about -serena-williams-body/.

112. David McCarthy, Robyn Lloyd Jones, and Paul Potrac, "Constructing Images and Interpreting Realities: The Case of the Black Soccer Player on Television," *International Review for the Sociology of Sport* 38 (2003): 217–38.

113. Dodai Stewart, "Is *Vogue's* 'LeBron Kong' Cover Offensive?," *Jezebel*, last modified March 17, 2008, http://jezebel.com/368655/is-vogues-lebron-kong-cover -offensive.

114. "Destroy This Mad Brute," *Digital Desk*, accessed July 5, 2015, http://www .digitaldesk.org/projects/secondary/propaganda/destroy_brute.html.

115. "NBC Air Racist Monkey Commercial After Gabby Douglas Olympics Gold Medal," YouTube video, 0:27, posted by "skatefan2009," August 2, 2012, https:// www.youtube.com/watch?v=OFBHjgpIq7I.

116. Jomills H. Braddock II, "Sport and Race Relations in American Society," *Sociological Symposium* 9 (1989) 53–76.

117. Lori Latrice Martin, "The Black Athletes and the Postracial Myth," in *Out of Bounds: Racism and the Black Athlete*, ed. Lori Latrice Martin (Santa Barbara, CA: Praeger, 2014), 3–28.

118. Jason Reitman, *Thank You for Smoking*, Film (Hollywood, CA: Paramount Pictures, 2005).

119. Sean Braswell, "Stephen Curry: Basketball's Ultimate Long Shot," *OZY*, last modified June 9, 2015, http://www.ozy.com/rising-stars-and-provocateurs/basket

balls-ultimate-long-shot/41292.article?utm_source=ddandutm_medium=email andutm_campaign=04162015.

120. Tristan Thornburgh, "Professional Dunker Jordan Kilganon Leaps 75," *Bleacher Report*, last modified April 21, 2015, http://m.bleacherreport.com/articles /2437447-professional-dunker-jordan-kilganon-leaps-75-box-jump-with-running -start?utm_source=facebook.comandutm_medium=referralandutm_campaign =programming-national?is_shared=true.

121. Gabe Zaldivar, "350-Pound Running Back David Fangupo Is Bigger and Faster Than You," *Bleacher Report*, last modified February 11, 2013, http://bleache rreport.com/articles/1524933-david-fangupo-is-a-350-pound-running-back-and -hes-bigger-and-faster-than-you.

122. Gregg Doyel, "Rice's 4-foot-9 Tailback Sensation Has a Big Future Ahead of Him," *CBS*, last modified October 30, 2013, http://www.cbssports.com/general /writer/gregg-doyel/24160988/rices-4foot9-tailback-sensation-has-a-big-future -ahead-of-him.

123. See Anne Bowker, Shannon Gadbois, and Becki Cornock, "Sports Participation and Self-Esteem: Variations as a Function of Gender and Gender Role Orientation," *Sex Roles* 49 (2003): 47–58; Emine Cağlar, "Similarities and Differences in Physical Self-Concept of Males and Females During Late Adolescence and Early Adulthood," *Adolescence* 44 (2009): 407–19; Sheryl Clark, "Being 'Good at Sport': Talent, Ability and Young Women's Sporting Participation," *Sociology* 46 (2012): 1178–93; Corentin Clément-Guillotin and Paul Fontayne, "Situational Malleability of Gender Schema: The Case of the Competitive Sport Context," *Sex Roles* 64 (2010): 426–39; Elizabeth Daniels and Campbell Leaper, "A Longitudinal Investigation of Sport Participation, Peer Acceptance, and Self-Esteem Among Adolescent Girls and Boys," *Sex Roles* 55 (2006): 875–80; Marizanne Grundlingh, "Boobs and Balls: Exploring Issues of Gender and Identity Among Women Soccer Players at Stellenbosch University," *Agenda* 24 (2010): 45–53; James C. Hannon and Thomas Ratliffe, "Physical Activity Levels in Coeducational and Single-Gender High School Physical Education Settings," *Journal of Teaching in Physical Education* 24 (2005): 149–64; Weidong Li, Amelia M. Lee, and Melinda A. Solomon, "Gender Differences in Beliefs About the Influence of Ability and Effort in Sport and Physical Activity," *Sex Roles* 54 (2006): 147–56; Michelle Mordaunt-Bexiga, "Rugby, Gender and Capitalism: 'Sportocracy' Up for Sale?," *Agenda: Empowering Women for Gender Equity* 25 (2011): 69–74; Sally R. Ross and Kimberly J. Shinew, "Perspectives of Women College Athletes on Sport and Gender," *Sex Roles* 58 (2008): 40–57; Samuel Y. Todd and Aubrey Kent, "Student Athletes' Perceptions of Self," *Adolescence* 38 (2003): 659–67.

124. Sarah M. Coyne et al., "It's a Bird! It's a Plane! It's a Gender Stereotype!: Longitudinal Associations Between Superhero Viewing and Gender Stereotyped Play," *Sex Roles* 70 (2014): 416–30; M. Francisca Del Rio and Katherine Strasser, "Preschool Children's Beliefs About Gender Differences in Academic Skills," *Sex Roles* 68 (2012): 231–38; Lisa DiDonato and JoNell Strough, "Contextual Influences

on Gender Segregation in Emerging Adulthood," *Sex Roles* 69 (2013): 632–43; Karen Dill and Kathryn Thill, "Video Game Characters and the Socialization of Gender Roles: Young People's Perceptions Mirror Sexist Media Depictions," *Sex Roles* 57 (2007): 851–64; Elizabeth H. Todd et al., "Respected or Rejected: Perceptions of Women Who Confront Sexist Remarks," *Sex Roles* 45 (2001): 567–77; Laura Doey, Robert J. Coplan, and Mila Kingsbury, "Bashful Boys and Coy Girls: A Review of Gender Differences in Childhood Shyness," *Sex Roles* 70 (2014): 255–66; Heidi Gazelle, Divya Peter, and Maedeh Aboutalebi Karkavandi, "Commentary: Bashful Boys and Coy Girls: A Review of Gender Differences in Childhood Shyness," *Sex Roles* 70 (2014): 285–308; Priscilla Goble et al., "Children's Gender-Typed Activity Choices Across Preschool Social Contexts," *Sex Roles* 67 (2012): 435–51; Shayla C. Holub, Marie S. Tisak, and David Mullins, "Gender Differences in Children's Hero Attributions: Personal Hero Choices and Evaluations of Typical Male and Female Heroes," *Sex Roles* 58 (2008): 567–78; Randall M. Jones et al., "Bedroom Design and Decoration: Gender Differences in Preference and Activity," *Adolescence* 42 (2006): 539–53; Ashley Smith Leavell et al., "African American, White and Latino Fathers' Activities with Their Sons and Daughters in Early Childhood," *Sex Roles* 66 (2012): 53–65; Anna C. Harrison and Susan A. O'Neill, "Preferences and Children's Use of Gender-Stereotyped Knowledge About Musical Instruments: Making Judgments About Other Children's Preferences," *Sex Roles* 49 (2003): 389–400; Kate M. Russell, "On Versus Off the Pitch: The Transiency of Body Satisfaction Among Female Rugby Players, Cricketers, and Netballers," *Sex Roles* 51 (2004): 561–74; Susan Sanderson and Vetta L. Sanders Thompson, "Factors Associated with Perceived Paternal Involvement in Childrearing," *Sex Roles* 46 (2002): 99–111; Michele Van Volkom, "The Relationships Between Childhood Tomboyism, Siblings' Activities, and Adult Gender Roles," *Sex Roles* 49 (2003): 609–18.

Chapter Five

1. Birch Brah, 117 CONG. REC. 30, 407 (1971).

2. For a comprehensive review of females' exclusion and inclusion in sports see Karen M. Appleby and Elaine Foster, "Gender and Sports Participation," in *Gender Relations in Sport*, ed. Emily A. Roper (The Netherlands: Sense Publishers), 1–20.

3. Marie Hardin and Jennifer D. Greer, "The Influence of Gender-Role Socialization, Media Use and Sports Participation on Perceptions of Gender-Appropriate Sports," *Journal of Sport Behavior* 32 (2009): 207–26; Ulrike Tischer, Ilse Hartmann-Tews, and Claudia Combrink, "Sport Participation of the Elderly—The Role of Gender, Age, and Social Class," *European Review of Aging and Physical Activity* 8 (2011): 83–91.

4. Jennifer A. Hargreaves, "Gender on the Sports Agenda," *International Review for the Sociology of Sport* 25 (1990): 287–307; Michael A. Messner, "Gender Ideologies, Youth Sports, and the Production of Soft Essentialism," *Sociology of Sport Journal* 28 (2011): 151–70.

5. Douglas E. Foley, "The Great American Football Ritual: Reproducing Race, Class, and Gender Inequality," *Sociology of Sport Journal* 7 (1990): 111–135.

6. Timothy P. O'Hanlon, "School Sports as Social Training: The Case of Athletics and the Crisis of World War I," *Journal of Sport History* 9(1982): 4–29.

7. Donald Sabo, "Sport, Patriarchy, and Male Identity: New Questions About Men and Sport," *Arena Review* 9 (1985): 1–30.

8. Jay Coakley, "The Good Father: Parental Expectations and Youth Sports," *Leisure Studies* 25 (2006): 153–63.

9. Mary Jo Kane, "The Female Athletic Role as a Status Determinant within the Social Systems of Adolescents," *Adolescence* 23 (1988): 253–64.

10. Nathalie Koivula, "Ratings of Gender Appropriateness of Sports Participation: Effects of Gender-Based Schematic Processing," *Sex Roles* 33 (1995): 543–57.

11. Mary Jo Kane and Eldon E. Snyder, "Sport Typing: The Social Containment of Women in Sport," *Arena Review* 13 (1989): 77.

12. Natalie Adams, Alison Schmitke, and Amy Franklin, "Tomboys, Dykes, and Girly Girls: Interrogating the Subjectivities of Adolescent Female Athletes," *Women's Studies Quarterly* 33 (2005): 18–34.

13. Jay Coakley, *Sports in Society: Issues and Controversies*, 10th ed. (Boston, MA: McGraw Hill, 2009), 248.

14. Hardin and Greer, "Influence of Socialization."

15. Cheryl M. Walter, Rosa Du Randt, and Daniel J. L. Venter, "The Physical Activity and Health Status of Two Generations of Black South African Professional Women: Original Research," *Health SA Gesondheid* 16 (2011): 1–9.

16. Adam Love and Kimberly Kelly, "Equity or Essentialism? U.S. Courts and the Legitimation of Girls' Teams in High School Sport," *Gender and Society* 25 (2011): 227–49; Michael A. Messner, "Sports and Male Domination: The Female Athlete as Contested Ideological Terrain," *Sociology of Sport Journal* 5 (1988) 197–211; Messner, "Gender Ideologies."

17. Messner, "Gender Ideologies."

18. Love and Kelly, "Equity or Essentialism?"

19. Michael A. Messner and Nancy M. Solomon, "Social Justice and Men's Interests: The Case of Title IX," *Journal of Sport and Social Issues* 31 (2007): 162–78.

20. Douglas E. Foley, "Rethinking School Ethnographies of Colonial Settings: A Performance Perspective of Reproduction and Resistance," *Comparative Education Review* (1991): 532–51; Foley, "Great American Football Ritual"; Hargreaves, "Gender on the Sports Agenda"; Ben Clayton and Barbara Humberstone, "Men's Talk: A (Pro)feminist Analysis of Male University Football Players' Discourse," *International Review for the Sociology of Sport* 41 (2006): 295–316.

21. Foley, "Rethinking School Ethnographies"; Foley, "Great American Football Ritual."

22. Foley, "Great American Football Ritual," 133.

23. Sabo, "Sport, Patriarchy, and Male Identity."

24. Ibid., 1.

25. Clayton and Humberstone, "Men's Talk," 296, 309.

26. Dorothy L. Schmaltz and Deborah L. Kerstetter, "Girlie Girls and Manly Men: Children's Stigma Consciousness of Gender in Sports and Physical Activities," *Journal of Leisure Research* 38 (2006): 536–57.

27. Sohaila Shakib and Michele D. Dunbar, "The Social Construction of Female and Male High School Basketball Participation: Reproducing the Gender Order Through a Two-Tiered Sporting Institution," *Sociological Perspectives* 45 (2002): 353–78.

28. Marie Hardin, Fuyuan Shen, and Nan Yu, "Sextyping of Sports: The Influence of Gender, Participation, and Mediated Sports Consumption on Responses to Visual Priming" (paper presented at the annual meeting of the Association for Education in Journalism and Mass Communication, Chicago, IL, August 6–9, 2008); Messner, "Sports and Male Domination."

29. Hardin, Shen, and Yu 2008, "Sextyping Sports"; Adams, Schmitke, and Franklin, "Tomboys"; Cheryl Cooky and Mary G. McDonald, "'If You Let Me Play': Young Girls' Insider-Other Narratives of Sport," *Sociology of Sport Journal* 22 (2005): 158–77; Laurel R. Davis-Delano et al., "Apologetic Behavior Among Female Athletes: A New Questionnaire and Initial Results," *International Review for the Sociology of Sport* 44 (2009): 131–50; Lisa A. Harrison and Amanda B. Lynch, "Social Role Theory and the Perceived Gender Role Orientation of Athletes," *Sex Roles* 52 (2005): 227–36.

30. B. Christine Green, "Building Sport Programs to Optimize Athlete Recruitment, Retention, and Transition: Toward a Normative Theory of Sport Development," *Journal of Sport Management* 19 (2005): 233–53.

31. Jennifer Hargreaves, *Sporting Females: Critical Issues in the History and Sociology of Women's Sport* (New York: Routledge, 1994); Michael A. Messner, *Power at Play: Sports and the Problems of Masculinity* (Boston, MA: Beacon Press, 1992).

32. Benjamin Rader, "'Matters Involving Honor': Region, Race, and Rank in the Violent Life of Tyrus Raymond Cobb," in *Baseball in America and America in Baseball*, ed. Donald G. Kyle and Robert B. Fairbanks (College Station: Texas A&M University Press, 2008), 189–222.

33. Allen R. Sanderson, "The Many Dimensions of Competitive Balance," *Journal of Sports Economics* 3 (2002): 204–28.

34. Jennifer E. Powell, "IX: Straining Toward an Elusive Goal," *Willamette Sports Law Journal* 1 (2004): 1–29.

35. Michael A. Messner, *Power at Play*.

36. For a timeline of girls playing football, see "A History of Girls Playing Tackle Football," Princesses of the Gridiron, last modified January 10, 2004, http://www.angelfire.com/sports/womenfootball/princesses/timeline.html.

37. Jonathan Lintner, "Indiana Girl Signs to Play College Football at Campbellsville," *USA Today*, last modified June 9, 2014, http://www.usatoday.com/story/sports/ncaaf/2014/06/05/jeffersonville-indiana-girl-shelby-osborne-college-football/10033155/.

38. Gary Libman, "Girls Put a Little Kick in Football: A Forgotten Chapter of Game's History Features Females," *Los Angeles Times*, last modified November 21, 1985, http://articles.latimes.com/1985-11-21/news/vw-1902_1_extra-points.

39. George Gipe, Thomas C. Jones, and Harriet B. Helmer, *The Great American Sports Book* (Geneva, IL: Hall of Fame Press, 1980), 250.

40. Associated Press, "First Female Football Player in Texas Recalls Glory Days," *Houston Chronicle*, last modified August 25, 2015, http://www.chron.com/sports /high-school/article/First-female-football-player-in-Texas-recalls-1673773.php.

41. Edward J. Rielly, *Football: An Encyclopedia of Popular Culture* (Lincoln, NE: University of Nebraska Press, 2009), 399.

42. "History of Girls Playing Tackle Football."

43. "The Feminist Chronicles, 1953–1993—1973—Feminist Majority Foundation," Feminist Majority Foundation, accessed August 24, 2015, http://www .feminist.org/research/chronicles/fc1973a.html.

44. "Sally Gutierrez Makes History," *Spokane Daily Chronicle*, last modified October 11, 1975, https://news.google.com/newspapers?nid=1338&dat=19751011 &id=K_AjAAAAIBAJ&sjid=yfgDAAAAIBAJ&pg=6790,2981953&hl=en.

45. "History of Girls Playing Tackle Football."

46. See Ibid.; Bonnie L. Parkhouse and Jackie Lapin, *Women Who Win: Exercising Your Rights in Sports* (Englewood Cliffs, NJ: Prentice-Hall, 1980), 47; "Earns Spot on Team," *The Free Lance-Star*, September 13, 1978, 10; Rielly, *Football*; *Christian Science Monitor*, Oct. 17, 1977: 2.

47. Stuart Miller, "Playing with the Big Boys," *Women's Sports and Fitness* 17 (1995): 75.

48. *Cohen v. Brown University*, 991 F.2d 888 (1st Cir. 1993).

49. "1969–2014 High School Athletics Participation Survey," National Federation of State High School Associations, accessed June 8, 2015, http://www.nfhs.org /ParticipationStatics/PDF/Participation%20Survey%20History%20Book.pdf.

50. See Andrew Carroll, "UWA's Tonya Butler Aims for NCAA History," *The Tuscaloosa News*, last modified September 13, 2003, http://www.tuscaloosanews.com /article/20030914/NEWS/309140367; Brian Christopherson, "Beanie Does It All," *Lincoln Journal Star*, last modified November 10, 2006, http://journalstar.com/news /local/beanie-does-it-all/article_49f86c25-0d9a-5b4d-8443-0219d373c072 .html; Adam Epstein, *Sports Law* (Boston, MA: Cengage Learning, 2002), 118; "Female Kicker Breaks Gender Barrier," *The New York Times,* last modified August 31, 2001, http://www.nytimes.com/2001/08/31/sports/football-college-female-kicker -breaks-gender-barrier.html; Elliott Jones, "Baker Gets Her Kicks, Sets Female Mark at D-III School," *USA Today*, last modified November 13, 2007, http://usa today30.usatoday.com/sports/college/football/2007-11-08-female-kicker_N.htm; John Grasso, *Historical Dictionary of Football* (Lanham, MD: Scarecrow Press, 2013), 431; "History of Girls Playing Tackle Football"; Lintner, "Indiana Girl Signs to Play College Football"; "Katie Hnida, American Football NCAA Kicker," *Barefoot Running Magazine* 10 (2013), 36; Rielly, *Football*; George Vecsey, "A Rare Kicker, but Simply a Player," *The New York Times*, last modified August 29, 2009, http://www .nytimes.com/2009/08/30/sports/ncaafootball/30vescey.html?_r=0.

51. Jennifer Ring, *Stolen Bases: Why American Girls Don't Play Baseball* (Champaign, IL: University of Illinois Press, 2000).

52. Alyson Footer, "Daughter of Former Big Leaguer to Make Her Pitch in College," *MLB*, accessed August 24, 2015, http://m.mlb.com/news/article/108733340/daughter-of-former-big-john-hudek-to-pitch-collegiately.

53. "Education Longitudinal Study of 2002 (ELS: 2002)," U.S. Department of Education Institute of Education Sciences National Center for Education Statistics, last modified August 2015, http://nces.ed.gov/surveys/els2002/.

54. See Kenneth J. Arrow, "The Theory of Discrimination," in *Discrimination in Labor Markets*, ed. Orley Ashenfelter and Albert Rees (Princeton, NJ: Princeton University Press, 1973), 3–33; Edmond S. Phelps, "The Statistical Theory of Racism and Sexism," *American Economics Review* 62 (1972): 659–61.

55. "Sports Sponsorship and Participation Rates Report, 1981–1982—2014–2015," NCAA, forthcoming, Indianapolis, IN.

56. A. Jerome Dees, "Access or Interest: Why Brown Has Benefited African-American Women More Than Title IX," *University of Missouri Kansas City Law Review* 76 (2008): 625–42.

57. Betsy Stevenson, "Beyond the Classroom: Using Title IX to Measure the Return to High School Sports," *Review of Economics and Statistics* 92 (2010): 284–301.

58. See D. Stanley Eitzen, "Upward Mobility Through Sport? Myths and Realities," in *Sport in Contemporary Society: An Anthology*, 6th ed., ed. D. Stanley Eitzen (New York: Worth Publishers, 1999), 256–63; Lawrence M. Kahn, "The Economics of Discrimination: Evidence from Basketball," in *The Oxford Handbook of Sports Economics: Volume 2: Economics Through Sports*, ed. Stephen Shmanske and Leo H. Kahane (New York: Oxford University Press, 2012), 21–38; Susan Welch and Lee Sigelman, "Who's Calling the Shots? Women Coaches in Division I Women's Sports," *Social Science Quarterly* 8 (2007): 1415–34.

59. Thurgood Marshall, *Brown v. Board of Education*, 347 U.S. 483 (1954).

Chapter Six

1. Mark Hinog, "More Americans Watched the Women's World Cup Final Than the NBA Finals or the Stanley Cup," *SB Nation*, last modified July 6, 2015, http://www.sbnation.com/2015/7/6/8900299/more-americans-watched-the-womens-world-cup-final-than-the-nba-finals.

2. Lindsey Adler, "U.S. Women's Soccer Team Will Get $33 Million Less Prize Money Than the Men's Winner," *BuzzFeed*, last modified July 6, 2015, http://www.buzzfeed.com/lindseyadler/us-womens-soccer-team-will-get-33-million-less-prize-money-m#.ekggRXAKq.

3. Jeff Kassouf, "NBC Sportsworld: NWSL Salaries and Chasing Dreams," *The Equalizer*, last modified April 13, 2015; Steve Keating, "Back to Obscurity for All but a Few After World Cup," *Yahoo*, last modified July 6, 2015, http://sports.yahoo.com/news/back-obscurity-few-world-cup-222354832—sow.html?soc_src=media contentsharebuttons&soc_trk=fb.

4. Susan Rinkunas, "The Sexist $33 Million World Cup Prize Gap," *New York Magazine*, last modified July 7, 2015, http://nymag.com/thecut/2015/07/sexist-33 -million-world-cup-prize-gap.html?mid=fb-share-thecut.

5. Maggie Mertens, "Women's Soccer Is a Feminist Issues: Female Athletes Have Historically Received Very Little Attention from Activists and Advocates for Gender Equality. Why?," *The Atlantic*, http://www.theatlantic.com/entertainment /archive/2015/06/womens-soccer-is-a-feminist-issue/394865/.

6. Beckett A. Broh, "Dumb Jock or Student Athlete? A Longitudinal Analysis of the Effects of Playing High School Interscholastic Sports on Academic Performance" (MA thesis, The Ohio State University, 1999); Benjamin G. Gibbs et al., "Extracurricular Associations and College Enrollment," *Social Science Research* 50 (2015): 367–81; Robert Sean Mackin and Carol S. Walther, "Race, Sport and Social Mobility: Horatio Alger in Short Pants?," *International Review for the Sociology of Sport* 47 (2011): 670–89; Jennifer Pearson, Sarah R. Crissey, and Catherine Riegle-Crumb, "Gendered Fields: Sports and Advanced Course Taking in High School," *Sex Roles* 61 (2009): 519–35.

7. Beverly A. Browne and Sally K. Francis, "Participants in School-Sponsored and Independent Sports: Perceptions of Self and Family," *Adolescence* 28 (1993): 383–91; Brianne L. Burr, "Do Extracurricular Activities Help Adolescents Develop Academic Self-Efficacy? Evidence for How and Why" (MA thesis, Brigham Young University, 2012); Wendy Deianey and Christina Lee, "Self-Esteem and Sex Roles Among Male and Female High School Students: Their Relationship to Physical Activity," *Australian Psychologist* 30 (1995): 84–87; David R. Shaffer and Erin Wittes, "Women's Precollege Sports Participation, Enjoyment of Sports, and Self-Esteem," *Sex Roles* 55 (2006): 225–32.

8. Sarah J. Donaldson and Kevin R. Ronan, "The Effects of Sports Participation on Young Adolescents' Emotional Well-Being," *Adolescence* 41 (2006): 369–89; Eva-Carin Lindgren, "The Impact of Sports on Young Women's Attitude to Physical Activity in Adult Life," *Women in Sport & Physical Activity Journal* 9 (2000): 65–86; Neely, Kacey C. and Nick Holt, "Parents' Perspectives on the Benefits of Sport Participation for Young Children," *Sport Psychologist* 28 (2014): 255–68; Christopher E. Sanders, "Moderate Involvement in Sports Is Related to Lower Depression Levels Among Adolescents," *Adolescence* 35 (2000): 793–97.

9. Mikaela J. Dufur, "Race and the NFL Draft: Views from the Auction Block," *Qualitative Sociology* 32 (2009): 53–73; Mikaela J. Dufur and Seth L. Feinberg, "Artificially Restricted Labor Markets and Worker Dignity in Professional Football," *Journal of Contemporary Ethnography* 36 (2007): 505–36; Ramón Spaaij, "Sport as a Vehicle for Social Mobility and Regulation of Disadvantaged Urban Youth: Lesson from Rotterdam," *International Review for the Sociology of Sport* 44 (2009): 247–64.

10. Edoardo G.F. Rosso and Richard McGrath, "Beyond Recreation: Personal Social Networks and Social Capital in the Transition of Young Players from Recreational Football to Formal Football Clubs," *International Review for the Sociology of Sport* 48 (2012): 453–70; Kaisa Snellman et al., "The Engagement Gap: Social

Mobility and Extracurricular Participation Among American Youth," *Annals of the American Academy of Political and Social Science* 657 (2014): 194–207; Carl Stempel, "Adult Participation Sports as Cultural Capital: A Test of Bourdieu's Theory of the Field of Sports," *International Review for the Sociology of Sport* 40 (2005): 411–32; Thomas C. Wilson, "The Paradox of Social Class and Sports Involvement: The Roles of Cultural and Economic Capital," *International Review for the Sociology of Sport* 37 (2002): 5–16.

11. Jacques M. Henry and Howard P. Comeaux, "Gender Egalitarianism in Coed Sport a Case Study of American Soccer," *International Review for the Sociology of Sport* 34 (1999): 277–90; Canan Koca, "Gender Interaction in Coed Physical Education: A Study in Turkey," *Adolescence* 44 (2008): 165–85.

12. Joyce L. Epstein, "After the Bus Arrives: Desegregation in Desegregated Schools," *Journal of Social Issues* 41 (1985): 23–43.

13. "1981–1982—2012–2013 NCAA Sports Sponsorship and Participation Rates Report," NCAA, last modified October 2014, http://www.ncaapublications .com/productdownloads/PR2014.pdf.

14. "University Asks Police to Look into Alleged Rape," *CNN*, last modified February 18, 2004, http://www.cnn.com/2004/US/Central/02/18/colorado.football/.

15. Kopano Ratele, "Gender Equality in the Abstract and Practice," *Men and Masculinities* 17 (2014): 513–14.

16. Bruce Kidd, "The Men's Cultural Center: Sports and the Dynamic of Women's Oppression/Men's Repression," in *Sport, Men and the Gender Order: Critical Feminist Perspectives*, ed. Michael A. Messner and Donald Sabo (Champaign, IL: Human Kinetics, 1990), 31–42; Michael A. Messner, "Boyhood, Organized Sports and the Construction of Masculinities," *Journal of Contemporary Ethnography* 18 (1990): 416–44; Michael A. Messner, *Power at Play: Sports and the Problems of Masculinity* (Boston, MA: Beacon Press, 1992).

17. B. Glenn George, "Fifty/Fifty: Ending Sex Segregation in School Sports," *Ohio State Law Journal* 63 (2002): 1107–64.

18. Larena Hoeber, "Gender Equity for Athletes: Multiple Understandings of an Organizational Value," *Sex Roles* 58 (2007): 58–71.

19. Lori Artinger et al., "The Social Benefits of Intramural Sports," *NASPA Journal* 43 (2006): 69–86; Francis O'Donnell, "Coed Adolescent Soccer Players in a Competitive Learning Milieu: An Ethnographic Assessment of Gender Attitudes, Perceptions and Sport Specific Component Testing" (PhD diss., University of Central Florida, 2004); Cheryl P. Stuntz, Julia K. Sayles, and Erin L. McDermott, "Same-Sex and Mixed-Sex Sport Teams: How the Social Environment Relates to Sources of Social Support and Perceived Competence," *Journal of Sport Behavior* 34 (2011): 98–120.

20. Ratele, "Gender Equality," 510–14.

21. Bob Pease, "'New Wine in Old Bottles?' A Commentary on 'What's in It for Men?' Old Question, New Data," *Men and Masculinities* 17 (2014): 549–51.

22. Eddie Bernice Johnson (Untitled speech given at the Ultimate Ladies Power Lunch, Birmingham, AL, March 23, 2012).

23. "Intimate Partner Violence: Consequences," Centers for Disease Control and Prevention (CDC), last modified March 3, 2015, http://www.cdc.gov/violence prevention/intimatepartnerviolence/consequences.html.

24. Adrienne N. Milner and Elizabeth H. Baker, "Athletic Participation and Intimate Partner Violence Victimization: Investigating Sport Involvement, Self-Esteem, and Abuse Patterns for Women and Men," *Journal of Intimate Partner Violence* (2015), DOI: 10.1177/0886260515585543; Kristine Newhall, "The Athlete Exception: Title IX, Sexual Assault, and Intercollegiate Athletics" (paper presented at the annual meeting for the Southern Sociological Society, New Orleans, LA, March 25–29, 2015).

25. Robin Bachin, Jan Sokol-Katz, and Jomills H. Braddock II, "Sport and Violence in American History," in *The Encyclopedia of Violence in the U.S.*, ed. Eric Foner (New York: Macmillan, 1999); Michael J. Merten, "Acceptability of Dating Violence Among Late Adolescents: The Role of Sports Participation, Competitive Attitudes, and Selected Dynamics of Relationship Violence," *Adolescence* 43 (2008): 31–56.

26. Jay Coakley, "The Sociological Perspective: Alternative Causations of Violence in Sport," *Arena* 5 (1981): 44–56; Kidd, "Men's Cultural Center"; Messner, "Boyhood"; Messner, *Power at Play*; Mariah Burton Nelson, *The Stronger Women Get the More Men Love Football: Sexism and the American Culture of Sports* (New York: Harcourt Brace, 1994); Donald Sabo and Ross Runfola, *Jock: Sports and the Male Identity* (Englewood Cliffs, NJ: Prentice-Hall, 1980); Peggy Reeves Sanday, "Rape-Prone Versus Rape-Free Campus Cultures," *Violence Against Women* 2 (1996): 191–208.

27. Todd W. Crosset, Jeffrey R. Benedict, and Mark A. McDonald, "Male Student-Athletes Reported for Sexual Assault: A Survey of Campus Police Departments and Judicial Affairs Offices," *Journal of Sport and Social Issues* 19 (1995): 126–40; Todd W. Crosset et al., "Male Student Athletes and Violence Against Women: A Survey of Campus Judicial Affairs Offices," *Violence Against Women* 2 (1996): 163–79; Mary Pat Fritner and Laurna Rubinson, "Acquaintance Rape: The Influence of Alcohol, Fraternity Membership and Sports Team Membership," *Journal of Sex Education and Therapy* 19 (1993): 272–84; Sarah K. Murnen, and Marla H. Kohlman, "Athletic Participation, Fraternity Membership, and Sexual Aggression Among College Men: A Meta-analytic Review," *Sex Roles* 57 (2007): 145–57; Michael Welch, "Violence Against Women by Professional Football Players: A Gender Analysis of Hypermasculinity, Positional Status, Narcissism, and Entitlement," *Journal of Sport and Social Issues* 21 (1997): 392–411.

28. Eric Anderson, "'I Used to Think Women Were Weak': Orthodox Masculinity, Gender Segregation, and Sport," *Sociological Forum* 23 (2008): 257–80; Ben Clayton and Barbara Humberstone, "Men's Talk: A (Pro)feminist Analysis of Male University Football Players' Discourse," *International Review for the Sociology of Sport* 41 (2006): 295–316; Derek Kreager, "Unnecessary Roughness? School Sports, Peer Networks, and Male Adolescent Violence," *American Sociological Review* 72 (2007): 705–24; Darlene R. Wright and Kevin M. Fitzpatrick, "Violence and Minority

Youth: The Effects of Risk and Asset Factors on Fighting Among African American Children and Adolescents," *Adolescence* 41 (2006): 251–62.

29. Anderson, "I Used to Think"; Janet Fink, "Challenging the Gender Binary: Male Practice Players' Views of Female Athletes and Women's Sports" (paper presented at the annual meeting for the North American Society for Sport Management, Tampa, FL, June 1–6, 2010).

30. "Declaration on the Elimination of Violence against Women," United Nations, last modified February 23, 1994, http://www.unhchr.ch/huridocda/huridoca .nsf/(Symbol)/A.RES.48.104.En?Opendocument.

31. "Sport and Gender: Empowering Girls and Women," United Nations, accessed July 7, 2015, http://www.un.org/wcm/webdav/site/sport/shared/sport /SDP%20IWG/Chapter4_SportandGender.pdf.

32. Amanda Roth and Susan Basow, "Femininity, Sports, and Feminism: Developing a Theory of Physical Liberation," *Journal of Sport and Social Issues* 28 (2004): 245–65.

33. Tonya Dodge and James Jaccard, "Participation in Athletics and Female Sexual Risk Behavior: The Evaluation of Four Causal Structures," *Journal of Adolescent Research* 17 (2002): 42–67.

34. Kathleen Miller et al., "Athletic Participation and Sexual Behavior in Adolescents: The Different Worlds of Boys and Girls," *Journal of Health and Social Behavior* 39 (1998): 108–23.

35. Jorunn Sundgot-Borgen et al., "Sexual Harassment and Eating Disorders in Female Elite Athletes—A Controlled Study," *Scandinavian Journal of Medicine & Science in Sports* 13 (2003): 330–35.

36. Milner and Baker, "Athletic Participation and IPV."

37. Mark Fainaru-Wada, "Documents Reveal New Details About Hope Solo's Actions Last June," *ESPN*, last modified June 7, 2015, http://espn.go.com/espn/otl /story/_/id/12976615/detailed-look-hope-solo-domestic-violence-case-includes -reports-being-belligerent-jail; Kevin Draper, "Britney Griner Files Annulment Papers Day After Wife Announces Baby," *Deadspin*, last modified June 6, 2015, http://deadspin.com/brittney-griner-files-annulment-papers-day-after-wife-a -1709523775.

38. George, "Fifty/Fifty."

39. Jean M. Twenge, "Status and Gender: The Paradox of Progress in an Age of Narcissism," *Sex Roles* 61 (2009): 338–40.

40. Will H. Courtenay, "Constructions of Masculinity and Their Influence on Men's Well Being: A Theory of Gender and Health," *Social Science and Medicine* 50 (2000): 1385–401.

41. Clare M. Mehta et al., "Associations Between Mixed-Gender Friendships, Gender Reference Group Identity and Substance Use in College Students," *Sex Roles* 70 (2013): 98–109.

42. Isabel Castillo et al., "Cross-Domain Generality of Achievement Motivation across Sport and the Classroom: The Case of Spanish Adolescents," *Adolescence* 44 (2009): 569–80.

43. Jason M. Breslow, "76 of 79 Deceased NFL Players Found to Have Brain Disease," last modified September 30, 2014, http://www.pbs.org/wgbh/pages /frontline/sports/concussion-watch/76-of-79-deceased-nfl-players-found-to-have -brain-disease/.

44. David Remnick, "Going the Distance: On and Off the Road with Barack Obama," *The New Yorker*, last modified January 27, 2014, http://www.newyorker .com/magazine/2014/01/27/going-the-distance-david-remnick.

45. "Malcolm Gladwell: Football Is a Moral Abomination," *Bloomberg* video, 3:51, November 12, 2014, http://www.bloomberg.com/news/videos/2014-11-13 /malcolm-gladwell-football-is-a-moral-abomination.

46. Mark Fainaru-Wada and Steve Fainaru, "Chris Borland Quits Over Safety Issues," *ESPN*, last modified March 17, 2015, http://espn.go.com/espn/otl/story/_ /id/12496480/san-francisco-49ers-linebacker-chris-borland-retires-head-injury -concerns.

47. Remnick, "Going the Distance."

48. Jacqueline McDowell and George B. Cunningham, "Reactions to Physical Contact Among Coaches and Players: The Influence of Coach Sex, Player Sex, and Attitudes Toward Women," *Sex Roles* 58 (2008): 761–67; Ashley Montagu, *The Natural Superiority of Women* (New York: Altamira Press, 1999); Howard L. Nixon II, "The Relationship of Friendship Networks, Sport Experiences, and Gender to Expressed Pain Thresholds," *Sociology of Sport Journal* 13 (1996): 78–86.

49. "Grambling Responds to Concerns," *ESPN*, last modified October 20, 2013, http://espn.go.com/college-football/story/_/id/9846943/grambling-state-tigers -players-send-letter-complaint-administration.

50. Steven Goff, "Women's World Cup Will Be Played on Lush, Green Artificial Turf," *The Washington Post*, last modified June 5, 2015, http://www.washingtonpost .com/sports/womens-world-cup-will-be-played-on-lush-green-artificial-turf /2015/06/05/a786a0ac-0b8d-11e5-951e-8e15090d64ae_story.html.

51. See George, "Fifty/Fifty"; Adam Love and Kimberly Kelly, "Equity or Essentialism? U.S. Courts and the Legitimation of Girls' Teams in High School Sport," *Gender and Society* 25 (2011): 227–49.

52. David Shields et al., "Predictors of Poor Sportspersonship in Youth Sports: Personal Attitudes and Social Influences," *Journal of Sport Exercise Psychology* 29 (2007): 747–62.

53. Linda B. Cottler et al., "Injury, Pain, and Prescription Opioid Use Among Former National Football League (NFL) Players," *Drug and Alcohol Dependence* 116 (2011): 188–94; Charles Cox, "Investigating the Prevalence and Risk-Factors of Depression Symptoms Among NCAA Division I Collegiate Athletes" (MS thesis, Southern Illinois University Edwardsville, 2015); Gregory D. Myer, "Injury Initiates Unfavourable Weight Gain and Obesity Markers in Youth," *British Journal of Sports Medicine* 48 (2014): 1477–81; Selcen Öztürk and Dilek Kılıç, "What Is the Economic Burden of Sports Injuries?," *Controversial Issues* 24 (2013): 108–11; Gary Vargas et al., "Predictors and Prevalence of Postconcussion Depression Symptoms in Collegiate Athletes," *Journal of Athletic Training* 50 (2015): 250–55.

54. Amy Slater and Marika Tiggemann, "'Uncool to Do Sport': A Focus Group Study of Adolescent Girls' Reasons for Withdrawing from Physical Activity," *Psychology of Sport and Exercise* 11 (2010): 619–26.

55. Amy Slater and Marika Tiggemann, "Time Since Menarche and Sport Participation as Predictors of Self-Objectification: A Longitudinal Study of Adolescent Girls," *Sex Roles* 67 (2012) 571–81.

56. Jean M. Lamont, "Trait Body Shame Predicts Health Outcomes in College Women: A Longitudinal Investigation," *Journal of Behavioral Medicine* (2015), DOI: 10.1007/s10865-015-9659-9.

57. Todd A. Migliaccio and Ellen C. Berg, "Women's Participation in Tackle Football: An Exploration of Benefits and Constraints," *International Review for the Sociology of Sport* 42 (2007): 271–87.

58. Sharon Wheeler, "The Significance of Family Culture for Sports Participation," *International Review for the Sociology of Sport* 47 (2011): 235–52; Sharon Wheeler and Ken Green, "Parenting in Relation to Children's Sports Participation: Generational Changes and Potential Implication," *Leisure Studies* 33 (2012): 267–84.

59. Nadira Faber, "Should Men and Women Be Segregated in Professional Sports?," Practical Ethics, last modified July 31, 2015, http://blog.practicalethics.ox .ac.uk/2012/07/should-men-and-women-be-segregated-in-professional-sports/.

60. Betsy Stevenson, "Beyond the Classroom: Using Title IX to Measure the Return to High School Sports," *Review of Economics and Statistics* 92 (2010): 284–301.

61. D. Stanley Eitzen, "Upward Mobility Through Sport? Myths and Realities," in *Sport in Contemporary Society: An Anthology*, 6th ed., ed. D. Stanley Eitzen (New York: Worth Publishers, 1999), 256–63; Lawrence M. Kahn, "The Economics of Discrimination: Evidence from Basketball," in *The Oxford Handbook of Sports Economics: Volume 2: Economics Through Sports*, ed. Stephen Shmanske and Leo H. Kahane (New York: Oxford University Press, 2012), 21–38; Susan Welch and Lee Sigelman, "Who's Calling the Shots? Women Coaches in Division I Women's Sports," *Social Science Quarterly* 8 (2007): 1415–34.

62. Kurt Badenhausen, The World's 50 Most Valuable Sports Teams 2014," *Forbes*, last modified July 16, 2014, http://www.forbes.com/sites/kurtbadenhausen /2014/07/16/the-worlds-50-most-valuable-sports-teams-2014/.

63. Collin R. Flake, Mikaela J. Dufur, and Erin L. Moore, "Advantage Men: The Sex Pay Gap in Professional Tennis," *International Review for the Sociology of Sport* 48 (2012): 366–76.

64. Matthew Linford, "Understanding the Relationship Between Interscholastic Sports Participation and Labor Market Outcomes: Interscholastic Sports as Cultural Capital" (MS thesis, Brigham Young University, 2009).

65. Warren A. Whisenant, Paul M. Pederson, and Bill L. Obenour, "Success and Gender: Determining the Rate of Advancement for Intercollegiate Athletic Directors," *Sex Roles* 47 (2002): 485–91.

66. Warren A. Whisenant, John Miller, and Paul M. Pedersen, "Systemic Barriers in Athletic Administration: An Analysis of Job Descriptions for Interscholastic Athletic Directors," *Sex Roles* 53 (2005): 916.

67. Warren A. Whisenant, "Sustaining Male Dominance in Interscholastic Athletics: A Case of Homologous Reproduction . . . or Not?," *Sex Roles* 58 (2008): 772–73.

68. Laura J. Burton et al., " 'Think Athletic Director, Think Masculine?': Examination of the Gender Typing of Managerial Subroles Within Athletic Administration Positions," *Sex Roles* 61 (2009): 416–26.

69. Newman Wadesango et al., "Nature and Effects of Women's Participation in Sporting Decision-making Structures in the Context of the 2010 FIFA World Cup," *Agenda: Empowering Women for Gender Equity* 24 (2011): 62–75.

70. Pamela Wicker, Christoph Breuer, and Tassilo Von Hanau, "Gender Effects on Organizational Problems—Evidence from Non-Profit Sports Clubs in Germany," *Sex Roles* 66 (2011): 105–16.

71. Nancy M. Carter, Ph.D., Senior Vice President, Research, Catalyst Inc. and by Harvey M. Wagner, "The Bottom Line: Corporate Performance and Women's Representation on Boards (2004–2008)," Catalyst, Inc., last modified March 1, 2011, http://www.catalyst.org/system/files/the_bottom_line_corporate_perfor mance_and_women%27s_representation_on_boards_%282004-2008%29.pdf; Julia Dawson, Richard Kersley, and Stefano Natella, "The CS Gender 3000: Women in Senior Management," Credit Suisse, last modified September 2014, https:// publications.credit-suisse.com/tasks/render/file/index.cfm?fileid=8128F3C0 -99BC-22E6-838E2A5B1E4366DF; Corinne Post, "When Is Female Leadership an Advantage? Coordination Requirements, Team Cohesion, and Team Interaction Norms," *Journal of Organizational Behavior* (2015), DOI: 10.1002/job.2031.

72. Kenneth N. Robinson, *From Vick-Tim to Vick-Tory: The Fall and Rise of Michael Vick* (Houston, TX: Strategic Book Publishing, 2013), 157–206.

73. Manase Chiweshe, "One of the Boys: Female Fans' Responses to the Masculine and Phallocentric Nature of Football Stadiums in Zimbabwe," *Critical African Studies* 6 (2014): 211–22.

74. Garry Crawford and Victoria K. Gosling, "The Myth of the 'Puck Bunny': Female Fans and Men's Ice Hockey," *Sociology* 38 (2004): 477–93.

75. Michael A. Messner, Margaret Carlisle Duncan, and Faye Linda Wachs, "The Gender of Audience Building: Televised Coverage of Women's and Men's NCAA Basketball," *Sociological Inquiry* 66 (1996): 422–40.

76. "Super Bowl XLVII Most-Watched TV Program in U.S. History," *NFL*, last modified February 3, 2014, http://www.nfl.com/superbowl/story/0ap200000032 3430/article/super-bowl-xlviii-mostwatched-tv-program-in-us-history.

77. "Super Bowl 2014: Seattle Trounces Denver, 43–48," *CBS*, last modified February 3, 2014, http://www.cbsnews.com/news/super-bowl-2014-seattle-trounces -denver-43-8/.

78. Cheryl Cooky, "Strong Enough to Be a Man, but Made a Woman: Discourses of Sports and Femininity in *Sports Illustrated for Women*," in *Sexual Sports Rhetoric*, ed. Linda K. Fuller (New York: Haworth Press, 2006), 97–106; Elizabeth A. Daniels and Heidi Wartena, "Athlete or Sex Symbol: What Boys Think of Media Representations of Female Athletes," *Sex Roles* 65 (2011): 566–79; Valarie Hanson,

"The Inequality of Sport: Women < Men," *Undergraduate Review: A Journal of Undergraduate Student Research* 13 (2013): 15–22; Marie Hardin, Erin Whiteside, and Erin Ash, "Ambivalence on the Front Lines? Attitudes Toward Title IX and Women's Sports Among Division I Sports Information Directors," *International Review for the Sociology of Sport* 49 (2014): 42–64; Emily R. Kaskan and Ivy K. Ho, "Microaggressions and Female Athletes," *Sex Roles* (2014), DOI: 10.1007/211199-014-0425-1; Michael A. Messner, Margaret Carlisle Duncan, and Nicole Willms, "This Revolution Is Not Being Televised," *Contexts: Understanding People in Their Social Worlds* 5 (2006): 34–38; Michael A. Messner, Margaret Carlisle Duncan, and Cheryl Cooky, "Silence, Sports Bras, and Wrestling Porn: The Treatment of Women in Televised Sports News and Highlights," *Journal of Sport and Social Issues* 27 (2003): 38–51; Hamidreza Mirsafian, Tamás Dóczi, and Azadeh Mohamadinejad, "Attitude of Iranian Female University Students to Sport and Exercise," *Iranian Studies* 47 (2013): 951–66; Olan K. M. Scott, Brad Hill, and Dwight Zakus, "Framing the 2007 National Basketball Association Finals: An Analysis of Commentator Discourse," *International Review for the Sociology of Sport* 49 (2012): 728–44; Portia Vann, "Changing the Game: The Role of Social Media in Overcoming Old Media's Attention Deficit Toward Women's Sport," *Journal of Broadcasting & Electronic Media* 58 (2014): 438–55; Jonetta D. Weber and Robert M. Carini, "Where Are the Female Athletes in *Sports Illustrated*? A Content Analysis of Covers (2000–2011)," *International Review for the Sociology of Sport* 48 (2012): 196–203; Sarah Marie Wolter, "Serving, Informing, and Inspiring Today's Female Athlete and Fan Postfeminist Discourse: A Critical Media Analysis of EspnW" (PhD diss., University of Minnesota, 2012).

79. Cheryl Cooky, Michael A. Messner, and Michela Musto, " 'It's Dude Time!': A Quarter Century of Excluding Women's Sports in Televised Sports News and Highlight Shows," *Communication and Sport* 3 (2015): 261–87.

80. Mary Jo Kane, "The Better Sportswomen Get, the More the Media Ignore Them," *Communication and Sport* 1 (2013): 231–36.

81. Catherine Adams et al., "Sport Is King: An Investigation into Local Media Coverage of Women's Sport in the UK East Midlands," *Journal of Gender Studies* 23 (2014): 422–39; Steph Mackay and Christine Dallaire, "Campus Newspaper Coverage of Varsity Sports: Getting Closer to Equitable and Sports-related Representations of Female Athletes?," *International Review for the Sociology of Sport* 44 (2009): 25–40.

82. Sarah K. Fields, "Hoover v. Meiklejohn: The Equal Protection Clause, Girls, and Soccer," *Journal of Sport History* 30 (2003): 309; Allie D. LeFeuvre, E. Frank Stephenson, and Sara M. Walcott, "Football Frenzy: The Effect of the 2011 World Cup on Women's Professional Soccer League Attendance," *Journal of Sports Economics* 14 (2013): 440–48.

83. Maya Moore, "(In)Visibility," *The Players' Tribune*, last modified April 30, 2015, http://www.theplayerstribune.com/maya-moore-wnba-visibility/.

84. Merrill J. Melnick and Steven J. Jackson, "Globalization American-Style and Reference Idol Selection: The Importance of Athlete Celebrity Others Among New Zealand Youth," *International Review for the Sociology of Sport* 37 (2002): 429–48.

85. Sumaya F. Samie et al., "Voices of Empowerment: Women from the Global South Re/negotiating Empowerment and the Global Sports Mentoring Programme," *Sport in Society* 18 (2015): 923–37.

86. Nadav Goldschmied and Jason Kowalczyk, "Gender Performance in the NCAA Rifle Championships: Where Is the Gap?," *Sex Roles* 71 (2014): 1–13; Mika Hämäläinen, "A Sport with Untapped Potential to Empower Women," *Journal of the Philosophy of Sport* 41 (2014): 53–63.

87. Cheryl Roberts, "Government Intervention Needed to Improve Status of Women in Sport," *Agenda: Empowering Women for Gender Equity* 24 (2011): 146–47.

88. Megan Townsend, "Laverne Cox Makes History with Daytime Creative Arts Emmy Win," GLAAD, last modified April 25, 2015, http://www.glaad.org/blog /laverne-cox-makes-history-daytime-creative-arts-emmy-win.

89. "Gender Neutral Housing," Human Rights Campaign, accessed July 23, 2015, http://www.hrc.org/resources/entry/gender-neutral-housing.

90. Aron Macarow, "Five Women's Colleges Now Admit Some Transgender People," *Attn:*, last modified February 23, 2015, http://www.attn.com/stories/521 /do-transgender-men-belong-womens-colleges.

91. Ray Locker and Tom Vanden Brook, "Pentagon Moves Closer to Allowing Transgender Troops to Serve," *USA Today*, http://www.usatoday.com/story/news /nation/2015/07/13/carter-defense-transgender-policy/30104403/.

92. Hayley Miller, "Hawaii Bill Allowing Transgender People to Amend Birth Certificates Signed into Law," Human Rights Campaign, last modified July 15, 2015, http://www.hrc.org/blog/entry/hawaii-bill-allowing-transgender-people-to -amend-birth-certificates-signed?utm_content=buffer4fbbf&utm_medium =social&utm_source=plus.google.com&utm_campaign=hrcsocialteam.

93. Cheryl Cooky and Shari L. Dworkin, "Policing the Boundaries of Sex: A Critical Examination of Gender Verification and the Caster Semenya Controversy," *Journal of Sex Research* 50 (2013): 103–11; Shari L. Dworkin and Cheryl Cooky, "Sport, Sex Segregation, and Sex Testing: Critical Reflections on This Unjust Marriage," *American Journal of Bioethics* 12 (2012): 1–3; Shari L. Dworkin, Amanda Lock Swarr, and Cheryl Cooky, "(In)Justice in Sport: The Treatment of South African Track Star Caster Semenya," *Feminist Studies* 39 (2013): 40–69; Bennett Foddy and Julian Savulescu, "Time to Re-Evaluate Gender Segregation in Athletics?," *British Journal of Sports Medicine* 45 (2011): 1184–88; Katrina Karkazis and Rebecca Jordan-Young, "Debating a 'Sex Gap' in Testosterone," *Science* 348 (2015): 858–60; Sarah Teetzel, "The Onus of Inclusivity: Sport Policies and the Enforcement of the Women's Category in Sport," *Journal of the Philosophy of Sport* 41 (2013): 113–27; Eric Vilain, "Gender Testing for Athletes Remains a Tough Call," *The New York Times*, last modified June 18, 2012, http://www.nytimes.com/2012/06/18/sports /olympics/the-line-between-male-and-female-athletes-how-to-decide.html?_r=0.

94. Phil Helsel, "Caitlyn Jenner Receives ESPY Arthur Ashe Award for Courage," *NBC*, last modified July 15, 2015, http://www.nbcnews.com/news/us-news /caitlyn-jenner-receives-espy-award-courage-n392911.

95. Mitch Kellaway, "Michigan's Planet Fitness 'Controversy' Echoes National Debate on Trans Access," *The Advocate*, http://abcnews.go.com/Health/planet-fit ness-revokes-womans-membership-transgender-complaint/story?id=29465983.

96. Zack Ford, "Transgender Woman Sues CrossFit After Being Denied Access to Competition," Think Progress, last modified March 7, 2014, http://thinkprogress .org/lgbt/2014/03/07/3378021/crossfit-transgender/.

97. Erin E. Buzuvis, "Transgender Student-Athletes and Sex-Segregated Sport: Developing Policies of Inclusion for Intercollegiate and Interscholastic Athletics," *Seton Hall Journal of Sports and Entertainment Law* 21 (2011): 1–59; Alice Dreger, "Sex Typing for Sport," *Hastings Center Report* 40 (2010): 22–24; Brendon Tagg, "Men's Netball or Gender-Neutral Netball," *International Review for the Sociology of Sport* (2014), DOI: 10.1177/1012690214524757.

98. Joseph Harry, "Sports Ideology, Attitudes Toward Women, and Anti-Homosexual Attitudes," *Sex Roles* 32 (1995): 109–16; Jay Johnson, "Are Sisters Doing It for Themselves? An Analysis of Gender and the Sport Initiation Ceremony," *Canadian Woman Studies* 21 (2002): 125–31; John Nauright, "African Women and Sport: The State of Play," *Sport in Society* 17 (2013): 1–12; John F. Zipp, "Sport and Sexuality: Athletic Participation by Sexual Minority and Sexual Majority Adolescents in the U.S," *Sex Roles* 64 (2011): 19–31.

99. Elaine M. Blinde and Diane E. Taub, "Women Athletes as Falsely Accused Deviants: Managing the Lesbian Stigma," *Sociological Quarterly* 33 (1992): 521–33; Pat Griffin, *Strong Women, Deep Closets: Lesbians and Homophobia in Sport* (Champaign, IL: Human Kinetics, 1998); Kerrie Krauer and Vikki Krane, " 'Scary Dykes' and 'Feminine Queens': Stereotypes and Female Collegiate Athletics," *Women in Sport and Physical Activity Journal* 15 (2006): 42–55; Vikki Krane, "Homonegativism Experienced by Lesbian Collegiate Athletes," *Women in Sport and Physical Activity Journal* 6 (1997): 165–88; Vikki Krane, "We Can Be Athletics and Feminine, but Do We Want to? Challenging Hegemonic Femininity in Women's Sport," *Quest* 53 (2001): 115–33; Elizabeth M. Mullin, "Scale Development: Heterosexist Attitudes in Women's Collegiate Athletics," *Measurement in Physical Education and Exercise Science* 17 (2012): 1–21; Darcy C. Plymire and Pamela L. Forman, "Breaking the Silence: Lesbian Fans, the Internet, and the Sexual Politics of Women's Sport," *International Journal of Sexuality and Gender Studies* 5 (2000): 141–53.

100. Eric Anderson, "Updating the Outcome: Gay Athletes, Straight Teams, and Coming Out in Educationally Based Sport Teams," *Gender and Society* 25 (2011): 250–68; Eric Anderson, " 'Being Masculine Is Not About Who You Sleep with . . .': Masculinity and the One-Time Rule of Homosexuality," *Sex Roles* 58(2007): 104–15; Thomas R. Alley and Catherine M. Hicks, "Peer Attitudes Toward Adolescent Participants in Male and Female Oriented Sports," *Adolescence* 40 (2005): 273–80; Britney G. Brinkman and Kathryn M. Rickard, "College Students' Descriptions of Everyday Gender Prejudice," *Sex Roles* 61 (2009): 461–75; Caroline Chimot and Catherine Louveau, "Becoming a Man While Playing a Female Sport: The Construction of Masculine Identity in Boys Doing Rhythmic Gymnastics," *International Review for the Sociology of Sport* 45 (2010): 436–56; Kelly Knez, Tansin Benn, and

Sara Alkhaldi, "World Cup Football as a Catalyst for Change: Exploring the Lives of Women in Qatar's First National Football Team—A Case Study," *International Journal of the History of Sport* 31 (2014): 1755–73; Todd A. Migliaccio and Ellen C. Berg, "Women's Participation in Tackle Football: An Exploration of Benefits and Constraints," *International Review for the Sociology of Sport* 42 (2007): 271–87; Jon Swain, "The Role of Sport in the Promotion of Masculinity in an English Independent Junior School," *Sport, Education and Society* 11 (2006): 317–35; Brendon Tagg, "'Imagine, a Man Playing Netball!': Masculinities and Sport in New Zealand," *International Review for the Sociology of Sport* 43 (2008): 409–30; Josh Tinley, "Why Do Boys Play Baseball and Girls Play Softball?" *Midwest Sports Fans*, last modified June 1, 2012, http://www.midwestsportsfans.com/2012/06/why-do-boys-play-baseball -and-girls-play-softball/.

101. Judith E. Owen Blakemore and Renee E. Centers, "Characteristics of Boys' and Girls' Toys," *Sex Roles* 53 (2005): 619–33.

102. "What's in Store: Moving Away from Gender-Based Signs," Target Corporation, last modified August 7, 2015, https://corporate.target.com/article/2015/08 /gender-based-signs-corporate.

103. Geoff Nichols, Richard Tacon, and Alison Muir, "Sport Clubs' Volunteers: Bonding in or Bridging Out?," *Sociology* 47 (2012): 350–67.

104. "Education Longitudinal Study of 2002 (ELS: 2002)," U.S. Department of Education Institute of Education Sciences National Center for Education Statistics, last modified August 2015, http://nces.ed.gov/surveys/els2002/.

105. Ashley Mikulyuk, Adrienne N. Milner, and Jomills Henry Braddock II, "Public Perceptions of Title IX: Evidence from a Recent National Poll" (paper presented at the annual meeting for the Southern Sociological Society, New Orleans, LA, March 21–24, 2012).

106. See "Stop and Frisk Facts," The New York Civil Liberties Union, accessed August 31, 2015, http://www.nyclu.org/node/1598.

107. Love and Kelly, "Equity or Essentialism?," 246.

Chapter Seven

1. Dennis Dodd, "California Passes Student-Athlete Bill of Rights," *CBS Sports*, last modified October 9, 2012, http://www.cbssports.com/collegefootball/writer /dennis-dodd/20525847/california-passes student-athlete-bill-of-rights.

2. Brian Bennet, "Northwestern Players Get Union Vote," *ESPN*, last modified March 27, 2014, http://espn.go.com/college-football/story/_/id/10677763/north western-wildcats-football-players-win-bid-unionize.

3. Joe Nocera, "Let's Start Paying College Athletes," *The New York Times Magazine*, last modified December 30, 2011, http://www.nytimes.com/2012/01/01 /magazine/lets-start-paying-college-athletes.html.

4. Victor Lipman, "Why Considering College Athletes Pro Athletes Is a Really Bad Idea," *Forbes*, last modified April 1, 2014, http://www.forbes.com/sites/victorlipman /2014/04/01/why-considering-college-athletes-pro-athletes-is-a-really-bad-idea/.

5. Clotilde Talleu, "Access for Girls and Women to Sport Practices," Counsel of Europe, last modified September 2011, http://www.coe.int/t/DG4/EPAS/Publications/Handbook_2%20_Gender_equality_in_sport.pdf.

6. "Sport and Gender: Empowering Girls and Women," United Nations, accessed July 7, 2015, http://www.un.org/wcm/webdav/site/sport/shared/sport/SDP%20 IWG/Chapter4_SportandGender.pdf (X) guide for improving women's access to and experience within sport.

7. Talleu, "Access"; United Nations, "Sport and Gender."

8. Newman Wadesango et al., "Nature and Effects of Women's Participation in Sporting Decision-Making Structures in the Context of the 2010 FIFA World Cup," *Agenda: Empowering Women for Gender Equity* 24 (2011): 62–75.

9. Donald Sabo and Philip Veliz, "The Decade of Decline: Gender Equity in High School Sports," Women's Sports Foundation, last modified October 8, 2012, http:// irwg.research.umich.edu/pdf/OCR.pdf.

10. Larena Hoeber, "Gender Equity for Athletes: Multiple Understandings of an Organizational Value," *Sex Roles* 58 (2007): 58–71; Leanne Norman, "The Impact of an 'Equal Opportunities' Ideological Framework on Coaches' Knowledge and Practice," *International Review for the Sociology of Sport* (2015): 1–30.

11. Lauren Rauscher and Cheryl Cooky, "Ready for Anything the World Gives Her? A Critical Look at Sports-Based Positive Youth Development for Girls," *Sex Roles* (2015), DOI: 10.1007/211199-014-0400-x.

12. "NCAA Women's Basketball Adopts New Rules, Including Four 10-Min. Quarters," NCAA, last modified June 10, 2015, http://www.ncaa.com/news /basketball-women/article/2015-06-08/ncaa-womens-basketball-adopts-new -rules-including-four-10.

13. Nicole Auerbach, "NCAA Adopts Men's Basketball Rules, Including Shorter Short Clock," *USA Today*, last modified June 8, 2015, http://www.usatoday.com /story/sports/ncaab/2015/06/08/rules-changes-mens-basketball-shot-clock -timeouts/28697577/.

14. Kevin Patra, "NFL Moves Extra Point to 15-Yard Line for 2015 Season," *NFL*, last modified May 20, 2015, http://www.nfl.com/news/story/0ap3000000493347 /article/nfl-moves-extra-point-to-15yard-line-for-2015-season.

15. Josh Tinley, "Why Do Boys Play Baseball and Girls Play Softball?," *Midwest Sports Fans*, last modified June 1, 2012, http://www.midwestsportsfans.com/2012 /06/why-do-boys-play-baseball-and-girls-play-softball/.

16. Zacharias Wood, "Administrator Perceptions of Intramural Coed Flag Football Modifications: A Qualitative Analysis" (MS thesis, Louisiana State University, 2014).

17. Harvey Araton, "A Coed Vision of Professional Basketball," *The New York Times*, last modified November 21, 2013, http://www.nytimes.com/2013/11/22 /sports/basketball/novel-league-would-insert-gender-into-the-game.html.

18. B. Glenn George, "Fifty/Fifty: Ending Sex Segregation in School Sports," *Ohio State Law Journal* 63 (2002): 1107–64.

19. Ivo van Hilvoorde, Agnes Elling, and Ruud Stokvis, "How to Influence National Pride? The Olympic Medal Index as a Unifying Narrative," *International Review for the Sociology of Sport* 45 (2010): 87–102.

20. Peter Donnelly and Michele K. Donnelly, "The London 2012 Olympics: A Gender Equality Audit," Center for Sport Policy Studies, last modified September 2013, http://physical.utoronto.ca/docs/csps-pdfs/donnelly-donnelly---olympic-gender-equality-report.pdf, 5–6.

21. "Approved FIH and USA Field Hockey Protective Eyewear," USA Field Hockey, last modified April 22, 2011, http://www.teamusa.org/USA-Field-Hockey/Features/2011/April/22/Approved-FIH-and-USA-Field-Hockey-protective-eyewear.aspx.

22. Donnelly and Donnelly, "London 2012 Olympics," 7.

23. Johanna Adriaanse and Toni Schofield, "The Impact of Gender Quotas on Gender Equality in Sport Governance," *Journal of Sport Management* 28 (2014): 495.

24. "State and Country QuickFacts," The United States Census Bureau, last modified June 8, 2015, http://quickfacts.census.gov/qfd/states/00000.html.

25. Donnelly and Donnelly, "London 2012 Olympics," 5.

26. Abeer Ahmed Alamri, "Participation of Muslim Female Students in Sporting Activities in Australian Public High Schools: The Impact of Religion," *Journal of Muslim Minority Affairs* 33 (2013): 418–29; Kristin Walseth and Kari Fasting, "Islam's View on Physical Activity and Sport: Egyptian Women Interpreting Islam," *International Review for the Sociology of Sport* 38 (2003): 45–60.

27. Ibid.

28. Mikaela J. Dufur and Seth L. Feinberg, "Artificially Restricted Labor Markets and Worker Dignity in Professional Football," *Journal of Contemporary Ethnography* 36 (2007): 505–36.

29. See DraftSite for eligibility requirements, accessed July 22, 2015, http://www.draftsite.com/.

30. Jeroen Schreeder et al., "Sports Participation Among Females from Adolescence to Adulthood," *International Review for the Sociology of Sport* 41 (2006): 413–30.

31. Barrie Thorne, *Gender Play: Girls and Boys in School* (New Brunswick, NJ: Rutgers University Press, 1993).

32. "Mixed Football Age Limit Raised to Under-16s," Club Website, last modified June 26, 2014, http://www.clubwebsite.co.uk/news/2014/06/26/mixed-football-age-limit-raised-to-under-16s/.

33. Adam Love and Kimberly Kelly, "Equity or Essentialism? U.S. Courts and the Legitimation of Girls' Teams in High School Sport," *Gender and Society* 25 (2011): 227–49; Ann Travers, "The Sport Nexus and Gender Injustice," *Studies in Social Justice* 2 (2008): 79–101.

34. Rebecca S. Bigler and Margaret L. Signorella, "Single-Sex Education: New Perspectives and Evidence on a Continuing Controversy," *Sex Roles* 65 (2011): 659–69.

35. Travers, "Sport Nexus," 92–93.

36. Rauscher and Cooky, "Ready for Anything."

37. Love and Kelly, "Equity or Essentialism?," 245–46.

38. Derrick Bell, *Silent Covenants: Brown v. Board of Education and the Unfulfilled Hopes for Racial Reform* (New York: Oxford University Press, 2004).

39. Sabo and Veliz, "Decade of Decline."

40. Rick Eckstein, Dana M. Moss, and Kevin J. Delaney, "Sports Sociology's Still Untapped Potential," *Sociological Forum* 25 (2010): 500–18.

41. For more information on stereotype threat, see ReducingStereotypeThreat .org, last modified June 6, 2009, http://www.reducingstereotypethreat.org/.

42. Núria Puig and Alan Ingham, "Sport and Space: An Outline of the Issue," *International Review for the Sociology of Sport* 28 (1993): 101–6.

43. Janet S. Fink, "Gender and Sex Diversity in Sport Organizations: Concluding Comments," *Sex Roles* 58 (2008): 146–47.

Selected Bibliography

Acosta, Vivian R., and Linda Jean Carpenter. "Women in Sport." In *Sport and Higher Education*, edited by Donald Chu, Jeffrey O. Segrave, and Beverly J. Becker, 313–25. Champaign, IL: Human Kinetics, 1985.

Adams, Catherine, Matthew Ashton, Hannah Lupton, and Hanne Pollack. "Sport Is King: An Investigation into Local Media Coverage of Women's Sport in the UK East Midlands." *Journal of Gender Studies* 23 (2014): 422–39.

Adams, Natalie, Alison Schmitke, and Amy Franklin. "Tomboys, Dykes, and Girly Girls: Interrogating the Subjectivities of Adolescent Female Athletes." *Women's Studies Quarterly* 33 (2005): 18–34.

Adriaanse, Johanna, and Toni Schofield. "The Impact of Gender Quotas on Gender Equality in Sport Governance." *Journal of Sport Management* 28 (2014): 485–97.

Alamri, Abeer Ahmed. "Participation of Muslim Female Students in Sporting Activities in Australian Public High Schools: The Impact of Religion." *Journal of Muslim Minority Affairs* 33 (2013): 418–29.

Alexander, Lisa Doris. "Race on First, Class on Second, Gender on Third, and Sexuality up to Bat: Intersectionality and Power in Major League Baseball, 1995–2005." PhD diss., Bowling Green State University, 2006.

Alley, Thomas R., and Catherine M. Hicks. "Peer Attitudes toward Adolescent Participants in Male and Female Oriented Sports." *Adolescence* 40 (2005): 273–80.

Anderson, Deborah J., John J. Cheslock, and Ronald G. Ehrenberg. "Gender Equity in Intercollegiate Athletics: Determinants of Title IX Compliance." *Journal of Higher Education* 77 (2006): 225–50.

Anderson, Eric. "'Being Masculine Is Not about Who You Sleep with . . .': Masculinity and the One-Time Rule of Homosexuality." *Sex Roles* 58 (2007): 104–15.

Anderson, Eric. "'I Used to Think Women Were Weak': Orthodox Masculinity, Gender Segregation, and Sport." *Sociological Forum* 23 (2008): 257–80.

Anderson, Eric. "Orthodox and Inclusive Masculinity: Competing Masculinities among Heterosexual Men in a Feminized Terrain." *Sociological Perspectives* 48 (2005): 337–55.

Anderson, Eric. "Updating the Outcome: Gay Athletes, Straight Teams, and Coming Out in Educationally Based Sport Teams." *Gender and Society* 25 (2011): 250–68.

Anderson, James D. *The Education of Blacks in the South 1860–1935*. Chapel Hill: University of North Carolina Press, 1988.

Anderson, Matthew R., Susan Moscou, Celestine Fulchon, and Daniel R. Neuspiel. "The Role of Race in the Clinical Presentation." *Family Medicine* 33 (2001): 430–34.

Appleby, Karen M., and Elaine Foster. "Gender and Sports Participation." In *Gender Relations in Sport*, edited by Emily A. Roper, 1–20. The Netherlands: Sense Publishers.

Artinger, Lori, Lisa Clapham, Carla Hunt, Matthew Meigs, Nadia Milord, Bryan Sampson, and Scott A. Forrester. "The Social Benefits of Intramural Sports." *NASPA Journal* 43 (2006): 69–86.

Bachin, Robin, Jan Sokol-Katz, and Jomills H. Braddock II. "Sport and Violence in American History." In *The Encyclopedia of Violence in the U.S.*, edited by Eric Foner. New York: Macmillan, 1999.

Baker, Elizabeth H., Michael S. Rendall, and Margaret M. Weden. "Epidemiological Paradox or Immigrant Vulnerability? Obesity Among Young Children of Immigrants." *Demography* 52 (2015): 1295–320.

Barnett, Lynn, and John J. Weber. "Perceived Benefits to Children from Participating in Different Types of Recreational Activities." *Journal of Park and Recreation Administration* 26 (2008): 1–20.

Bell, Derrick. *Silent Covenants: Brown v. Board of Education and the Unfulfilled Hopes for Racial Reform*. New York: Oxford University Press, 2004.

Bell, Derrick. *Faces at the Bottom of the Well: The Permanence of Racism*. New York: Basic Books, 1992.

Berenbaum, Sheri A., Judith E. Owen Blakemore, and Adriene M. Beltz. "A Role for Biology in Gender-Related Behavior." *Sex Roles* 64 (2011): 804–25.

Best, Deborah L. "Another View of the Gender-Status Relation." *Sex Roles* 61 (2009): 341–51.

Bigler, Rebecca S., and Margaret L. Signorella. "Single-Sex Education: New Perspectives and Evidence on a Continuing Controversy." *Sex Roles* 65 (2011): 659–69.

Bird, Anne Marie. "Nonreactive Research: Applications for Sociological Analysis of Sport." *International Review for the Sociology of Sport* 11 (1976): 83–89.

Birke, Lynda, and Gail Vines. "A Sporting Chance: The Anatomy of Destiny?" *Women's Studies International Forum* 10 (1987): 337–58.

Blakemore, Judith E. Owen, and Renee E. Centers. "Characteristics of Boys' and Girls' Toys." *Sex Roles* 53 (2005): 619–33.

Blinde, Elaine M., and Diane E. Taub. "Women Athletes as Falsely Accused Deviants: Managing the Lesbian Stigma." *The Sociological Quarterly* 33 (1992): 521–33.

Bloch, Herman D. *The Circle of Discrimination: An Economic and Social Study of the Black Man in New York*. New York: New York University Press, 1969.

Blumer, Herber. "Race Prejudice as a Sense of Group Position." *Pacific Sociological Review* 1 (1958): 37.

Bobo, Lawrence D., James R. Kluegel, and Ryan A. Smith. "Laissez-Faire Racism: The Crystallization of a Kinder, Gentler Antiblack Ideology." In *Racial Attitudes in the 1990s: Continuity and Change*, edited by Steven A. Tuch and Jack K. Martin, 15–44. Westport, CT: Praeger, 1997.

Bonilla-Silva, Eduardo. *Racism Without Racists: Color-Blind Racism and the Persistence of Racial Inequality in the United States*. New York: Rowman and Littlefield, 2003.

Bonilla-Silva, Eduardo. *White Supremacy and Racism in the Post-Civil Rights Era*. Boulder, CO: Lynne Rienner Publishers, 2001.

Bordo, Susan. "Pills and Power Tools." *Men and Masculinities* 1 (1998): 87–90.

Bouffard, Suzanne, Christopher Wimer, Pia Caronongan, Priscilla Little, Eric Dearing, and Sandra Simpkins. "Demographic Differences in Patterns of Youth Out-of-School Time Activity Participation." *Journal of Youth Development* 1 (2006): 24–39.

Bowker, Anne, Shannon Gadbois, and Becki Cornock. "Sports Participation and Self-Esteem: Variations as a Function of Gender and Gender Role Orientation." *Sex Roles* 49 (2003): 47–58.

Braathen, Eli Torild, and Sven Svebak. "Motivational Differences among Talented Teenage Athletes: The Significance of Gender, Type of Sport and Level of Excellence." *Scandinavian Journal of Medicine* 2 (2007): 153–59.

Braddock II, Jomills Henry. "Sport and Race Relations in American Society." *Sociological Symposium* 9 (1989): 53–76.

Braddock II, Jomills Henry, Christine Sanchez-Weston, Adrienne N. Milner, Ashley Mikulyuk, and Marvin Dawkins. "Gender Diversity and U.S. Olympic Team Success at the 2012 London Games." Paper presentation at the annual meetings for the Southern Sociological Society, Atlanta, GA, April 24–27, 2013.

Braddock II, Jomills Henry, Jan H. Sokol-Katz, Anthony Greene, and Lorrine Basinger-Fleischman. "Uneven Playing Fields: State Variations in Boy's and Girl's Access to and Participation in High School Interscholastic Sports." *Sociological Spectrum* 25 (2005): 231–50.

Brake, Deborah L. *Getting in the Game: Title IX and the Women's Sports Revolution*. New York: New York University Press, 2010.

Brinkman, Britney G., and Kathryn M. Rickard. "College Students' Descriptions of Everyday Gender Prejudice." *Sex Roles* 61 (2009): 461–75.

Broh, Beckett A. "Dumb Jock or Student Athlete? A Longitudinal Analysis of the Effects of Playing High School Interscholastic Sports on Academic Performance." Master's thesis, The Ohio State University, 1999.

Brown, Jill, and Gordon Bear. "Minorities in Major League Baseball 1952–1987." *International Review for the Sociology of Sport* 34 (1999): 411–22.

Brown, Michael K., Martin Carnoy, Elliott Currie, Troy Duster, David B. Oppen-
heimer, Marjorie M. Schultz, and David Wellman. *Whitewashing Race: The
Myth of a Color-Blind Society.* Berkeley: University of California Press, 2003.
Browne, Beverly A., and Sally K. Francis. "Participants in School-Sponsored and
Independent Sports: Perceptions of Self and Family." *Adolescence* 28 (1993):
383–91.
Budhwani, Henna, Kristine Ria Hearld, and Daniel Chavez-Yenter. "Depression in
Racial and Ethnic Minorities: The Impact of Nativity and Discrimination."
Journal of Racial and Ethnic Health Disparities 2 (2015): 34–42.
Bunji, Sawanobori. "Brown v. Board of Education: Its Continuing Significance."
Nanzan Review of American Studies 26 (2004): 27–41.
Burke, Michael. "Women's Standpoints and Internalism in Sport." *Journal of the Phi-
losophy of Sport* 41 (2013): 39–52.
Burr, Brianne L. "Do Extracurricular Activities Help Adolescents Develop Academic
Self-Efficacy? Evidence for How and Why." MA thesis, Brigham Young Uni-
versity, 2012.
Burton, Laura J., Carol A. Barr, Janet S. Fink, and Jennifer E. Bruening. "'Think
Athletic Director, Think Masculine?': Examination of the Gender Typing of
Managerial Subroles within Athletic Administration Positions." *Sex Roles* 61
(2009): 416–26.
Butler, Judith. *Gender Trouble: Feminism and the Subversion of Identity.* New York:
Routledge, 2006.
Buzuvis, Erin E. "Transgender Student-Athletes and Sex-Segregated Sport: Devel-
oping Policies of Inclusion for Intercollegiate and Interscholastic Athletics."
Seton Hall Journal of Sports and Entertainment Law 21 (2011): 1–59.
Cağlar, Emine. "Similarities and Differences in Physical Self-Concept of Males and
Females During Late Adolescence and Early Adulthood." *Adolescence* 44
(2009): 407–19.
Cancian, Francesca M. "The Feminization of Love." *Signs* 11 (1983): 692–709.
Carmichael, Stokely, and Charles V. Hamilton. *Black Power: The Politics of Libera-
tion in America.* New York: Random House, 1967.
Carr, Benjamin P. "Can Separate Be Equal? Single-Sex Classrooms, the Constitu-
tion, and Title IX." *Notre Dame Law Review* 83 (2007): 409–42.
Carr, C. Lynn. "Where Have All the Tomboys Gone? Women's Accounts of Gender
in Adolescence." *Sex Roles* 56 (2007): 439–48.
Castillo, Isabel, Joan L. Duda, Isabel Balaguer, and Inés Thomás. "Cross-Domain
Generality of Achievement Motivation across Sport and the Classroom: The
Case of Spanish Adolescents." *Adolescence* 44 (2009): 569–80.
Castine, Sandra C., and Glyn C. Roberts. "Modeling in the Socialization Process
of the Black Athlete." *International Review for the Sociology of Sport* 9 (1974):
59–74.
Chae, David H., Sean Clouston, Mark L. Hatzenbuehler, Michael R. Kramer, Han-
nah L. F. Cooper, Sacoby M. Wilson, Seth I. Stephens-Davidowitz, Robert S.
Gold, and Bruce G. Link. "Association between an Internet-Based Measure

of Area Racism and Black Mortality." *PLoS One* 10 (2015). DOI: 10.1371/journal.pone.0122963.

Chae, David H., Karen D. Lincoln, Nancy E. Adler, and S. Leonard Syme. "Do Experiences of Racial Discrimination Predict Cardiovascular Disease among African American Men? The Moderating Role of Internalized Negative Racial Group Attitudes." *Social Science & Medicine* 71 (2010): 1182–88.

Chae, David H., Amani M. Nuru-Jeter, Nancy E. Adler, Gene H. Brody, Jue Lin, Elizabeth H. Blackburn, and Elissa S. Epel. "Discrimination, Racial Bias, and Telomere Length in African-American Men." *American Journal of Preventive Medicine* 46 (2014): 103–11.

Chimot, Caroline, and Catherine Louveau. "Becoming a Man While Playing a Female Sport: The Construction of Masculine Identity in Boys Doing Rhythmic Gymnastics." *International Review for the Sociology of Sport* 45 (2010): 436–56.

Chiweshe, Manase. "One of the Boys: Female Fans' Responses to the Masculine and Phallocentric Nature of Football Stadiums in Zimbabwe." *Critical African Studies* 6 (2014): 211–22.

Chomitz, Virginia R., Meghan M. Slining, Robert J. McGowan, Suzanne E. Mitchell, Glen F. Dawson, and Karen A. Hacker. "Is There a Relationship Between Physical Fitness, and Academic Achievement? Positive Results from Public School Children in the Northeastern United States." *Journal of School Health* 79 (2009): 30–37.

Clark, Kenneth B. "The *Brown* Decision: Racism, Education, and Human Values." *Journal of Negro Education* 57 (1988): 125–32.

Clark, Kenneth B. "Some Principles Related to the Problem of Desegregation." *Journal of Negro Education* 23 (1954): 339–47.

Clark, Sheryl. "Being 'Good at Sport': Talent, Ability and Young Women's Sporting Participation." *Sociology* 46 (2012): 1178–93.

Clayton, Ben, and Barbara Humberstone. "Men's Talk: A (Pro)feminist Analysis of Male University Football Players' Discourse." *International Review for the Sociology of Sport* 41 (2006): 295–316.

Clement, Dorothy, Margaret Eisenhart, and John R. Wood. "School Desegregation and Educational Inequality: Trends in the Literature 1960–1975." In *The Desegregation Literature: A Critical Appraisal*, edited by David Mathews, Harold L. Hodgkinson, Harold Delany, and Ray C. Rist, 1–77. Washington, D.C.: National Institute of Education, 1976.

Clément-Guillotin, Corentin, and Paul Fontayne. "Situational Malleability of Gender Schema: The Case of the Competitive Sport Context." *Sex Roles* 64 (2010): 426–39.

Coakley, Jay. "The Good Father: Parental Expectations and Youth Sports." *Leisure Studies* 25 (2006): 153–63.

Coakley, Jay. "The Sociological Perspective: Alternative Causations of Violence in Sport." *Arena* 5 (1981): 44–56.

Coakley, Jay. *Sports in Society: Issues and Controversies*, 10th edition. Boston, MA: McGraw Hill, 2009.

Coleman, James S., Ernest Q. Campbell, Carol J. Hobson, James McPartland, Alexander M. Mood, Frederic D. Weinfeld, and Robert York. *Equality of Educational Opportunity*. Washington, D.C.: U.S. Government Printing Office, 1966.

Collins, Patricia Hill. *Black Feminist Thought: Knowledge, Consciousness and the Politics of Empowerment*. New York: Routledge, 1991.

Combahee River Collective Staff. *The Combahee River Collective Statement: Black Feminist Organizing in the Seventies and Eighties*. Brooklyn: Kitchen Table/Women of Color Press, 1986.

Connell, Raewyn. "Masculinity Construction and Sports in Boys' Education: A Framework for Thinking about the Issue." *Sport, Education and Society* 13 (2008): 131–45.

Cooky, Cheryl. "Strong Enough to Be a Man, but Made a Woman: Discourses of Sports and Femininity in *Sports Illustrated for Women*." In *Sexual Sports Rhetoric*, edited by Linda K. Fuller, 97–106. New York: Haworth Press, 2006.

Cooky, Cheryl, and Shari L. Dworkin. "Policing the Boundaries of Sex: A Critical Examination of Gender Verification and the Caster Semenya Controversy." *Journal of Sex Research* 50 (2013): 103–11.

Cooky, Cheryl, and Mary G. McDonald. "'If You Let Me Play': Young Girls' Insider-Other Narratives of Sport." *Sociology of Sport Journal* 22 (2005): 158–77.

Cooky, Cheryl, Michael A. Messner, and Michela Musto. "'It's Dude Time!': A Quarter Century of Excluding Women's Sports in Televised Sports News and Highlight Shows." *Communication and Sport* 3 (2015): 261–87.

Cooper, Richard S., Charles N. Rotimi, Jay S. Kaufman, Eme E. Owoaje, Henry Fraser, Terrence Forrester, Rainford Wilks, Lisa K. Riste, and J. Kennedy Cruickshank. "Prevalence of NIDDM among Populations of the African Diaspora." *Diabetes Care* 20 (1997): 343–48.

Cottler, Linda B., Arbi Ben Abdallah, Simone M. Cummings, John Barr, Rayna Banks, and Ronnie Forchheimer. "Injury, Pain, and Prescription Opioid Use among Former National Football League (NFL) Players." *Drug and Alcohol Dependence* 116 (2011): 188–94.

Courtenay, Will H. "Constructions of Masculinity and Their Influence on Men's Well Being: A Theory of Gender and Health." *Social Science and Medicine* 50 (2000): 1385–401.

Cox, Charles. "Investigating the Prevalence and Risk-Factors of Depression Symptoms among NCAA Division I Collegiate Athletes." MS thesis, Southern Illinois University Edwardsville, 2015.

Coyne, Sarah M., Jennifer Ruh Linder, Eric E. Rasmussen, David A. Nelson, and Kevin M. Collier. "It's a Bird! It's a Plane! It's a Gender Stereotype!: Longitudinal Associations Between Superhero Viewing and Gender Stereotyped Play." *Sex Roles* 70 (2014): 416–30.

Crawford, Garry, and Victoria K. Gosling. "The Myth of the 'Puck Bunny': Female Fans and Men's Ice Hockey." *Sociology* 38 (2004): 477–93.

Crenshaw, Kimberle, Neil Gotanda, Gary Peller, and Kendall Thomas (eds). *Critical Race Theory: The Key Writings That Formed the Movement.* New York: New Press, 1988.

Crosset, Todd W., Jeffrey R. Benedict, and Mark A. McDonald. "Male Student-Athletes Reported for Sexual Assault: A Survey of Campus Police Departments and Judicial Affairs Offices." *Journal of Sport and Social Issues* 19 (1995): 126–40.

Crosset, Todd W., James Ptacek, Mark A. McDonald, and Jeffrey R. Benedict. "Male Student Athletes and Violence Against Women: A Survey of Campus Judicial Affairs Offices," *Violence Against Women* 2 (1996): 163–79.

Cunningham, George B., Kathi Miner, and Jennifer McDonald. "Being Different and Suffering the Consequences: The Influence of Head Coach–Player Racial Dissimilarity on Experienced Incivility." *International Review for the Sociology of Sport* 48 (2013): 689–705.

Cunningham, George B., and Michael R. Regan. "Political Activism, Racial Identity and the Commercial Endorsement of Athletes: Athlete Activism." *International Review for the Sociology of Sport* 47 (2011): 657–69.

Daniel, Philip T. K. "The Not So Strange Path of Desegregation in America's Public Schools." *Negro Educational Review* 56 (2005): 57–66.

Daniels, Elizabeth, and Campbell Leaper. "A Longitudinal Investigation of Sport Participation, Peer Acceptance, and Self-Esteem Among Adolescent Girls and Boys." *Sex Roles* 55 (2006): 875–80.

Daniels, Elizabeth A., and Heidi Wartena. "Athlete or Sex Symbol: What Boys Think of Media Representations of Female Athletes." *Sex Roles* 65 (2011): 566–79.

Davis-Delano, Laurel R., April Pollock, and Jennifer Ellsworth Vose. "Apologetic Behavior among Female Athletes: A New Questionnaire and Initial Results." *International Review for the Sociology of Sport* 44 (2009): 131–50.

Dees, A. Jerome. "Access or Interest: Why Brown Has Benefited African-American Women More Than Title IX." *University of Missouri Kansas City Law Review* 76 (2008): 625–42.

Deianey, Wendy, and Christina Lee. "Self-Esteem and Sex Roles among Male and Female High School Students: Their Relationship to Physical Activity." *Australian Psychologist* 30 (1995): 84–87.

Del Rio, M. Francisca, and Katherine Strasser. "Preschool Children's Beliefs about Gender Differences in Academic Skills." *Sex Roles* 68 (2012): 231–38.

Delsahut, Fabrice, and Thierry Terret. "First Nations Women, Games, and Sport in Pre-and Post-Colonial North America." *Women's History Review* 23 (2014): 976–95.

DiDonato, Lisa, and JoNell Strough. "Contextual Influences on Gender Segregation in Emerging Adulthood." *Sex Roles* 69 (2013): 632–43.

Diefenbeck, Cythnia, Barret Michalec, and Robbi Alexander. "Lived Experiences of Racially and Ethnically Underrepresented Minority BSN Students: A Case

Study Specifically Exploring Issues Related to Recruitment and Retention." *Nursing Education Perspectives* (2015). DOI: http://dx.doi.org/10.5480/13 -1183.

Dill, Karen, and Kathryn Thill. "Video Game Characters and the Socialization of Gender Roles: Young People's Perceptions Mirror Sexist Media Depictions." *Sex Roles* 57 (2007): 851–64.

Dodd, Elizabeth H., Traci A. Giuliano, Jori M. Boutell, and Brooke E. Moran. "Respected or Rejected: Perceptions of Women Who Confront Sexist Remarks." *Sex Roles* 45 (2001): 567–77.

Dodge, Tonya, and James Jaccard. "Participation in Athletics and Female Sexual Risk Behavior: The Evaluation of Four Causal Structures." *Journal of Adolescent Research* 17 (2002): 42–67.

Doey, Laura, Robert J. Coplan, and Mila Kingsbury. "Bashful Boys and Coy Girls: A Review of Gender Differences in Childhood Shyness." *Sex Roles* 70 (2014): 255–66.

Donaldson, Sarah J., and Kevin R. Ronan. "The Effects of Sports Participation on Young Adolescents' Emotional Well-Being." *Adolescence* 41 (2006): 369–89.

Donnelly, Peter, and Michele K. Donnelly. "The London 2012 Olympics: A Gender Equality Audit." Center for Sport Policy Studies. Last modified September 2013. http://physical.utoronto.ca/docs/csps-pdfs/donnelly-donnelly---olympic -gender-equality-report.pdf.

Dreber, Anna, Emma von Essen, and Eva Ranehill. "Outrunning the Gender Gap— Boys and Girls Compete Equally." *Experimental Economics* 14 (2011): 567–82.

Dufur, Mikaela. "Race Logic and 'Being Like Mike': Representations of Athletes in Advertising 1985–1994." *Sociological Focus* 30 (1997): 345–56.

Dufur, Mikaela J. "Race and the NFL Draft: Views from the Auction Block." *Qualitative Sociology* 32 (2009): 53–73.

Dufur, Mikaela J., and Seth L. Feinberg. "Artificially Restricted Labor Markets and Worker Dignity in Professional Football." *Journal of Contemporary Ethnography* 36 (2007): 505–36.

Dundes, Alan. "Into the Endzone for a Touchdown: A Psychoanalytic Consideration of American Football." *Western Folklore* 37 (1978): 75–88.

Dworkin, Jodi B., Reed Larson, and David Hansen. "Adolescents' Accounts of Growth Experiences in Youth Activities." *Journal of Youth and Adolescence* 32 (2003): 17–26.

Dworkin, Shari L. "'Holding Back': Negotiating a Glass Ceiling on Women's Muscular Strength." *Sociological Perspectives* 44 (2001): 333–50.

Dworkin, Shari L., and Cheryl Cooky. "Sport, Sex Segregation, and Sex Testing: Critical Reflections on This Unjust Marriage." *American Journal of Bioethics* 12 (2012): 1–3.

Dworkin, Shari L., Amanda Lock Swarr, and Cheryl Cooky. "(In)Justice in Sport: The Treatment of South African Track Star Caster Semenya." *Feminist Studies* 39 (2013): 40–69.

Eccles, Jacquelynne S., Bonnie L. Barber, Margaret Stone, and James Hunt. "Extra-curricular Activities and Adolescent Development." *Journal of Social Issues* 59 (2003): 865–89.

Eccles, Jacquelynne S., and Rena D. Harold. "Gender Differences in Sport Involvement: Applying the Eccles' Expectancy-Value Model." *Journal of Applied Sport Psychology* 3 (1991): 7–35.

Eckstein, Rick, Dana M. Moss, and Kevin J. Delaney. "Sports Sociology's Still Untapped Potential." *Sociological Forum* 25 (2010): 500–18.

Eder, Donna, and David A. Kinney. "The Effect of Middle School Extra Curricular Activities on Adolescents' Popularity and Peer Status." *Youth and Society* 26 (1995): 298–324.

Edwards, Harry. *The Revolt of the Black Athlete*. New York: Free Press, 1969.

Eime, Rochelle, Jack T. Harvey, Wendy J. Brown, and Warren Payne. "Does Sports Club Participation Contribute to Health-Related Quality of Life?" *Medicine and Science in Sports and Exercise* 42 (2010): 1022–28.

Eitle, Tamela McNulty. "Do Gender and Race Matter? Explaining the Relationship between Sports Participation and Achievement." *Sociological Spectrum* 25 (2005): 177–95.

Eitzen, D. Stanley. "Upward Mobility through Sport? Myths and Realities." In *Sport in Contemporary Society: An Anthology*, 6th edition, edited by D. Stanley Eitzen, 256–63. New York: Worth Publishers, 1999.

English, Ashley. "Restoring Equal Opportunity in Education: An Analysis of Arguments for and Against the Bush Administration Single-Sex Education Regulations." *Institute for Women's Policy Research*. Last modified July 30, 2009. http://files.eric.ed.gov/fulltext/ED556716.pdf.

Epstein, Joyce L. "After the Bus Arrives: Desegregation in Desegregated Schools." *Journal of Social Issues* 41 (1985): 23–43.

Fausto-Sterling, Anne. "The Five Sexes, Revisited." *The Sciences* 40 (2000): 18–23.

Fausto-Sterling, Anne. "The Five Sexes: Why Male and Female Are Not Enough." *The Sciences* 33 (1993): 20–24.

Fausto-Sterling, Anne. "Nature." In *Critical Terms for the Study of Gender*, edited by Catherine R. Stimpson and Gilbert Herdt, 295–315. Chicago: University of Chicago Press, 2014.

Fausto-Sterling, Anne. *Sex/Gender: Biology in a Social World*. New York: Routledge, 2012.

Feagin, Joe R. *Systemic Racism: A Theory of Oppression*. New York: Routledge, 2006.

Fejgin, Naomi. "Participation in High School Competitive Sports: A Subversion of School Mission or Contribution to Academic Goals?" *Sociology of Sport Journal* 11 (1995): 211–30.

Feldman, Amy F., and Jennifer L. Matjasko. "The Role of School-Based Extracurricular Activities in Adolescent Development: A Comprehensive Review and Future Directions." *Review of Educational Research* 75 (2005): 159–210.

Fields, Sarah K. "Hoover v. Meiklejohn: The Equal Protection Clause, Girls, and Soccer." *Journal of Sport History* 30 (2003): 309–21.

Fink, Janet. "Challenging the Gender Binary: Male Practice Players' Views of Female Athletes and Women's Sports." Paper presented at the annual meeting for the North American Society for Sport Management, Tampa, Florida, June 1–6, 2010.

Fink, Janet S. "Gender and Sex Diversity in Sport Organizations: Concluding Comments." *Sex Roles* 58 (2008): 146–47.

Fishel, Andrew, and Janice Pottker. *National Politics and Sex Discrimination in Education.* Lexington, MA: Lexington Books, 1977.

Flake, Collin R., Mikaela J. Dufur, and Erin L. Moore. "Advantage Men: The Sex Pay Gap in Professional Tennis." *International Review for the Sociology of Sport* 48 (2012): 366–76.

Foddy, Bennett, and Julian Savulescu. "Time to Re-Evaluate Gender Segregation in Athletics?" *British Journal of Sports Medicine* 45 (2011): 1184–88.

Foley, Douglas E. "The Great American Football Ritual: Reproducing Race, Class, and Gender Inequality." *Sociology of Sport Journal* 7 (1990): 111–35.

Foley, Douglas E. "Rethinking School Ethnographies of Colonial Settings: A Performance Perspective of Reproduction and Resistance." *Comparative Education Review* (1991): 532–51.

Forman, Tyrone A. "Color-Blind Racism and Racial Indifference: The Role of Racial Apathy in Facilitating Enduring Inequalities." In *The Changing Terrain of Race and Ethnicity*, edited by Maria Krysan and Amanda Lewis, 43–66. New York: Russel Sage, 2004.

Forseth, Renee, Jennifer Karam, and Eric J. Sobocinski. "Progress in Gender Equity: An Overview of the History and Future of Title IX of the Education Amendments Act of 1972." *Villanova Sports and Entertainment Law Forum* 2 (1995): 51–98.

Fox, Claudia K., Daheia Barr-Anderson, Dianne Neumark-Sztainer, and Melanie Wall. "Physical Activity and Sports Team Participation: Associations with Academic Outcomes in Middle School and High School Students." *Journal of School Health* 80 (2010): 31–37.

Friedl, Ernestine. "Society and Sex Roles." *Human Nature* 1 (1978): 8–75.

Fritner, Mary Pat, and Laurna Rubinson. "Acquaintance Rape: The Influence of Alcohol, Fraternity Membership and Sports Team Membership." *Journal of Sex Education and Therapy* 19 (1993): 272–84.

Gazelle, Heidi, Divya Peter, and Maedeh Aboutalebi Karkavandi. "Commentary: Bashful Boys and Coy Girls: A Review of Gender Differences in Childhood Shyness." *Sex Roles* 70 (2014): 285–308.

George, B. Glenn "Fifty/Fifty: Ending Sex Segregation in School Sports." *Ohio State Law Journal* 63 (2002): 1107–64.

Gerard, Harold B. "School Desegregation: The Social Science Role." *American Psychologist* 38 (1983): 869–77.

Gibbs, Benjamin G., Lance D. Erickson, Mikaela J. Dufur, and Aaron Miles. "Extracurricular Associations and College Enrollment." *Social Science Research* 50 (2015): 367–81.

Glenn, Evelyn Nakano. *Unequal Freedom: How Race and Gender Shaped American Citizenship and Labor.* Cambridge, MA: Harvard University Press, 2002.

Goble, Priscilla, Carol Lynn Martin, Laura D. Hanish, and Richard A. Fabes. "Children's Gender-Typed Activity Choices Across Preschool Social Contexts." *Sex Roles* 67 (2012): 435–51.

Goldschmied, Nadav, and Jason Kowalczyk. "Gender Performance in the NCAA Rifle Championships: Where Is the Gap?" *Sex Roles* 71 (2014): 1–13.

Goldsmith, Pat António. "Race Relations and Racial Patterns in School Sports Participation." *Sociology of Sport Journal* 20 (2003): 147–71.

Graves, Fatima Goss, Neena Chaudhry, Katharine Gallagher Robbins, Anne Morrison, Lauren Frohlich, Adaku Onyeka-Crawford, Philip Tegeler, Michael Hilton, and Silva Mathema. "Finishing Last: Girls of Color and School Sports Opportunities." National Women's Law Center and Poverty and Race Research Action Council. Last modified April, 2015. http://www.nwlc.org/sites/default/files/pdfs/final_nwlc_girlsfinishinglast_report.pdf.

Green, B. Christine. "Building Sport Programs to Optimize Athlete Recruitment, Retention, and Transition: Toward a Normative Theory of Sport Development." *Journal of Sport Management* 19 (2005): 233–53.

Grieser, Mira, Dianne Neumark-Sztainer, Brit I. Saksvig, Jung-Sun Lee, Gwen M. Felton, and Martha Y. Kubik. "Black, Hispanic, and White Girls' Perceptions of Environmental and Social Support and Enjoyment of Physical Activity." *Journal of School Health* 78 (2008): 314–20.

Griffin, Pat. *Strong Women, Deep Closets: Lesbians and Homophobia in Sport.* Champaign, IL: Human Kinetics, 1998.

Grundlingh, Marizanne. "Boobs and Balls: Exploring Issues of Gender and Identity among Women Soccer Players at Stellenbosch University." *Agenda* 24 (2010): 45–53.

Hall, Ann M. "How Should We Theorize Sport in a Capitalist Patriarchy?" *International Review for the Sociology of Sport* 20 (1985): 109–16.

Hall, Ronald E. "The Ball Curve: Calculated Racism and the Stereotype of African American Men." *Journal of Black Studies* 32 (2002): 104–19.

Hallinan, Maureen T. "Ability Group Effects on High School Learning Outcomes." Paper presented at the annual meeting of the American Sociological Association, Washington, DC, August 12–15, 2000.

Hämäläinen, Mika. "A Sport with Untapped Potential to Empower Women." *Journal of the Philosophy of Sport* 41 (2013): 53–63.

Hannon, James C., and Thomas Ratliffe. "Physical Activity Levels in Coeducational and Single-Gender High School Physical Education Settings." *Journal of Teaching in Physical Education* 24 (2005): 149–64.

Hansen, David M., Reed W. Larson, and Jodi B. Dworkin. "What Adolescents Learn in Organized Youth Activities: A Survey of Self-Reported Developmental Experiences." *Journal of Research on Adolescence* 13 (2003): 25–55.

Hanson, Sandra L., and Rebecca S. Kraus. "Science Experiences among Female Athletes: Race Makes a Difference." *Journal of Women and Minorities in Science and Engineering* 9 (2003): 287–323.

Hanson, Sandra L., and Rebecca S. Kraus. "Women, Sports, and Science: Do Female Athletes Have an Advantage?" *Sociology of Education* 71 (1998): 93–110.

Hanson, Valarie. "The Inequality of Sport: Women < Men." *Undergraduate Review: A Journal of Undergraduate Student Research* 13 (2013): 15–22.

Hardin, Marie, and Jennifer D. Greer. "The Influence of Gender-Role Socialization, Media Use and Sports Participation on Perceptions of Gender-Appropriate Sports," *Journal of Sport Behavior* 32 (2009): 207–26.

Hardin, Marie, Fuyuan Shen, and Nan Yu. "Sextyping of Sports: The Influence of Gender, Participation, and Mediated Sports Consumption on Responses to Visual Priming." Paper presented at the annual meeting of the Association for Education in Journalism and Mass Communication, Chicago, IL, August 6–9, 2008.

Hardin, Marie, Erin Whiteside, and Erin Ash. "Ambivalence on the Front Lines? Attitudes toward Title IX and Women's Sports among Division I Sports Information Directors." *International Review for the Sociology of Sport* 49 (2014): 42–64.

Hargreaves, Jennifer. *Sporting Females: Critical Issues in the History and Sociology of Women's Sport.* New York: Routledge, 1994.

Hargreaves, Jennifer A. "Gender on the Sports Agenda." *International Review for the Sociology of Sport* 25 (1990): 287–307.

Harrison, Anna C., and Susan A. O'Neill. "Preferences and Children's Use of Gender-Stereotyped Knowledge about Musical Instruments: Making Judgments about Other Children's Preferences." *Sex Roles* 49 (2003): 389–400.

Harrison, Lisa A., and Amanda B. Lynch. "Social Role Theory and the Perceived Gender Role Orientation of Athletes." *Sex Roles* 52 (2005): 227–36.

Harry, Joseph. "Sports Ideology, Attitudes toward Women, and Anti-Homosexual Attitudes." *Sex Roles* 32 (1995): 109–16.

Hattery, Angela J., Earl Smith, and Ellen Staurowsky. "They Play Like Girls: Gender Equity in NCAA Sports." *Journal for the Study of Sports and Athletes in Education* 1 (2007): 249–72.

Henry, Jacques M., and Howard P. Comeaux. "Gender Egalitarianism in Coed Sport a Case Study of American Soccer." *International Review for the Sociology of Sport* 34 (1999): 277–90.

Hilvoorde, Ivo van, Agnes Elling, and Ruud Stokvis. "How to Influence National Pride? The Olympic Medal Index as a Unifying Narrative." *International Review for the Sociology of Sport* 45 (2010): 87–102.

Hines, Ralph H. "Social Expectations and Cultural Deprivation." *Journal of Negro Education* 33 (1964): 136–42.

Ho, Arnold K., Jim Sidanius, Daniel T. Levin, and Mahzarin R. Banaji. "Evidence for Hypodescent and Racial Hierarchy in the Categorization and Perception of Biracial Individuals." *Journal of Personality and Social Psychology* 100 (2011): 492–506.

Hoeber, Larena. "Gender Equity for Athletes: Multiple Understandings of an Organizational Value." *Sex Roles* 58 (2007): 58–71.

Holmes, Morgan. "Re-Membering a Queer Body." *Undercurrents* 6 (1994): 11–13.

Holub, Shayla C., Marie S. Tisak, and David Mullins. "Gender Differences in Children's Hero Attributions: Personal Hero Choices and Evaluations of Typical Male and Female Heroes." *Sex Roles* 58 (2008): 567–78.

hooks, bell. *Feminist Theory: From Margin to Center*. Boston: South End Press, 1984.

hooks, bell. *Talking Back: Thinking Feminist, Thinking Black*. Boston: South End Press, 1989.

Howell, Susan E., Huey L. Perry, and Matthew Vile. "Black Cities/White Cities: Evaluating the Police." *Political Behavior* 26(1): 45–68.

Hoxby, Caroline. "Peer Effects in the Classroom: Learning from Gender and Race Variation." National Bureau of Economic Research. Accessed July 12, 2015, http://www.nber.org/papers/w7867.pdf.

Johnson, Jay. "Are Sisters Doing It for Themselves? An Analysis of Gender and the Sport Initiation Ceremony." *Canadian Woman Studies* 21 (2002): 125–31.

Jones, Randall M., Denise E. Taylor, Andrew J. Dick, Archana Singh, and Jerry L. Cook. "Bedroom Design and Decoration: Gender Differences in Preference and Activity." *Adolescence* 42 (2006): 539–53.

Jordan, Will J. "Black High School Students' Participation in School-Sponsored Sports Activities." *Journal of Negro Education* 68 (1999): 54–71.

Kahn, Lawrence M. "The Economics of Discrimination: Evidence from Basketball." In *The Oxford Handbook of Sports Economics: Volume 2: Economics through Sports*, edited by Stephen Shmanske, and Leo H. Kahane, 21–38. New York: Oxford University Press, 2012.

Kane, Mary Jo. "The Better Sportswomen Get, the More the Media Ignore Them." *Communication and Sport* 1 (2013): 231–36.

Kane, Mary Jo. "The Female Athletic Role as a Status Determinant within the Social Systems of High School Adolescents." *Adolescence* 23 (1988): 253–64.

Kane, Mary Jo, and Eldon E. Snyder. "Sport Typing: The Social Containment of Women in Sport." *Arena Review* 13 (1989): 77–96.

Karkazis, Katrina, and Rebecca Jordan-Young. "Debating a 'Sex Gap' in Testosterone." *Science* 348 (2015): 858–60.

Kaskan, Emily R., and Ivy K. Ho. "Microaggressions and Female Athletes." *Sex Roles* (2014): 1–13.

Kaufman, Jay S., Lena Dolman, Dinela Rushani, and Richard S. Cooper. "The Contribution of Genomic Research to Explaining Racial Disparities in Cardiovascular Disease: A Systematic Review." *American Journal of Epidemiology* 187 (2015): 464–72.

Kaufman, Peter. "Boos, Bans, and Backlash: The Consequences of Being an Activist Athlete." *Humanity and Society* 32 (2008): 215–37.

Kaufman, Peter, and Eli A. Wolff. "Playing and Protesting: Sport as a Vehicle for Social Change." *Journal of Sport and Social Issues* 34 (2010): 154–75.

Kavoura, Anna, Marja Kokkonen, and Tatiana Ryba. "The Female Fighter Phenomenon in Denmark and Greece: Exploring Gender Dynamics in Judo." In *Fighting: Intellectualising Combat Sports*, edited by Keith Gilbert, 87–96. Champaign, IL: Common Ground Publishing, 2014.

Kawachi, Ichiro, Norman Daniels, and Dean E. Robinson. "Health Disparities By Race and Class: Why Both Matter." 24 *Health Affairs* (2005): 343–52.

Khaleberg, Richard D. "From All Walks of Life: New Hope for School Integration," *American Educator* 36 (2013): 2–7, 10–14.

Kidd, Bruce. "The Men's Cultural Center: Sports and the Dynamic of Women's Oppression/Men's Repression." In *Sport, Men and the Gender Order: Critical Feminist Perspectives*, edited by Michael A. Messner and Donald Sabo, 31–42. Champaign, IL: Human Kinetics, 1990.

Kidd, Bruce. "A New Social Movement: Sport for Development and Peace." *Sport in Society* 11 (2008): 370–80.

Kidd, Bruce, and Peter Donnelly. "Human Rights in Sports." *International Review for the Sociology of Sport* 35 (2000): 131–48.

Kinder, Donald R., and David O. Sears. "Prejudice and Politics: Symbolic Racism versus Racial Threats to the Good Life." *Journal of Personality and Social Psychology* 40 (1981): 414–31.

King, C. Richard, and Charles Fruehling Springwood. "Fighting Spirits: The Racial Politics of Sports Mascots." *Journal of Sport and Social Issues* 24 (2000): 282–304.

Klomsten, Anne Torhild, Herb W. Marsh, and Einar M. Skaalvik. "Adolescents' Perceptions of Masculine and Feminine Values in Sport and Physical Education: A Study of Gender Differences." *Sex Roles* 52 (2005): 625–36.

Knez, Kelly, Tansin Benn, and Sara Alkhaldi. "World Cup Football as a Catalyst for Change: Exploring the Lives of Women in Qatar's First National Football Team—A Case Study." *The International Journal of the History of Sport* 31 (2014): 1755–73.

Knifsend, Casey A., and Sandra Graham. "Too Much of a Good Thing? How Breadth of Extracurricular Participation Relates to School-Related Affect and Academic Outcomes during Adolescence." *Journal of Youth and Adolescence* 41 (2012a): 379–89.

Knifsend, Casey A., and Sandra Graham. "Unique Challenges Facing Female Athletes in Urban High Schools." *Sex Roles* 67 (2012b): 236–46.

Koca, Canan. "Gender Interaction in Coed Physical Education: A Study in Turkey." *Adolescence* 44 (2008): 165–85.

Koivula, Nathalie. "Ratings of Gender Appropriateness of Sports Participation: Effects of Gender-Based Schematic Processing." *Sex Roles* 33 (1995): 543–57.

Krane, Vikki. "Homonegativism Experienced by Lesbian Collegiate Athletes." *Women in Sport and Physical Activity Journal* 6 (1997): 165–88.

Krane, Vikki. "We Can Be Athletic and Feminine, but Do We Want To? Challenging Hegemonic Femininity in Women's Sport." *Quest* 53 (2001): 115–33.

Krauer, Kerrie, and Vikki Krane. "'Scary Dykes' and 'Feminine Queens': Stereotypes and Female Collegiate Athletics." *Women in Sport and Physical Activity Journal* 15 (2006): 42–55.

Kreager, Derek. "Unnecessary Roughness? School Sports, Peer Networks, and Male Adolescent Violence." *American Sociological Review* 72 (2007): 705–24.

Kuznick, Lexie, and Megan Ryan. "Changing Social Norms? Title IX and Legal Activism: Comments from the Spring 2007 *Harvard Journal of Law and Gender* Conference." *Harvard Journal of Law and Gender* 31 (2008): 367–406.

Lamont, Jean M. "Trait Body Shame Predicts Health Outcomes in College Women: A Longitudinal Investigation." *Journal of Behavioral Medicine* (2015). DOI: 10.1007/s10865-015-9659-9.

Leahy, Crista D. "The Title Bout: A Critical Review of the Regulation and Enforcement of Title IX in Intercollegiate Athletics." *Journal of College and University Law* 24 (1998): 489–583.

Leavell, Ashley Smith, Catherine S. Tamis-LeMonda, Diane N. Ruble, Kristina M. Zosuls, and Natasha J. Cabrera. "African American, White and Latino Fathers' Activities with Their Sons and Daughters in Early Childhood." *Sex Roles* 66 (2012): 53–65.

Leonard, David J. "The Next M. J. or the Next O. J.? Kobe Bryant, Race, and the Absurdity of Colorblind Rhetoric." *Journal of Sport and Social Issues* 28 (2004): 284–313.

Lewis, Debra A., Eliezer Kamon, and James L. Hodgson. "Physiological Differences between Genders Implications for Sports Conditioning." *Sports Medicine* 3 (1986): 357–69.

Li, Weidong, Amelia M. Lee, and Melinda A. Solmon. "Gender Differences in Beliefs About the Influence of Ability and Effort in Sport and Physical Activity." *Sex Roles* 54 (2006): 147–56.

Lindgren, Eva-Carin. "The Impact of Sports on Young Women's Attitude to Physical Activity in Adult Life." *Women in Sport & Physical Activity Journal* 9 (2000): 65–86.

Linford, Matthew. "Understanding the Relationship between Interscholastic Sports Participation and Labor Market Outcomes: Interscholastic Sports as Cultural Capital." MS thesis, Brigham Young University, 2009.

Link, Bruce G., and Jo C. Phelan. "Social Conditions as Fundamental Causes of Disease." *Journal of Health and Social Behavior* 35 (1995): 80–94.

Lobel, Thalma E., Michelle Slone, and Gil Winch. "Masculinity, Popularity, and Self-Esteem among Israeli Preadolescent Girls." *Sex Roles* 36 (1997): 395–408.

Loewen, James. *Lies My Teacher Told Me: Everything Your American History Textbook Got Wrong.* New York: Touchstone, 1995.

Lopiano, Donna. "Gender Equity and the Black Female in Sport." Women's Sports Foundation. Last Modified 2001. http://www.womenssportsfoundation.org

/en/home/research/articles-and-reports/athletes-of-color/gender-equity-and
-the-black-female-athlete.

Lorber, Judith. *'Night to His Day': The Social Construction of Gender.* New Haven, CT: Yale University Press, 1994.

Love, Adam, and Kelly, Kimberly. "Equity or Essentialism? U.S. Courts and the Legitimation of Girls' Teams in High School Sport." *Gender and Society* 25 (2011): 227–49.

Mackay, Steph, and Christine Dallaire. "Campus Newspaper Coverage of Varsity Sports: Getting Closer to Equitable and Sports-related Representations of Female Athletes?" *International Review for the Sociology of Sport* 44 (2009): 25–40.

Mackin, Robert Sean, and Carol S. Walther. "Race, Sport and Social Mobility: Horatio Alger in Short Pants?" *International Review for the Sociology of Sport* (2011): 670–89.

MacKinnon, Catherine. "Difference and Dominance: On Sex Discrimination." In *Feminist Legal Theory*, edited by Katharine Bartlett and Rosanne Kennedy, 81–94. Boulder, CO: Westview Press, 1991.

Madden, Janice Fanning. "Differences in the Success of NFL Coaches by Race, 1990–2002 Evidence of Last Hire, First Fire." *Journal of Sports Economics* 5 (2004): 6–19.

Marini, Margaret Mooney. "Sex and Gender: What Do We Know?" *Sociological Focus* 5 (1990): 95–120.

Marsh, Herbert W., and Susan A. Jackson. "Multidimensional Self-Concepts, Masculinity, and Femininity as a Function of Women's Involvement in Athletics." *Sex Roles* 15 (1986): 391–415.

Martin, Emily. "The Egg and the Sperm: How Science Has Constructed a Romance Based on Stereotypical Male-Female Roles" *Signs* 16 (1991): 485–501.

Martin, Lori Latrice. "The Black Athletes and the Postracial Myth." In *Out of Bounds: Racism and the Black Athlete*, edited by Lori Latrice Martin, 3–28. Santa Barbara, CA: Praeger, 2014.

Massey, Douglas, and Nancy Denton. *American Apartheid.* Chicago: University of Chicago Press, 1993.

Mayeda, David Tokiharu. "From Model Minority to Economic Threat: Media Portrayals of Major League Baseball Pitchers Hideo Nomo and Hideki Irabu." *Journal of Sport and Social Issues* 23 (1999): 203–17.

McCarthy, David, and Robyn Lloyd Jones. "Speed, Agression, Strength, and Tactical Naivete: The Portrayal of the Black Soccer Player on Television." *Journal of Sport and Social Issues* 21 (1997): 348–62.

McCarthy, David, Robyn Lloyd Jones, and Paul Potrac. "Constructing Images and Interpreting Realities: The Case of the Black Soccer Player on Television." *International Review for the Sociology of Sport* 38 (2003): 217–38.

McCreary, Donald R. "The Male Role and Avoiding Femininity." *Sex Roles* 31 (1994): 517–31.

McDonagh, Eileen, and Laura Pappano. *Playing with the Boys: Why Separate Is Not Equal in Sports*. New York: Oxford University Press, 2008.

McDowell, Jacqueline, and George B. Cunningham. "Reactions to Physical Contact among Coaches and Players: The Influence of Coach Sex, Player Sex, and Attitudes toward Women." *Sex Roles* 58 (2008): 761–67.

McGrath, Shelly A., and Ruth A. Chananie-Hill. " 'Big Freaky-Looking Women': Normalizing Gender Transgression through Bodybuilding." *Sociology of Sport Journal* 26 (2009): 235–54.

McNeal, Jr., Ralph B. "Extracurricular Activities and High School Dropouts," *Sociology of Education* 68 (1995): 62–81.

McNeal, Jr., Ralph B. "Participation in High School Extracurricular Activities: Investigating School Effects," *Social Science Quarterly* 80 (1999): 291–309.

Mehta, Clare M., Jacqueline Alfonso, Rebecca Delaney, and Brian J. Ayotte. "Associations between Mixed-Gender Friendships, Gender Reference Group Identity and Substance Use in College Students." *Sex Roles* 70 (2013): 98–109.

Melnick, Merrill J., and Steven J. Jackson. "Globalization American-Style and Reference Idol Selection: The Importance of Athlete Celebrity Others among New Zealand Youth." *International Review for the Sociology of Sport* 37 (2002): 429–48.

Mernissi, Fatema. "Size 6: The Western Women's Harem." In *Scheherazade Goes West: Different Cultures, Different Harems*, edited by Fatima Mernissi, 208–20. New York: Washington Square Press, 2001.

Merten, Michael J. "Acceptability of Dating Violence Among Late Adolescents: The Role of Sports Participation, Competitive Attitudes, and Selected Dynamics of Relationship Violence." *Adolescence* 43 (2008): 31–56.

Messner, Michael A. "Boyhood, Organized Sports and the Construction of Masculinities." *Journal of Contemporary Ethnography* 18 (1990): 416–44.

Messner, Michael A. "Gender Ideologies, Youth Sports, and the Production of Soft Essentialism." *Sociology of Sport Journal* 28 (2011): 151–70.

Messner, Michael A. *Power at Play: Sports and the Problems of Masculinity*. Boston: Beacon Press, 1992.

Messner, Michael A. "Sports and Male Domination: The Female Athlete as Contested Ideological Terrain." *Sociology of Sport Journal* 5 (1988): 197–211.

Messner, Michael A. "Still a Man's World? Studying Masculinities and Sport." In *Handbook of Studies on Men and Masculinities*, edited by Michael S. Kimmel, Jeff Hearn, and R. W. Connell, 313–25. Thousand Oaks, CA: Sage, 2005.

Messner, Michael A. *Taking the Field: Women, Men, and Sports*. Minneapolis: University of Minnesota Press, 2002.

Messner, Michael A., Margaret Carlisle Duncan, and Cheryl Cooky. "Silence, Sports Bras, and Wrestling Porn: The Treatment of Women in Televised Sports News and Highlights." *Journal of Sport and Social Issues* 27 (2003): 38–51.

Messner, Michael A., Margaret Carlisle Duncan, and Faye Linda Wachs. "The Gender of Audience Building: Televised Coverage of Women's and Men's NCAA Basketball." *Sociological Inquiry* 66 (1996): 422–40.

Messner, Michael A., Margaret Carlisle Duncan, and Nicole Willms. "This Revolution Is Not Being Televised." *Contexts: Understanding People in Their Social Worlds* 5 (2006): 34–38.

Messner, Michael A., and Nancy M. Solomon. "Social Justice and Men's Interests: The Case of Title IX." *Journal of Sport and Social Issues* 31 (2007): 162–78.

Mickelson, Roslyn Arlin. "Subverting Swann: First- and Second-Generation Segregation in the Charlotte-Mecklenburg Schools." *American Educational Research Journal* 38 (2001): 215–52.

Migdal, Ariela, Emily J. Martin, Mie Lewis, and Lenora M. Lapidus. "The Need to Address Equal Educational Opportunities for Women and Girls." *Human Rights* 35 (2008): 16–25.

Migliaccio, Todd A., and Ellen C. Berg. "Women's Participation in Tackle Football: An Exploration of Benefits and Constraints." *International Review for the Sociology of Sport* 42 (2007): 271–87.

Mikulyuk, Ashley, Adrienne N. Milner, and Jomills Henry Braddock II. "Public Perceptions of Title IX: Evidence from a Recent National Poll." Paper presented at the annual meeting for the Southern Sociological Society, New Orleans, Louisiana, March 21–24, 2012.

Miller, Kathleen E., Donald F. Sabo, Michael P. Farrell, Grace M. Barnes, and Merrill J. Melnick. "Athletic Participation and Sexual Behavior in Adolescents: The Different Worlds of Boys and Girls." *Journal of Health and Social Behavior* 39 (1998): 108–23.

Miller, Stuart. "Playing with the Big Boys." *Women's Sports and Fitness* 17 (1995): 72–76.

Milner, Adrienne N., and Elizabeth H. Baker. "Athletic Participation and Intimate Partner Violence Victimization: Investigating Sport Involvement, Self-Esteem, and Abuse Patterns for Women and Men." *Journal of Intimate Partner Violence* (2015). DOI: 10.1177/0886260515585543.

Mirsafian, Hamidreza, Tamás Dóczi, and Azadeh Mohamadinejad. "Attitude of Iranian Female University Students to Sport and Exercise." *Iranian Studies* 47 (2013): 951–66.

Mitten, Matthew, Timothy Davis, Rodney Smith, and N. Jeremi Duru. *Sports Law and Regulation: Cases, Materials, and Problems*, 2nd edition. New York: Aspen Publishers, 2009.

Montagu, Ashley. *The Natural Superiority of Women*. New York: Altamira Press, 1999.

Mordaunt-Bexiga, Michelle. "Rugby, Gender and Capitalism: 'Sportocracy' Up for Sale?" *Agenda: Empowering Women for Gender Equity* 25 (2011): 69–74.

Mullin, Elizabeth M. "Scale Development: Heterosexist Attitudes in Women's Collegiate Athletics." *Measurement in Physical Education and Exercise Science* 17 (2012): 1–21.

Murnen, Sarah K., and Marla H. Kohlman. "Athletic Participation, Fraternity Membership, and Sexual Aggression among College Men: A Meta-analytic Review." *Sex Roles* 57 (2007): 145–57.

Myer, Gregory D. "Injury Initiates Unfavourable Weight Gain and Obesity Markers in Youth." *British Journal of Sports Medicine* (2014): 1477–81.

National Collegiate Athletic Association. "1999–00—2005–06 NCAA Student-Athlete Race and Ethnicity Report." Last modified April 2006. http://www.ncaapublications.com/productdownloads/ETHN06.pdf.

National Collegiate Athletic Association. "1999–00—2006–07 NCAA Student-Athlete Race and Ethnicity Report." Last modified January 2008. http://www.ncaapublications.com/productdownloads/RE2008N.pdf.

National Collegiate Athletic Association. "1981–82—2007–08 NCAA Sports Sponsorship and Participation Report." Last modified April 2009. http://www.ncaapublications.com/productdownloads/PR2009.pdf.

National Collegiate Athletic Association. "1981–82—2012–13 NCAA Sports Sponsorship and Participation Rates Data." Last modified October 2014. http://www.ncaapublications.com/productdownloads/PR2014.pdf.

National Collegiate Athletic Association. Forthcoming. "Sports Sponsorship and Participation Rates Report, 1981–1982—2014–15." Indianapolis, IN.

National Collegiate Athletic Association. "Sport Sponsorship, Participation and Demographics Search." Accessed September 14, 2015. http://web1.ncaa.org/rgdSearch/exec/main.

National Federation of State High School Associations. "1969–2014 High School Athletics Participation Survey." Accessed June 8, 2015. http://www.nfhs.org/ParticipationStatics/PDF/Participation%20Survey%20History%20Book.pdf.

Nauright, John. "African Women and Sport: The State of Play." *Sport in Society* 17 (2013): 1–12.

Nauright, John. *Long Run to Freedom: Sport, Cultures and Identities in South Africa.* Morgantown, WV: Fitness Information Technology, 2010.

Neely, Kacey C., and Nick Holt. "Parents' Perspectives on the Benefits of Sport Participation for Young Children." *The Sport Psychologist* 28 (2014): 255–68.

Nelson, Jack K., Jerry R. Thomas, Karyn R. Nelson, and Penny C. Abraham. "Gender Differences in Children's Throwing Performance: Biology and Environment." *Research Quarterly for Exercise and Sport* 57 (1986): 280–87.

Nelson, Mariah Burton. *The Stronger Women Get the More Men Love Football: Sexism and the American Culture of Sports.* New York: Harcourt Brace, 1994.

Newhall, Kristine. "The Athlete Exception: Title IX, Sexual Assault, and Intercollegiate Athletics." Paper presented at the annual meeting for the Southern Sociological Society, New Orleans, Louisiana, March 25–29, 2015.

Nichols, Geoff, Richard Tacon, and Alison Muir. "Sport Clubs' Volunteers: Bonding in or Bridging Out?" *Sociology* 47 (2012): 350–67.

Nixon II, Howard L. "The Relationship of Friendship Networks, Sport Experiences, and Gender to Expressed Pain Thresholds." *Sociology of Sport Journal* 13 (1996): 78–86.

Norman, Leanne. "The Impact of an 'Equal Opportunities' Ideological Framework on Coaches' Knowledge and Practice." *International Review for the Sociology of Sport* (2015). DOI: 10.1177/1012690214565377.

Nygård, Håvard Mokleiv, and Scott Gates. "Soft Power at Home and Abroad: Sport Diplomacy, Politics and Peace-Building." *International Area Studies Review* 16 (2013): 235–43.

Oakes, Jeannie. "Two Cities' Tracking and Within-School Segregation." *Teachers College Record* 96 (1996): 681–90.

Oakes, Jeannie. "Within-School Integration, Grouping Practices, and Educational Quality in Rockford Schools." Report prepared in conjunction with *People Who Care et al. v. Rockford, IL. Independent School District*, 2000.

O'Donnell, Francis. "Coed Adolescent Soccer Players in a Competitive Learning Milieu: An Ethnographic Assessment of Gender Attitudes, Perceptions and Sport Specific Component Testing." PhD diss., University of Central Florida, 2004.

O'Hanlon, Timothy P. "School Sports as Social Training: The Case of Athletics and the Crisis of World War I." *Journal of Sport History* 9(1982): 4–29.

Oliver, Melvin L., and Thomas M. Shapiro. *Black/Wealth/White Wealth: A New Perspective on Racial Inequality.* New York: Routledge, 1995.

Olsen, Jack. *The Black Athlete: A Shameful Story: The Myth of Integration in American Sport.* New York: Time-Life Books, 1968.

Omi, Michael, and Howard Winant. *Racial Formation in the United States: From the 1960s to the 1990s,* 2nd Edition. New York: Routledge, 1994.

Orfield, Gary, and Erica Frankenberg. "Brown at 60: Great Progress, a Long Retreat and an Uncertain Future." The Civil Rights Project. Last modified May 15, 2014. http://civilrightsproject.ucla.edu/research/k-12-education/integration-and-diversity/brown-at-60-great-progress-a-long-retreat-and-an-uncertain-future/Brown-at-60-051814.pdf.

Orfield, Gary, John Kucsera, and Genevieve Siegel-Hawley. "E Pluribus . . . Separation: Deepening Double Segregation for More Students." The Civil Rights Project. Last modified September 19, 2012. http://civilrightsproject.ucla.edu/research/k-12-education/integration-and-diversity/mlk-national/e-pluribus . . . separation-deepening-double-segregation-for-more-students/orfield_epluribus_revised_omplete_2012.pdf.

Orfield, Gary, and Chungmei Lee. Why Segregation Matters: Poverty and Education Inequality. The Civil Rights Project. Last modified January 13, 2005. http://civilrightsproject.ucla.edu/research/k-12-education/integration-and-diversity/why-segregation-matters-poverty-and-educational-inequality

Öztürk, Selcen, and Dilek Kılıç. "What Is the Economic Burden of Sports Injuries?" *Controversial Issues* 24 (2013): 108–11.

Palmer, Catherine. "Drinking Like a Guy? Women and Sport-Related Drinking." *Journal of Gender Studies* 19 (2013): 1–13.

Paoletti, Jo B. *Pink and Blue: Telling the Boys from the Girls in America.* Bloomington: Indiana University Press, 2012.

Parker, Wendy. *Beyond Title IX: The Cultural Laments of Women's Sports.* June 20, 2012. http://www.amazon.com/Beyond-Title-IX-Wendy-Parker-ebook/dp/B008DFZV9E.

Pearson, Jennifer, Sarah R. Crissey, and Catherine Riegle-Crumb. "Gendered Fields: Sports and Advanced Course Taking in High School." *Sex Roles* 61 (2009): 519–35.

Pease, Bob. "'New Wine in Old Bottles?' A Commentary on 'What's in It for Men?' Old Question, New Data." *Men and Masculinities* 17 (2014): 549–51.

Pelak, Cynthia Fabrizo. "Athletes as Agents of Change: An Examination of Shifting Race Relations within Women's Netball in Post-Apartheid South Africa." *Sociology of Sport Journal* 21 (2005): 59–77.

Pfister, Gertrud. "Appropriation of the Environment, Motor Experiences and Sporting Activities of Girls and Women." *International Review for the Sociology of Sport* 28 (1993): 159–72.

Phillips, Lynn. *The Girls Report: What We Know and Need to Know about Growing Up Female.* New York: National Council for Research, 1998.

Pickett, Moneque Walker. "The Invisible Black Woman in the Title IX Shuffle: An Empirical Analysis and Critical Examination of Gender Equity Policy in Assessing Access and Participation of Black and White High School Girls in Interscholastic Sports." PhD diss., University of Miami, 2009.

Pickett, Moneque Walker, Marvin P. Dawkins, and Jomills Henry Braddock, II. "The Effect of Title IX on Participation of Black and White Females in High School Sports: Evidence from National Longitudinal Surveys." *The Journal of Race and Policy* 5 (2009): 79–90.

Pickett, Moneque Walker, Marvin P. Dawkins, and Jomills Henry Braddock, II. "Race and Gender Equity in Sports: Have White and African American Females Benefited Equally from Title IX?" *American Behavioral Scientist* 56 (2012): 1581–603.

Pisu, Maria, Kelly Kenzic, Robert Oster, Patricia Drentea, Kimlin Ashing, Mona Fouad, and Michelle Martin. "Economic Hardship of Minority and Non-Minority Cancer Survivors One Year after Diagnosis: Another Long Term Effect of Cancer?" *Cancer* (2015). DOI: 10.1002/cncr.29206.

Plymire, Darcy C., and Pamela L. Forman. "Breaking the Silence: Lesbian Fans, the Internet, and the Sexual Politics of Women's Sport." *International Journal of Sexuality and Gender Studies* 5 (2000): 141–53.

Post, Corinne. "When Is Female Leadership an Advantage? Coordination Requirements, Team Cohesion, and Team Interaction Norms." *Journal of Organizational Behavior* (2015). DOI: 10.1002/job.2031.

Powell, Jennifer E. "IX: Straining Toward an Elusive Goal." *Willamette Sports Law Journal* 1 (2004): 1–29.

Puig, Núria, and Alan Ingham. "Sport and Space: An Outline of the Issue." *International Review for the Sociology of Sport* 28 (1993): 101–6.

Rader, Benjamin. "'Matters Involving Honor': Region, Race, and Rank in the Violent Life of Tyrus Raymond Cobb." In *Baseball in America and America in*

Baseball, edited by Donald G. Kyle, and Robert B. Fairbanks, 189–222. College Station: Texas A&M University Press, 2008.

Ratele, Kopano. "Gender Equality in the Abstract and Practice." *Men and Masculinities* (2014): 510–14.

Rauscher, Lauren, and Cheryl Cooky. "Ready for Anything the World Gives Her? A Critical Look at Sports-Based Positive Youth Development for Girls." *Sex Roles* (2015). DOI: 10.1007/s11199-014-0400-x.

Richmond, Tracy K., Rodney A. Hayward, Sheila Gahagan, Alison E. Field, and Michele Heisler. "Can School Income and Racial/Ethnic Composition Explain the Racial/Ethnic Disparity in Adolescent Physical Activity Participation?" *Pediatrics* 117 (2006): 2158–66.

Ring, Jennifer. *Stolen Bases: Why American Girls Don't Play Baseball*. Champaign, IL: University of Illinois Press, 2000.

Roberts, Celia. "Biological Behavior? Horomones, Psychology, and Sex." *National Women's Studies Association Journal* 12 (2000): 1–20.

Roberts, Cheryl. "Government Intervention Needed to Improve Status of Women in Sport." *Agenda: Empowering Women for Gender Equity* 24 (2011): 146–47.

Robinson, Kenneth N. *From Vick-Tim to Vick-Tory: The Fall and Rise of Michael Vick*. Houston: Strategic Book Publishing, 2013.

Roscigno, Vincent J. *The Face of Discrimination: How Race and Gender Impact Work and Home Lives*. Lanham, MD: Rowman and Littlefield, 2007.

Ross, Sally R., and Kimberly J. Shinew. "Perspectives of Women College Athletes on Sport and Gender." *Sex Roles* 58 (2008): 40–57.

Ross, Terris, Grace Kena, Amy Rathbun, Angelina Kewal Ramani, Jijun Zhang, Paul Kristapovich, and Eileen Manning. "Higher Education: Gaps in Access and Persistence Study Statistical Analysis Report." U.S. Department of Education Institute of Education Sciences National Center for Education Statistics. Last modified August, 2012. http://files.eric.ed.gov/fulltext/ED534691 .pdf, 81.

Rosso, Edoardo G. F., and Richard McGrath. "Beyond Recreation: Personal Social Networks and Social Capital in the Transition of Young Players from Recreational Football to Formal Football Clubs." *International Review for the Sociology of Sport* 48 (2012): 453–70.

Roth, Amanda, and Susan Basow. "Femininity, Sports, and Feminism: Developing a Theory of Physical Liberation." *Journal of Sport and Social Issues* 28 (2004): 245–65.

Russell, Kate M. "On Versus Off the Pitch: The Transiency of Body Satisfaction Among Female Rugby Players, Cricketers, and Netballers." *Sex Roles* 51 (2004): 561–74.

Sabo, Donald. "Sport, Patriarchy, and Male Identity: New Questions about Men and Sport." *Arena Review* 9 (1985): 1–30.

Sabo, Donald, and Ross Runfola. *Jock: Sports and the Male Identity*. Englewood Cliffs, NJ: Prentice-Hall, 1980.

Sabo, Donald, and Philip Veliz. "The Decade of Decline: Gender Equity in High School Sports." Women's Sports Foundation. Last modified October 8, 2012. http://irwg.research.umich.edu/pdf/OCR.pdf.

Sabo, Donald, and Philip Veliz. "Go Out and Play: Youth Sports in America." Women's Sports Foundation. Last modified October 8, 2008. http://www.womenssportsfoundation.org/home/research/articles-and-reports/mental-and-physical-health/go-out-and-play.

Sabo, Donald, Kathleen Miller, Michael Farrell, Grace Barnes, and Merrill Melnick. "Sport and Teen Pregnancy." Women's Sports Foundation. Last modified October 5, 1998. http://www.womenssportsfoundation.org/home/research/articles-and-reports/mental-and-physical-health/sport-and-teen-pregnancy.

Sabo, Donald F., Kathleen E. Miller, Merill J. Melnick, and Leslie Heywood. "Her Life Depends on It: Sport, Physical Activity and the Health and Well-Being of American Girls." Women's Sports Foundation. Last modified December 8, 2004. http://celticfl.net/wp-content/uploads/2012/09/Her-life-depends-on-it.pdf.

Sailes, Gary A. "The African American Athlete: Social Myths and Stereotypes." In *African Americans in Sport: Contemporary Themes*, edited by Gary A. Sails, 183–98. New Brunswick, NJ: Transaction Publishers, 1998.

Sailes, Gary A. "An Investigation of Campus Stereotypes: The Myth of Black Athletic Superiority and the Dumb Jock Stereotype." *Sociology of Sport Journal* 10 (1993): 88–97.

Samie, Sumaya F., Alicia J. Johnson, Ashleigh M. Huffman, and Sarah J. Hillyer. "Voices of Empowerment: Women from the Global South Re/negotiating Empowerment and the Global Sports Mentoring Programme." *Sport in Society* 18 (2015): 923–37.

Sanday, Peggy Reeves. "Rape-Prone versus Rape-Free Campus Cultures." *Violence Against Women* 2 (1996): 191–208.

Sanders, Christopher E. "Moderate Involvement in Sports Is Related to Lower Depression Levels Among Adolescents." *Adolescence* 35 (2000): 793–97.

Sanderson, Allen R. "The Many Dimensions of Competitive Balance." *Journal of Sports Economics* 3 (2002): 204–28.

Sanderson, Susan, and Vetta L. Sanders Thompson. "Factors Associated with Perceived Paternal Involvement in Childrearing." *Sex Roles* 46 (2002): 99–111.

Sandler, Bernice R. "'Too Strong for a Woman'—The Five Words That Created Title IX." *Equity and Excellence in Education* 33 (2000): 9–13.

Sapir, Edward. *Culture, Language and Personality*. Berkeley: University of California Press, 1958.

Saylor, Roger. "Black College Football." *College Football Historical Society Newsletter* 13 (2000): 4–7.

Scheerder, Jeroen, Martine Thomis, Bart Vanreusel, Johan Lefevre, Roland Renson, Bart Vanden Eynde, and Gaston P. Beunen. "Sports Participation among Females from Adolescence to Adulthood." *International Review for the Sociology of Sport* 41 (2006): 413–30.

Schmaltz, Dorothy L., and Deborah L. Kerstetter. "Girlie Girls and Manly Men: Children's Stigma Consciousness of Gender in Sports and Physical Activities." *Journal of Leisure Research* 38 (2006): 536–57.

Schulz, David A. *Coming up Black: Patterns of Ghetto Socialization.* Upper Saddle River, NJ: Prentice Hall, 1969.

Scott, Olan K. M., Brad Hill, and Dwight Zakus. "Framing the 2007 National Basketball Association Finals: An Analysis of Commentator Discourse." *International Review for the Sociology of Sport* 49 (2012): 728–44.

Scriven, Michael. "The Methodology of Evaluation." In *Perspectives of Curriculum Evaluation,* edited by Ralph W. Tyler, Robert M. Gagne, and Michael Scriven, 39–83. Chicago: Rand McNally and Co., 1967.

Sewell, Abigail A. "Disaggregating Ethnoracial Disparities in Physician Trust." *Social Science Research* 54 (2015): 1–20.

Shaffer, David R., and Erin Wittes. "Women's Precollege Sports Participation, Enjoyment of Sports, and Self-Esteem." *Sex Roles* 55 (2006): 225–32.

Shakib, Sohaila, and Michele D. Dunbar. "The Social Construction of Female and Male High School Basketball Participation: Reproducing the Gender Order through a Two-Tiered Sporting Institution." *Sociological Perspectives* 45 (2002): 353–78.

Shakib, Sohalia, Phillip Veliz, Michele D. Dunbar, and Donald Sabo. "Athletics as a Source for Social Status among Youth: Examining Variation by Gender, Race/Ethnicity, and SES." *Sociology of Sport Journal* 28 (2011): 303–28.

Shen, Bo, Tamara Rinehart-Lee, Nate McCaughtry, and Xiaoming Li. "Urban African-American Girls' Participation and Future Intentions Toward Physical Education." *Sex Roles* 67 (2012): 323–33.

Shields, David Light, Nicole M. LaVoi, Brenda Light Bredemeier, and F. Clark Power. "Predictors of Poor Sportspersonship in Youth Sports: Personal Attitudes and Social Influences." *Journal of Sport Exercise Psychology* 29 (2007): 747–62.

Silverman, Irwin W. "Sex Differences in Simple Visual Reaction Time: A Historical Meta-Analysis." *Sex Roles* 54 (2006): 57–68.

Simons, Herbert D. "Race and Penalized Sports Behaviors." *International Review for the Sociology of Sport* 38 (2003): 5–22.

Sisjord, Mari Kristin, and Elsa Kristiansen. "Elite Women Wrestlers' Muscles: Physical Strength and a Social Burden." *International Review for the Sociology of Sport* 44 (2009): 231–46.

Slater, Amy, and Marika Tiggemann. "Time since Menarche and Sport Participation as Predictors of Self-Objectification: A Longitudinal Study of Adolescent Girls." *Sex Roles* 67 (2012): 571–81.

Slater, Amy and Marika Tiggemann. "'Uncool to Do Sport': A Focus Group Study of Adolescent Girls' Reasons for Withdrawing from Physical Activity." *Psychology of Sport and Exercise* 11 (2010): 619–26.

Smiler, Andrew P. "Thirty Years after the Discovery of Gender: Psychological Concepts and Measures of Masculinity." *Sex Roles* 50 (2004): 15–26.

Smith-Evans, Leticia, Janel George, Fatima Goss Graves, Lara S. Kaufmann, and Lauren Frohlich. "Unlocking Opportunity for African American Girls: A Call to Educational Equity." NAACP Legal Defense Fund and the National Women's Law Center. Last modified September 19, 2014. http://www.nwlc.org/sites/default/files/pdfs/unlocking_opportunity_for_african_american_girls_report.pdf.

Snellman, Kaisa, Jennifer M. Silva, Carl B. Frederick, and Robert D. Putnam. "The Engagement Gap: Social Mobility and Extracurricular Participation among American Youth." *The Annals of the American Academy of Political and Social Science* (2014): 194–207.

Spaaij, Ramón. "Sport as a Vehicle for Social Mobility and Regulation of Disadvantaged Urban Youth: Lesson from Rotterdam." *International Review for the Sociology of Sport* 44 (2009): 247–64.

Spatig-Amerikaner, Ary. "Unequal Education: Federal Loophole Enables Lower Spending on Students of Color." Center for American Progress. Last modified August, 2012. https://cdn.americanprogress.org/wp-content/uploads/2012/08/UnequalEduation-1.pdf.

Spencer, Nancy E. "Sister Act IV: Venus and Serena Williams at Indian Wells: Sincere Fictions and White Racism." *Journal of Sport and Social Issues* 28 (2004): 115–35.

Spivey, Donald. *Fire from the Soul: A History of the African-American Struggle.* Durham, NC: Carolina Academy Press, 2003.

Stainback, Kevin, Corre L. Robinson, and Donald Tomaskovic-Devey. "Race and Workplace Integration: A Politically Mediated Process?" *American Behavioral Scientist* 48 (2005): 2000–28.

Steinberg, Stephen. *The Ethnic Myth.* New York: Plenum Press, 1981.

Steinem, Gloria. "If Men Could Menstruate." *Ms. Magazine* 7 (1978): 110.

Steinfeldt, Jesse A., Hailee Carter, Emily Benton, and Matthew Clint Steinfeldt. "Muscularity Beliefs of Female College Student-Athletes." *Sex Roles* 64 (2011): 543–54.

Stempel, Carl. "Adult Participation Sports as Cultural Capital: A Test of Bourdieu's Theory of the Field of Sports." *International Review for the Sociology of Sport* 40 (2005): 411–32.

Stepanikova, Irena. "Racial and Ethnic Biases, Time Pressure, and Medical Decisions." *Journal of Health and Social Behavior* (2012): 329–43.

Stevenson, Betsey. "Title IX and the Evolution of High School Sports." *Contemporary Economic Policy* 25 (2007): 486–505.

Stevenson, Betsy. "Beyond the Classroom: Using Title IX to Measure the Return to High School Sports." *The Review of Economics and Statistics* 92 (2010): 284–301.

Stoddart, Mark C. J. "Constructing Masculinized Sportscapes: Skiing, Gender and Nature in British Columbia, Canada." *International Review for the Sociology of Sport* 46 (2010): 108–24.

Stoltenberg, John. *Refusing to be a Man: Essays on Sex and Justice.* New York: Routledge, 1999.

Stuntz, Cheryl P., Julia K. Sayles, and Erin L. McDermott. "Same-Sex and Mixed-Sex Sport Teams: How the Social Environment Relates to Sources of Social Support and Perceived Competence." *Journal of Sport Behavior* 34 (2011): 98–120.

Suggs, Welch. *A Place on the Team: The Triumph and Tragedy of Title IX.* Princeton, NJ: Princeton University Press, 2006.

Sullivan, Claire F. "Gender Verification and Gender Policies in Elite Sport: Eligibility and 'Fair Play.'" *Journal of Sport and Social Issues* 35 (2011): 400–19.

Sundgot-Borgen, Jorunn, Kari Fasting, Celia Brackenridge, Monica Klungland Torstveit, and Bo Berglund. "Sexual Harassment and Eating Disorders in Female Elite Athletes—A Controlled Study." *Scandinavian Journal of Medicine & Science in Sports* 13 (2003): 330–35.

Swain, Jon. "The Role of Sport in the Promotion of Masculinity in an English Independent Junior School." *Sport, Education and Society* 11 (2006): 317–35.

Tagg, Brendon. "'Imagine, a Man Playing Netball!': Masculinities and Sport in New Zealand." *International Review for the Sociology of Sport* 43 (2008): 409–30.

Tagg, Brendon. "Men's Netball or Gender-Neutral Netball." *International Review for the Sociology of Sport* (2014). DOI: 10.1177/1012690214524757.

Taliaferro, Lindsay A., Barbara A. Rienzo, M. David Miller, R. Morgan Pigg, Jr., and Virginia J. Dodd. "High School Youth and Suicide Risk: Exploring Protection Afforded through Physical Activity and Sport Participation." *Journal of School Health* 78 (2008): 545–53.

Talleu, Clotilde. "Access for Girls and Women to Sport Practices." Counsel of Europe. Last modified September 2011. http://www.coe.int/t/DG4/EPAS/Publications/Handbook_2%20_Gender_equality_in_sport.pdf.

Taylor, Judith. "Who Manages Feminist-Inspired Reform? An In-Depth Look at Title IX Coordinators in the United States." *Gender and Society* 19 (2005): 358–75.

Teetzel, Sarah. "The Onus of Inclusivity: Sport Policies and the Enforcement of the Women's Category in Sport." *Journal of the Philosophy of Sport* 41 (2013): 113–27.

Tiggemann, Marika. "Person x Situation Interactions in Body Dissatisfaction." *International Journal of Eating Disorders* 29 (2001): 65–70.

Tischer, Ulrike, Ilse Hartmann-Tews, and Claudia Combrink. "Sport Participation of the Elderly—The Role of Gender, Age, and Social Class." *European Review of Aging and Physical Activity* 8 (2011): 83–91.

Thomeer, Stipica Mudrazija, and Jacqueline L. Angel. "How Do Race and Hispanic Ethnicity Affect Nursing Home Admission? Evidence from the Health and Retirement Study." *The Journals of Gerontology: Social Sciences* 70 (2015): 628–38.

Thorne, Barrie. *Gender Play: Girls and Boys in School.* New Brunswick, NJ: Rutgers University Press, 1993.

Todd, M. Kent, Greg Czyszczon, Julie Wallace Carr, and Casey Pratt. "Comparison of Health and Academic Indices between Campus Recreation Facility Users and Nonusers." *Recreational Sports Journal* 33 (2009): 43–53.

Todd, Samuel Y., and Aubrey Kent. "Student Athletes' Perceptions of Self." *Adolescence* 38 (2003): 659–67.

Tong, Rosemarie. "Feminist Perspectives on Empathy as an Epistemic Skill and Caring as a Moral Value." *Journal of Medical Humanities* 18 (1997): 153–58.

Travers, Ann. "The Sport Nexus and Gender Injustice." *Studies in Social Justice* 2 (2008): 79–101.

Trujillo, Nick. "Machines, Missiles, and Men: Images of the Male Body on ABC's *Monday Night Football*." *Sociology of Sport Journal* 12 (1995): 403–23.

Turnbull, Oliver, Victoria E. Lovett, Jackie Chaldecottc, and Marilyn D. Lucasc. "Reports of Intimate Touch: Erogenous Zones and Somatosensory Cortical Organization." *Cortex* 53 (2014): 146–54.

Twenge, Jean M. "Status and Gender: The Paradox of Progress in an Age of Narcissism." *Sex Roles* 61 (2009): 338–40.

United Nations. "Sport and Gender: Empowering Girls and Women." Accessed July 7, 2015. http://www.un.org/wcm/webdav/site/sport/shared/sport/SDP%20IWG/Chapter4_SportandGender.pdf.

U.S. Department of Education Institute of Education Sciences National Center for Education Statistics. "Education Longitudinal Study of 2002 (ELS: 2002)." Last modified August 2015. http://nces.ed.gov/surveys/els2002/.

Vann, Portia. "Changing the Game: The Role of Social Media in Overcoming Old Media's Attention Deficit toward Women's Sport." *Journal of Broadcasting & Electronic Media* 58 (2014): 438–55.

Vargas, Gray, Amanda Rabinowitz, Jessica Meyer, and Peter A. Arnett. "Predictors and Prevalence of Postconcussion Depression Symptoms in Collegiate Athletes." *Journal of Athletic Training* 50 (2015): 250–55.

Venetsanou, Fontini, and Antonia Kambas. "Environmental Factors Affecting Preschoolers' Motor Development." *Early Childhood Education Journal* 37 (2009): 319–27.

Verdun, Vincene. "The Big Disconnect Between Segregation and Integration." *Journal of Negro Education* 56 (2005): 67–82.

Videon, Tami M. "Who Plays and Who Benefits: Gender, Interscholastic Athletics, and Academic Outcomes." *Sociological Perspectives* 45(4): 415–44.

Volkom, Michele Van. "The Relationships Between Childhood Tomboyism, Siblings' Activities, and Adult Gender Roles." *Sex Roles* 49 (2003): 609–18.

Wacquant, Loïc. "Deadly Symbiosis: Rethinking Race and Imprisonment in Twenty-First Century America." *Boston Review* 27 (2002): 21–31.

Wadesango, Newman, Severino Machingambi, Gladys Ashu, and Regis Chireshe. "Nature and Effects of Women's Participation in Sporting Decision-Making Structures in the Context of the 2010 FIFA World Cup." *Agenda: Empowering Women for Gender Equity* 24 (2011): 62–75.

Walseth, Kristin, and Kari Fasting. "Islam's View on Physical Activity and Sport: Egyptian Women Interpreting Islam." *International Review for the Sociology of Sport* 38 (2003): 45–60.

Walter, Cheryl M., Rosa Du Randt, and Daniel J. L. Venter. "The Physical Activity and Health Status of Two Generations of Black South African Professional Women: Original Research." *Health SA Gesondheid* 16 (2011): 1–9.

Weber, Jonetta D., and Robert M. Carini. "Where are the Female Athletes in *Sports Illustrated*? A Content Analysis of Covers (2000–2011)." *International Review for the Sociology of Sport* 48 (2012): 196–203.

Weinberg, Meyer. *Minority Students: A Research Appraisal.* Washington, DC: National Institute of Education, 1978.

Weiss, Carol H. *Evaluation Research: Methods of Assessing Program Effectiveness.* Englewood Cliffs, NJ: Prentice-Hall, 1972.

Welch, Michael. "Violence against Women by Professional Football Players: A Gender Analysis of Hypermasculinity, Positional Status, Narcissism, and Entitlement." *Journal of Sport and Social Issues* 21 (1997): 392–411.

Welch, Susan, and Lee Sigelman. "Who's Calling the Shots? Women Coaches in Division I Women's Sports." *Social Science Quarterly* 8 (2007): 1415–34.

Wells, Amy Stuart. "The 'Consequences' of School Desegregation: The Mismatch between the Research and the Rationale." *Hastings Constitutional Law Quarterly* 28 (2002): 771–97.

Wells, Amy Stuart, Jennifer Jellison Holme, Anita Tijerina Revilla, and Awo Korantemaa Atanda. "How Society Failed School Desegregation Policy: Looking Past the Schools to Understand Them." *Review of Research in Education* 28 (2004): 47–99.

Welschen, Saskia Irene. "Making Sense of being South African: The Analysis of National Identity Construction in Talk." Paper presented at the ISA World Congress of Sociology, Gothenburg, Sweden, July 11–17, 2010.

Wheeler, Sharon. "The Significance of Family Culture for Sports Participation." *International Review for the Sociology of Sport* 47 (2011): 235–52.

Wheeler, Sharon, and Ken Green. "Parenting in Relation to Children's Sports Participation: Generational Changes and Potential Implication." *Leisure Studies* 33 (2012): 267–84.

Whisenant, Warren A. "Sustaining Male Dominance in Interscholastic Athletics: A Case of Homologous Reproduction . . . or Not?" *Sex Roles* 58 (2008): 768–75.

Whisenant, Warren A., John Miller, and Paul M. Pedersen. "Systemic Barriers in Athletic Administration: An Analysis of Job Descriptions for Interscholastic Athletic Directors." *Sex Roles* 53 (2005): 911–18.

Whisenant, Warren A., Paul M. Pederson, and Bill L. Obenour. "Success and Gender: Determining the Rate of Advancement for Intercollegiate Athletic Directors." *Sex Roles* 47 (2002): 485–91.

Whorf, Benjamin. In *Language, Thought, and Reality: Selected Writings of Benjamin Lee Whorf*, edited by John B. Carroll. Cambridge, MA: MIT Press, 1956.

Wicker, Pamela, Christoph Breuer, and Tassilo Von Hanau. "Gender Effects on Organizational Problems—Evidence from Non-Profit Sports Clubs in Germany." *Sex Roles* 66 (2011): 105–16.

Wilson, Thomas C. "The Paradox of Social Class and Sports Involvement: The Roles of Cultural and Economic Capital." *International Review for the Sociology of Sport* 37 (2002): 5–16.

Wittig, Monique. "One Is Not Born a Woman." In *The Lesbian and Gay Studies Reader*, edited by Henry Abelove, Michele Aina Barale, and David M. Halperin, 103–09. New York: Routledge, 1993.

Wolter, Sarah Marie. "Serving, Informing, and Inspiring Today's Female Athlete and Fan Postfeminist Discourse: A Critical Media Analysis of EspnW." PhD diss., University of Minnesota, 2012.

Wood, Zacharias. "Administrator Perceptions of Intramural Coed Flag Football Modifications: A Qualitative Analysis." MS thesis, Louisiana State University, 2014.

Wright, Darlene R., and Kevin M. Fitzpatrick. "Violence and Minority Youth: The Effects of Risk and Asset Factors on Fighting among African American Children and Adolescents." *Adolescence* 41 (2006): 251–62.

Zipp, John F. "Sport and Sexuality: Athletic Participation by Sexual Minority and Sexual Majority Adolescents in the U.S." *Sex Roles* 64 (2011): 19–31.

Index

race (*cont.*)
  differences, 5, 23, 57, 69–70, 72,
    74; divisions, 31, 71; groups, 2, 54,
    74; minorities, 2, 7, 38, 45–47, 69,
    72, 99, 109–110; profiling, 115;
    progress, 33, 73, 126; violence, 97
racism, 5, 10, 31, 57, 69–74, 77, 96
rape, 70, 100, 108
reaction time, 63–64
religion, 1, 3, 10
role modeling, 74, 76, 110, 118
Rousey, Ronda, 51–52
rugby, 26–27, 33, 83, 92–93
rule changes, 119–121, 123

Sabo, Donald F., 79, 81, 127
safety, 96, 102–104, 121
Sails, Gary A., 72
salaries, 95, 107
Sam, Michael, 8–9
Sapir–Whorf hypothesis, 55, 57
scholarships, 19–20, 27, 89;
  allocation, 117; collegiate, 34;
  opportunities, 26, 99
science, 7, 16, 29, 45, 47–49, 69
science, technology, engineering, and
  math (STEM), 7, 16, 49, 99
segregation, 6, 12, 20, 23, 33, 38,
  41–42, 70, 97–98, 125–126; legal,
  4, 42; maintaining sex, 41, 93;
  racial, 72–73, 84. *See also*
  desegregation; integration
self-efficacy, 10, 77
self-esteem, 10, 67, 77, 96
sex, 1–6, 15–16, 18, 22–23, 33–35,
  41–44, 51–61, 63–71, 73–77,
  79–80, 82–83, 111–114, 118,
  120, 122; categories, 54–56,
  58–59, 68, 71, 82, 95, 97, 99, 101,
  103, 105, 107, 109, 111–113, 115;
  desegregation, 99, 104, 108, 127
  (*see also* sex integration); differences,
  2, 62–65, 67–68, 79–80, 93, 102;
  discrimination, 1–2, 17, 19, 28,

42; disparities, 15–16, 45, 67, 101,
  106, 110–111, 113; equality, 6, 41,
  56–57, 111, 120; equity, 6, 20, 22,
  26, 28, 30–31, 33, 35, 41–42,
  45–49, 94, 99–100, 115, 118,
  120–121; and gender, 55, 57, 59,
  66, 70; ideology, 37, 49, 52, 67,
  82, 97, 113; inequalities, 10, 17,
  37–38, 41, 81, 118, 120
sexed language, 57, 118
sex integration, 1, 6, 12–13, 41, 84,
  87, 91–94, 96–101, 103–105,
  107–108, 110–112, 116–119,
  121–125, 127; evaluating, 126–127;
  initiating, 126; modeling, 111;
  potential benefits of, 13, 99, 102,
  104, 109; in sports, 6–7, 11–12,
  87, 91, 93, 100–101, 104–105,
  112–113, 117–118, 122, 126–128.
  See also sex segregation
sexism, 9–10, 30, 57, 62–63, 73, 77,
  96, 98–99, 103, 125
sexist ideology, 5, 54, 56, 58, 60, 63,
  65, 71, 74, 77, 79, 98–99, 102–103,
  120, 127
sex segregation, 1–2, 4–8, 10, 12,
  15–16, 18, 20, 40–42, 62–64, 90,
  98, 104–106, 110–114, 120, 124.
  See also sex integration
sexual activity, 10, 61, 67;
  harassment, 16, 97, 101;
  intercourse, 60, 100
sexuality, 1, 8, 56, 59, 66–68, 112,
  127; heterosexuality, 66–67,
  112; homoeroticism, 66, 80;
  homosexuality, 66, 68
sexual orientation, 1–2, 66–68;
  bisexual, 1, 11, 66; gay, 1, 8, 11,
  66, 82, 99; lesbian, gay, bisexual,
  transgender (LGBT), 11, 96,
  109–112
sex verification, 96, 111
skating, 66, 80
skiing, 97

ABOUT THE AUTHORS

Adrienne N. Milner is an assistant professor in the Department of Sociology at the University of Alabama at Birmingham (UAB). Dr. Milner's research addresses issues of equity in terms of race/ethnicity and sex/gender in sports and political contexts. Specifically, she examines racial and sexual attitudes, policy preferences, and inequality in the Obama era. Her other work focuses on disparities in access to sport involvement and analyzes the costs and benefits of athletic participation for individuals with complex and diverse identities. She has 10 years of experience teaching sport and society and other courses to college students and student-athletes at two diverse universities, has published both peer-reviewed research articles and teaching materials related to sport and physical activity and racial and sexual disparities, and is a recipient of an American Heart Association Worksite Innovation Award. At UAB, Dr. Milner holds a secondary appointment in the African American Studies Program and the position of associate scientist in the Minority Health and Health Disparities Research Center and the Center for the Study of Community Health.

Jomills Henry Braddock II is a professor in the Department of Sociology at the University of Miami. Dr. Braddock has been researching and teaching about sport and social issues for over 35 years at top sociology institutions. His research focuses on sport and race/ethnicity, sex/gender equity, and results and reactions to social policy. For over 10 years, Professor Braddock served as the director in the Center for Research on Sport in Society at the University of Miami. Dr. Braddock has published more than 20 articles on sport in top sociology journals and served as PI on grants focusing on sport research that totaled more than $5.25 million. He was given the honor of serving as the outside representative to the NFL Players Association and is the recipient of the James E. Blackwell Founders Award for distinguished service and lifetime achievement from the Association of Black Sociologists. Dr. Braddock has organized, presented, and served as a panelist and discussant at over 50 professional conferences and also served as an expert witness at the Congressional Oversight Hearing on Equal Employment Opportunity in the NFL.